Spanish Captives in North Africa in the Early Modern Age

Spain in the sixteenth century was the dominant European power. Yet, along the coasts, Spanish farmers and fishermen lived in constant fear, the victims of regular kidnapping raids by North African corsairs. In this detailed study, Ellen G. Friedman examines this undeclared state of siege that would continue for two hundred years and perpetuate the centuries-old struggle of Christianity and Islam. Drawing on original archival sources, anecdotal materials, and computer analysis, she vividly documents the North African dependence on Spanish hostages, the experiences of Christian captives, and the officially-sanctioned efforts to free them. The result is a fresh perspective on Spain in its Golden Age, and a seminal study of European slaves in Africa.

Spanish Captives in North Africa in the Early Modern Age

Ellen G. Friedman

The University of Wisconsin Press

Published 1983

The University of Wisconsin Press
114 North Murray Street
Madison, Wisconsin 53715

The University of Wisconsin Press, Ltd.
1 Gower Street
London WC1E 6HA, England

First printing

Printed in the United States of America

For LC CIP information see the colophon

ISBN 0–299–09380–8

For Elisabeth
and to the memory of
Willa Sack Elton
and
Sara H. Sack

Contents

Tables

Abbreviations

ACA: Archivo de la Corona de Aragón

AGS: Archivo General de Simancas

AHB: Archivo Histórico de la Ciudad de Barcelona (Arxiu historic de la Ciutat de Barcelona)

AHN: Archivo Histórico Nacional

ATM: Archivo, Monasterio de la orden SS. Trinidad, Madrid

BNM: Biblioteca Nacional, Madrid

MN: Archivo General de la Marina (Museo Naval)

RAHM: Real Academia de Historia, Madrid

SIHMA: *Sources inédites de l'histoire du Maroc*, 1re Série: *Angleterre*

SIHME: *Sources inédites de l'histoire du Maroc*, 1re Série: *Espagne*

SIHMF: *Sources inédites de l'histoire du Maroc*, 1re Série: *France*

SIHMPB: *Sources inédites de l'histoire du Maroc*, 1re Série: *Pays-Bas*

SIHMP: *Sources inédites de l'histoire du Maroc*, 1re Série: *Portugal*

Monetary Equivalents

Castilian Coinage:

    Escudo: 400 maravedís until 1609

               440 maravedís from 1609 onward

    Ducat: 375 maravedís

    Peso: 450 maravedís

    Real: 34 maravedís

Libra: A Valencian coin worth approximately one Castilian ducat

Dobla: An Algerian coin worth approximately 160 maravedís

Acknowledgments

One of the most enduring impressions of the years spent on this study has been the support and generosity of teachers, friends, and colleagues, both in this country and in Spain. To them I have accumulated many more debts than I can ever repay.

Ruth Pike first suggested the possibility of captives as a fruitful research topic, and directed the doctoral dissertation from which this book sprang. Over the years she has provided support, encouragement, and inspiration. She has been a mentor in the best sense of the word.

During the early stages of this project, Albert J. Loomie, S.J., recommended new lines of research that have contributed to widening the scope of the work, and I am grateful to him. Andrew C. Hess read portions of the study as it progressed and made valuable suggestions that have been integrated into it.

Several friends and colleagues gave generously of their own time to read drafts of the present work. Their critiques were of substantial value in helping me deal with conceptual and organizational problems. For this assistance I am deeply indebted to Raymond F. Betts, John F. Guilmartin, Richard L. Kagan, Helen Nader, Carla Rahn Phillips, Joan Connelly Ullman, and John B. Wolf. I did not always take their advice, and any errors or defects in the work are entirely my responsibility.

The assistance of the staffs of Spanish archives and libraries has been indispensable. In nearly all cases, I have found them at least interested and eager to be of assistance, sometimes enthusiastic. They are dedicated professionals, who deserve more credit than they are usually given for their contributions to scholarship. I am grateful to all of them, but should like to mention especially Don Luis Vázquez de Parga of the Biblioteca Nacional in Madrid, who provided critical assistance during the early stages of my research. I am obliged as well to Father Buenaventura Ginarte (O.SS.T.), who took an interest in my work and helped me gain access to the archive of the Trinitarian monastery in Madrid.

Several organizations and institutions have provided research grants for this project. I wish to thank the University of Kentucky Research Foundation for a travel grant in the summer of 1976; the Graduate School of Arts and Sciences of the University of Kentucky for a faculty fellowship in 1977; and the Joint Spanish-United States Committee for Educational and Cultural Affairs for a postdoctoral research grant that enabled me to spend eighteen months in Spain in 1978 and 1979.

Finally, I should like to thank my colleagues at Boston College for creating an environment that is supportive and nurturing of scholarly activity.

Portions of this work have been published in the *Sixteenth Century Journal*, 6 (1975); *The International History Review*, 1 (1979); *The Catholic Historical Review*, 66 (1980); and *The International Journal of African Historical Studies*, 13 (1980). My thanks to the editors and publishers of these journals for their permission to use this material.

Cambridge, Massachusetts
March 8, 1982

Introduction and Historical Background

In 1614 city officials of Gibraltar wrote to Philip III of Spain, requesting relief from the financial exactions of the crown. In support of their claim, the petitioners pointed out that the inhabitants of Gibraltar were already making a substantial contribution to the struggle with the North African corsairs. The city paid from its own treasury the salaries of forty-two guards who served in the port's nine towers. During the summer and at times when there were warnings of approaching Muslim ships, Gibraltar's citizens would join the guards at their posts to assist them, or make sorties on horseback outside the walls. The people of Gibraltar never felt secure—"neither at night nor during the day, neither in bed nor at mealtimes, neither in the fields nor in our homes."[1] Despite all the efforts to defend themselves, many captives were seized, and the city had to raise large sums of money to ransom them.

Gibraltar, because of its geographical position, was more susceptible to attack than any other place in Spain. The burden of combat with North African corsairs, however, was felt no less keenly in other places along the coast. The ruins of watchtowers standing on the Spanish coastline today serve as mute testimony to Spain's preoccupation with the corsair conflict, a new chapter of an old struggle.

The confrontation between Christianity and Islam has traditionally been regarded as a phenomenon primarily of the Middle Ages. Hostilities reached a peak in the sixteenth century, when the medieval holy war merged with the clash between the two great superpowers of the age, the Spanish and Ottoman empires, and then, in the last quarter of the century, faded, as the adversaries turned to other concerns. For Spain, however, the struggle with the Muslim world did not end. It entered a new phase, in which its principal enemies were the North African states, and the dominant form of warfare was piracy. This "little war" of piracy had always been present, but only as an adjunct of the larger conflict. Now the great battles were fought elsewhere. In the Mediterranean, the corsair war came to the forefront.[2] It is to the era of the corsairs, from the end of the great Spanish-Ottoman struggle to the late eighteenth century, when North African corsairing was but a shadow of what it had once been, that this book is devoted.

This study examines the effect on Spanish society of the prolonged, but frequently ignored, "little war" with the corsair states of North Africa. It is concerned with the response of that society and the reasons why it responded as it did. The work approaches the topic from the point of view of the problem of those who were taken captive by the corsairs, individually and collectively the most tangible manifestation for Spaniards of this continuing confrontation.

Piracy in the western Mediterranean was, of course, by no means a new phenomenon in the sixteenth century, nor was it the exclusive preserve of the Muslims. The activities of medieval Italian and Spanish corsairs in the eastern Maghrib, of the Knights of Malta, and, later, of corsairs from western and northern Europe, are all well known. As Fernand Braudel has pointed out, the Mediterranean was historically an area of "constant conflict between two warring civilizations, in which war was a permanent reality, excusing and justifying piracy."[3] Neither did the Muslims have a monopoly on the enslavement of captives and prisoners. From the Middle Ages, this had been a common characteristic of both sides in the wars between Christians and Muslims, and many of the slaves in early modern Spain were Muslims who had been seized by Spanish corsairs. This study does not deal, except peripherally, with that side of the story, nor does it represent an attempt to write North African history. Such an effort is precluded both by the absence of substantial North African sources on the subject and by my own interests. My focus is on the consequences of the conflict as part of the early modern Spanish experience.

Background

From the late fourteenth century, corsairs from the coasts of North Africa had engaged in organized privateering against Christian vessels and coastlines, activity that found its ideological base in the holy war.[4] The anti-Christian, and especially anti-Spanish, attitudes of these corsairs were given impetus by the defeat of the Hispano-Muslims in Granada in 1492, their subsequent forced conversion to Christianity, and the immigration of many of them to North Africa. Their presence there not only strengthened the ideological prop for corsairing, but also provided for the corsairs a group of embittered exiles who had an intimate knowledge of Spanish coastal regions and who could frequently pass as Spaniards.

In the face of increasing depredations by the Barbary corsairs, King Ferdinand of Spain acceded to the pleas of the Archbishop of Toledo, Francisco Cardinal Jiménez de Cisneros, that he carry the crusade against Islam into North Africa. From 1497 to 1510 Spain seized a number of key ports on the Maghribian coast, including Melilla, Mers el-Kebir, El Peñón de Vélez, Orán, Bougie, and Tripoli. This impressive string of victories persuaded Algiers, in 1510, to surrender one of four small islands at the entrance to the city, where the Spaniards erected the fortress of El Peñón.

These successes placed Spain in control of the principal points on the North African coast and in a position to undertake the conquest of the central Maghrib. But the campaign was never made. Ferdinand's interests lay in Italy, not Africa, so Spain contented itself with a system of limited occupation, erecting fortified *presidios* (garrisons) at the conquered places.[5]

Ferdinand's failure to carry the campaign into North Africa must be regarded as an important missed opportunity, one that had significant long-term implications for Spain. North Africa at the time was, as one contemporary described it, a region in which "disorder is the rule."[6] It was rent by differences between the regions, as well as by tribal disputes, conflicting claims of various princes, and the independent status of the *marabouts* (religious men), who frequently intervened in politics.[7] These conditions made the moment ripe for Spanish action.

As it was, Spain's limited measures along the coast not only failed to curb corsair activity, but also provided a pretext and an opportunity for Ottoman penetration into North Africa. Many Algerians resented the establishment of the Spanish fortress El Peñón at the entrance to their city and turned for assistance to the Ottoman corsair, Oruç, who entered Algiers in 1516 and, after executing the legitimate ruler of the city, had himself proclaimed sultan by his soldiers. The Ottoman presence in Algiers was secured after Oruç died in 1518 and was succceeded by his brother, Hayreddin, known to his western contemporaries as Barbarossa. In order to cement his position in Algiers, where his political opponents far outnumbered his supporters, Barbarossa turned to the Ottoman sultan for assistance. He became a vassal of the sultan, who in turn made Algiers a regency of the Ottoman empire, appointed Barbarossa *beylerbey* (regent, or governor), and provided him with a military force. This force solidified Barbarossa's power by driving his opponents from Algiers and, in 1525, the Spaniards from El Peñón. These victories were followed by others, which expanded the territory of the regency.

With this westward movement of the Ottoman frontier, the Maghrib and its corsair fleets came to play an increasingly important role in the struggle in the western Mediterranean. The corsairs of the new and expanding North African regency contributed to the Ottoman struggle against Spain in the sixteenth century on two levels: as an integral component of the Ottoman naval establishment, and as privateers against Spanish coasts and shipping.

Both Charles V and Philip II made several attempts, mostly unsuccessful, to neutralize the North African coasts. In July 1535 Charles captured Tunis, seized the year before by Barbarossa. This was not followed, however, by the establishment of a strong Spanish presence in Tunis. Instead, Charles limited himself to restoring the Ḥafṣid sultan deposed by Barbarossa, creating a Spanish protectorate over Tunisia, and erecting a fortress, which would always be poorly manned, at the Tu-

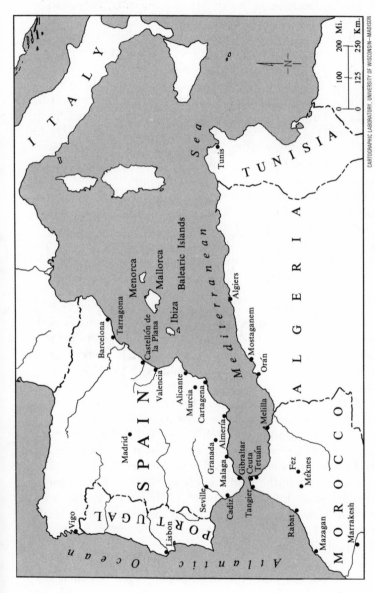

Iberian Peninsula and North Africa

nisian port of La Goletta. An effort by Charles, in 1541, to solidify his position in North Africa by seizing Algiers itself failed when the Spanish forces were driven back by storms.

In the course of the next three decades, years in which the Ottomans seemed invincible in the western Mediterranean, the role of the Maghrib in Spanish-Ottoman confrontations continued to be a vital one.[8] During this period, the regency added important territories. In 1551 the Ottoman corsair Turgut Reis, known to Europeans as Dragut, took Tripoli from the Knights of Malta, whom Charles V had installed there in 1530. Then, in 1569, Uluç Ali Paşa, the Algerian governor, took advantage of the uprising of the Moriscos (Hispano-Muslims converted to Christianity) in Spain to capture Tunis. It was retaken by Don Juan of Austria in 1573, but this victory was short-lived; in 1574 Uluç Ali again seized Tunis, as well as the Spanish fortress at La Goletta, ending Spanish influence there once and for all. Both Tunis and Tripoli were incorporated into the Turkish regency in North Africa, under the jurisdiction of the governor of Algiers.[9]

The end of an era in Spanish-Ottoman relations came in 1580. In 1571, Spain and her allies in the Holy League had broken the Turkish stranglehold in the Mediterranean with their victory at Lepanto. This did not mark the beginning of a Turkish withdrawal, however, since the Porte soon recovered and was able to secure its western flank with the 1574 victory at Tunis. Then both sides began to disengage themselves from the Mediterranean. Negotiations for a truce, which had begun in 1573, culminated in an agreement signed in 1580 which left Spain with her presidios at Melilla, Mers el-Kebir, and Orán.

The age of the crusades was over. Philip II was occupied with European concerns. Faced with the threat of Protestant-inspired revolts in the Netherlands and France, the notion of a crusade against Islam lost much of its force. At the same time, the Turks, too, were drawn away from the western Mediterranean. For them, the center of gravity shifted eastward, to internal conflicts within their own empire.[10]

The beginning of détente between the two great empires did not mark the end of Spanish-Muslim confrontation. On the contrary, the truce ushered in an era of corsair expansion, especially in Algiers, where corsairing reached its peak in the seventeenth century and continued well into the eighteenth.

Muslim corsair activity against Spain was not confined to those states that moved within the Ottoman orbit. Tetuán and other coastal cities of Morocco, which came under the Porte's influence briefly in the sixteenth century but never under its control, were also active corsair ports. During the course of the sixteenth century Morocco's sovereignty was threatened repeatedly by the Ottomans and their North African regency. This resulted in an ambivalent Moroccan foreign policy, in which its rulers frequently allied themselves with their traditional adversary, Spain, against the Turks. The great Moroccan victory over the Portuguese at Alcazar in 1578, however, brought such wealth and status to the new sultan, al-Manṣūr— a putative Ottoman client when the victory was won—that it paradoxically ended the threat of Ottoman subjection of Morocco for the remainder of the sixteenth century. Al-Manṣūr abandoned his predecessors' policy of allying with Spain against the Turks. Even as he resisted incorporation into the Ottoman sphere, he emphasized his dynasty's religious character and hatred of Catholic Spain.[11] The scale of Moroccan corsairing never approached that of Algiers, but with the breakdown of central government after the death of al-Manṣūr at the beginning of the seventeenth century, Moroccan corsairs became more aggressive at sea and came to play an increasingly important role in politics at home.[12]

Another element in this corsair aggression against Spain was the role of the Moriscos. The nature of the Morisco problem in sixteenth-century Spain cannot be understood without considering the international situation. Faced with what was regarded as a deadly threat from the Ottomans, Spain could not tolerate the existence within its boundaries of a group whose first loyalties were believed to be, and often were, to Islam. Many Spaniards considered the Moriscos a security risk and, to a degree, this perception was correct. Substantial documentation has been found of subversive contacts between the Moriscos and Spain's enemies, including not only the Ottomans and North Africans, but also the Protestants of Northern Europe.[13] In part, it was to eliminate what was regarded as a serious internal danger that the Moriscos were expelled from Spain in 1609. Their role as collaborators, however, did not end with their expulsion. The evidence strongly suggests a direct relationship between the expulsion and the significant increase in corsair activity on Spain's coasts in the seventeenth century.

A corollary development of the early seventeenth century—one that various factors gave rise to but in which the Moriscos were implicated—was the movement, in large numbers, of Muslim corsairs into the Atlantic, where they threatened the northwest coasts of Spain and Portugal, as well as the Indies fleet and other Atlantic navigation. As a result, whereas in the sixteenth century the Spanish-Muslim struggle had been confined to the Mediterranean, in the seventeenth the theater of war widened to include the Atlantic.

What were the motives of the corsairs? Certainly the obvious ones were economic—the need to make a living—and perhaps, at times, religious. Did they go deeper? Andrew Hess argues that the intensification of corsair warfare was but one manifestation of a kind of cultural disengagement, of the decline of the Hispano-Muslim frontier as a point of cultural interchange, a process that had been taking place during much of the sixteenth century. In the same vein, John Guilmartin attributes the ferocity of the corsair attack to their unconscious realization that the struggle was one of different social and economic systems, as well as of incompatible cultures and values. Perhaps so. Braudel sees positive factors at work in this phenomenon, suggesting that piracy was a means by which the North Africans might gain access to the superior technology of the west.[14] It is a fact that corsair activities, and especially the seizure of captives, were a source of both income and valuable services that helped to right the difference between the developing technologies and economies of western Europe and the static ones of North Africa.

The "little war" with the North Africans was brought home to more Spaniards in a more direct and personal way, and may have stirred up more religious and national feeling, than any of the major wars in which Spain was involved in the sixteenth and seventeenth centuries. It affected Spanish society in many ways—in the constant threat to Spanish coasts and shipping, in the resources that were regularly mobilized, especially by coastal localities, to defend against corsair attacks and for the ransom of captives.

From the early years of the sixteenth century, thousands of Spaniards were captured by the North Africans, as a result of piracy as well as military and naval engagements. Many of them spent the rest of their lives as slaves in North Africa, but a good number were ransomed, primarily through the work of two orders of religious redemptionists, the Order of Our Lady of Mercy (Mercedarians) and the Order of the Holy Trinity. There is little doubt that the efforts of the redemptionist fathers helped make corsairing a profitable endeavor. The intensification of the activities of the Maghribian corsairs in the seventeenth century was accompanied by an expansion of the activities of the friars, both in ransoming and in providing a variety of services that were intended to ease the plight of those captives who were left behind.

Perhaps more important, though less tangible than the economic outlay, was the influence of the conflict on Spanish attitudes. It created a climate of fear and led to the development of a siege mentality, especially but not only in the coastal regions, where the anticipation of attack and captivity had as much impact as the reality. It contributed to the xenophobia of which Spaniards have often been accused, by making them suspicious and wary of people of different cultures and religions, who might be a threat to the Spanish way of life. It was inevitable that this suspicion, as well as the actual conflict, would embitter relations between old Christians and Moriscos throughout Spain in the sixteenth century.

Captivity in North Africa was a real concern of people from all sectors of Spanish society. Although those who dwelt in coastal regions faced the greatest threat, residents of inland provinces were also affected, for they too took voyages by sea, or served in the military, or had friends or relatives who became captives. No socioeconomic group was immune from captivity. The lists of captives reveal that they ranged from agricultural workers and fishermen to members of the royal councils. Finally, the prominence of the activities of the redemptionist orders served as constant reminders to all Spaniards of the problem of captives in North Africa.

The concern of contemporary Spanish society for the captives was indicated by the generosity with which Spaniards contributed funds for their rescue. But fear, an even more powerful motivator than generosity, may have been behind many of the contributions. The campaigns to raise money for the ransoms were accompanied by propaganda that dwelt on the alleged horrors of captivity in North Africa. The effect of this was to intensify the hatred that many Spaniards already felt toward Muslims.

The literature of the period (especially that of Cervantes and Lope de Vega and the romances of the eighteenth century), in which captivity by the infidel is a recurring theme, also reflects this preoccupation with the problem. As Albert Mas has pointed out, the French literature of the sixteenth and seventeenth centuries deals with Muslims in the context of such themes as the rivalries of the seraglio. But when the infidel is the subject of Spanish Golden Age literature, the captive is nearly always central to the plot.[15] For most Spaniards, the association of Muslims and captivity was inescapable.

Sources

The sources for this study are primarily archival. They include the records of some eighty ransoming expeditions made by the redemptionist friars, compiled by the official notaries who accompanied them to North Africa. These can be found in the Archivo Histórico Nacional and the Biblioteca Nacional, both in Madrid, and in the Archivo de la Corona de Aragón, in Barcelona, and usually contain all the documents pertaining to the redemption, including complete financial information, detailed accounts of negotiations with the North Africans for the rescues, and descriptions of procedures. In addition, they list the captives who were rescued and include biographical data on each one. This material provided the basis for a computer-aided quantitative survey of the Spanish captive population. Other important sources were found in various sections of the Archivo General de Simancas, the Archivo Histórico Nacional, the Archivo de la Corona de Aragón, the Archivo Histórico de la Ciudad de Barcelona, and the libraries of the Museo Naval and the Real Academia de la Historia in Madrid.

I have made use, as well, of redemptionist writings, captive memoirs, and contemporary literature, especially that of Cervantes, who was himself a captive. In utilizing such sources I have tried to remain alert to the bias that is inevitably present in works of this nature.

PART 1
THE CONFLICT

Chapter 1

The Captives and Their Captors

From the sixteenth century, Christian captives played a vital role in the economies and societies of the North African states.[1] They were important both as slave labor and for the substantial sums paid to rescue them. Spaniards were especially prominent among the captive population, and may even have constituted a majority. Certainly they were the most sought after, primarily because expeditions by the Spanish redemptionist orders were so frequent and Spanish captives were likely to command the best ransom prices.

Captives were obtained by various means. Many were military men, most of them captured during major engagements or while on duty at the Spanish presidios in North Africa. Individuals such as these were prisoners of war in the traditional sense—they were the participants in the continuous war waged between Spain and the North African states during the early modern period. But there were other captives as well, most of whom were not participants, but onlookers, in the war. These were the victims of piracy and raids against the Spanish coasts and on the high seas.

Through the use of a computer, a survey has been made of more than 9,500 captives who were rescued by the Spanish redemptionist orders. The survey is based on the records of fifty-three redemptions made by the orders between 1575 and 1769.[2] Those surveyed came from a broad spectrum of Spanish society and from all parts of Spain, and probably represent a fair sampling of all Spaniards in captivity, with certain exceptions. One limitation of these lists is that most of the records found represent the efforts of the Castilian and Andalusian branches of the redemptionist orders. Although these friars rescued many captives from other parts of Spain, they preferred those from their own regions. For that reason, it is not possible to assume that the geographical makeup of the surveyed group is that of all Spaniards in captivity. A second problem is that priority was given to the redemption of certain categories of captives whose rescue was regarded as most beneficial to the state: military men and, from the seventeenth century, those from the *carrera de las Indias* (the Indies fleet). Thus, the proportion of these captives would be higher in the group surveyed than in the actual captive population. At the same time, the percentage seized under other circumstances would be lower in the sample group than in the actual captive population.[3] In evaluating apparent fluctuations in the representation of captives from different categories, it is also necessary to examine the proportion of those from the two preferred groups. Despite the shortcomings of the data, it is still possible to utilize this survey to determine changes in the composition of the captive population and the geographic locations and circumstances under which captives were seized. It can also be used to determine the characteristics of the group rescued.

The analysis of the data shows that during most of the period studied the largest single element in the Spanish captive population was not those taken prisoner in military or naval engagements, but individuals who had been seized on the coasts of Spain. At least one-fifth of these had been captured on land.[4] The nature of the problem is underscored by the fact that a large percentage of the victims (more than 40 percent in the seventeenth century) were taken captive right in their home regions, either on land or in the immediate coastal waters.

Clearly, piracy was a threat to all residents of the coasts of peninsular Spain, whether they ventured out on the high seas or remained close to home. To those for whom the sea was a factor in earning a living, the danger was especially great. Information on the circumstances of captivity was available in about 43 percent of the cases. Of these, 26.6 percent were seized while fishing and 12.3 percent while transporting merchandise along the coast. An additional 3.7 percent had been captured on land while tending livestock or working in the fields. Thus, more than 40 percent of those for whom such information was given were taken captive right on the coasts while engaged in work that was basic to the economies of Spain's coastal regions.

Although the data shows that throughout the two centuries in question individuals seized by corsairs on Spain's coasts were at all times prominent in the captive population, it also demonstrates that the nature of the Spanish-North African conflict was not static, but changed over time. The most dramatic of these changes occurred in the early seventeenth century, when the direct military confrontations between Spain and the Ottomans that had characterized the sixteenth century had all but ceased.

The Aftermath of the Battle of Lepanto

The first redemption for which a record book has been found took place in 1575 and was executed by the Mercedarian order. Calculations show that the average time in captivity for rescued captives was slightly more than five years. Thus, most of those taken earlier than 1570 who were going to be ransomed had already gained their freedom by 1575. This was especially true of military captives, to whom priority was shown. For this reason, statistics available for the period prior to the Battle of Lepanto, which took place in 1571, cannot be considered representative of those captured or even of those rescued. Nevertheless, it is worth looking at these figures.

Information was found on eighty-five people taken captive during the ten years prior to Lepanto. Nearly 60 percent had been seized by corsairs, either on Spain's Mediterranean coasts or at sea. Keeping in mind the fact that many military captives from this period would have been rescued by 1575, this figure still suggests that even during a period of active warfare between Spain and the North African states, in their capacity as the western flank of the Ottoman Empire, many, and perhaps most, of the Spanish captives in North Africa were victims of piracy rather than of direct military confrontations. It is well known, of course, that prior to the Battle of Lepanto piracy was a serious problem in the Mediterranean and on the Spanish coasts from the Strait of Gibraltar to Catalonia.[5]

The unfortunate absence of more detailed information for the period prior to Lepanto makes it difficult to evaluate the effect that the Christian victory there had on piracy in the Mediterranean, and particularly along Spain's coasts. It has already been noted that the years following the battle saw a general disengagement of forces in the Mediterranean by Spain and the Ottoman Empire. But while the threat from the Porte itself may have diminished, that from the North African corsairs did not.

A survey of ninety-nine people captured during the three years following Lepanto, 1572–1574, shows that about 70 percent had been taken prisoner in 1574 when Spain lost Tunis, the site of the major Turkish effort during this period (see table 1). Another 18 percent were captured at sea in the Mediterranean. Only 5 percent were seized on the Spanish littoral. While it is not possible to say with certainty, the small percentage of captives from the coasts probably indicates a decline in corsair activity in Spanish waters during these three years. This may have been due to the fact that in 1572 many of the regency's corsair vessels, which escaped extensive damage at Lepanto, as well as its experienced corsair captains, were transferred to Constantinople to aid in the restoration of the Ottoman fleet.[6]

The picture changed considerably during the next years. Of 252 people in the survey who were captured between 1575

Table 1. Seizure of Captives, 1572–1589

Years	Total Surveyed	Percentage Captured on Spanish Coasts	Percentage Captured at Sea — Mediterranean	Percentage Captured in North Africa	Percentage Captured between Africa and Spain
1572–1574	99	5.0	18.0	70.0	2.0
1575–1581	252	30.0	21.4	31.3	6.3
1582–1589	99	34.3	21.2	4.0	9.0

and 1581, over 31 percent had been taken in North Africa, nearly all during the Portuguese war in Morocco in 1578. But almost as many, 30 percent, were seized along the Spanish coasts, half of these on land. An additional 21 percent were captured at sea in the Mediterranean. Taking the rescue statistics as a reflection of the composition of the entire population of Spanish captives at this time—except for the skew toward military captives—this represents a substantial increase in successful corsair activity on Spain's coasts over the three years immediately following Lepanto. Thus, the long-term effect on coastal security of the victory at Lepanto seems to have been negligible. Although it may have given coastal Spain a few years of relative security, it was not long before North African corsairs were once again a threat to that region.

The subsequent truce between Spain and the Porte did not alter the situation either, as Spain's coasts continued to suffer from repeated raids. Indeed, the Hispano-Turkish détente ushered in a new offensive by the North African corsairs, who were no longer distracted by the need to serve in imperial armadas. Albert Tenenti, writing of the decade from 1580 to 1590, remarked that "there was no harbour and no coastline belonging to the Catholic states which escaped their attacks."[7]

In Spain the 1580s saw a series of attempts against the coastline, especially that of Valencia. At the beginning of 1583 a corsair assault on Calpe was driven off. But the North African pirates were successful in September against Chilches, in northern Valencia, and in November against Moraira. The offensive continued in 1584, when Altea was attacked in February and Polop and Moraira again in March. In July of that year the viceroy put the entire Valencian coast on a war footing because of the threat posed by twenty-four Algerian vessels that were hovering about the region after having attacked Cadaqués in Catalonia. In spite of the special precautions, the defenders were not able to prevent the corsairs from disembarking and assaulting Callosa in July and Altea and Cabo Martín in August.[8]

The statistical survey supports the impression of an intensification of corsair activity against Spain's coasts during the years following the truce. Of those surveyed for 1582–1589, 34 percent had been captured on the coasts, nearly half of these on land, and 21 percent at sea in the Mediterranean. In contrast, only 4 percent had been captured in North Africa, underscoring the decline in Spanish-Muslim confrontations within that region.

Thus, in the two decades after Lepanto, at least 23 percent of the captives in the survey had been captured on the coasts of Spain and another 20 percent at sea in the Mediterranean. Some of those in the latter category were military men traveling on troop transport vessels that were attacked by the corsair fleet, while others were fishermen or people engaged in trade. About 5 percent of the captives were seized between Spain and North Africa, most of them while transporting supplies to Spain's North African garrisons. Prisoners taken in North Africa, almost all military men, represent about one-third of the captives surveyed. Most came from major engagements, such as the struggle for Tunis and the Portuguese war in Morocco. Only a small number of captives were seized during minor skirmishes in this region.

Although there was some corsair activity in the Atlantic during this period, it accounted for only 3 percent of all the captives surveyed. None of the captives were from the Indies fleet.

In the final analysis, then, neither the Christian victory at Lepanto, nor the Hispano-Turkish truce, nor the Ottoman withdrawal from the western Mediterranean following the truce resulted in a contraction of North African corsairing against Spain. Other events of the late sixteenth and the seventeenth centuries, however, did have an effect on this activity.

During the regency of Barbarossa, from 1518 to 1534, Algiers had become the dominant corsair port in the Maghrib and the most important city of North Africa. We possess numerous contemporary descriptions of its flourishing commerce. In spite of the city's growth, its economy suffered from basic structural defects, primarily due to the fact that it depended so heavily on corsair activity. While Algiers was an active commercial center, most of its trade was carried on by

Europeans, and piracy, which provided the basis for this trade, was the most important source of revenue. There was little manufacturing activity in Algiers and goods produced there were not a significant factor in its commerce. Furthermore, Algiers, like the rest of North Africa, was underpopulated; this manpower shortage was undoubtedly an element in the prominence in Algerian society of Christian renegades and captives.[9]

The heavy dependence of Algiers on corsairing made the *ta'ifa* (corporation) of the *reis* (corsair captains) a powerful element in its government and society. The other dominant group was the janissary corps, also established by Barbarossa. The janissaries of Algiers, recruited primarily from among renegade Christians and Anatolian Turks, were by the latter part of the sixteenth century a military aristocracy. They elected their own *ağa* (commander) and *divan* (governing council), which protected the interests of the group.

The beylerbeys of Algiers were appointed for life by the sultan in Constantinople and were theoretically responsible only to him. The *paşas* (rulers) of Tunis and Tripoli, the other Ottoman provinces in North Africa, were subordinate to the beylerbeys. These rulers were all loyal to the Porte, and under them Turkish dominance over the North African regency was effective.[10] Within Algiers, the powerful corsairs generally supported the government, while the janissaries, who aspired to control of the state, frequently challenged the rule of the beylerbeys.

The last beylerbey was the great Uluç Ali, who until 1587 served as both ruler of Algiers and commander of the Ottoman fleet. After his death the sultan, in an effort to increase his control over the North African provinces, transformed them into three separate regencies, each governed by a paşa who was appointed for a three-year term. These officials never had the authority or stature of the beylerbeys. This change, the general weakening of Ottoman power in the western Mediterranean, the desire of the janissaries to control the government, and a series of revolts in North Africa in the late 1580s and the 1590s combined to reduce Ottoman control in the region, a process that continued throughout the seventeenth century.

Morocco, too, underwent important political upheavals at the turn of the century. After the Moroccan victory over Portugal in 1578, al-Manṣūr reorganized and unified the Moroccan state, which up to that time had consisted of many feuding principalities. But when al-Manṣūr died in 1603, the situation in Morocco once again deteriorated, with his sons vying for power and turning alternatively to either the Spaniards or Algerians for support. By 1613, two separate kingdoms had developed in Morocco, with the rival sultans having very little authority in either.

This situation permitted the corsair ports of Morocco to become quasi-independent republics. While the growth of Moroccan corsairing was part of a general trend at this time, it was encouraged by the chaotic conditions in Morocco. The political upheaval and strife continued until the last third of the seventeenth century, when a new dynasty gained the throne and Mawlay Ismāᶜēl (1672–1727) conquered and subjected virtually the entire country.

The political instability and absence of central authority in the states of the Maghrib brought greater independence to the corsairs of both regions. This was especially true of Algiers; events in the regency toward the end of the sixteenth century had the effect of finally freeing the Algerian corsairs, always the most numerous and active, from whatever restraints the Porte's truce with Spain may have imposed on them.

Almost simultaneously, large numbers of English and Dutch pirates appeared in North Africa, where they augmented the ranks of the Muslim corsairs and introduced a new naval technology, against which traditional Mediterranean naval defenses were inadequate. By the early seventeenth century, the northerners' contributions had revolutionized Algerian corsairing, transformed the corsair war in the Mediterranean, and opened the Atlantic to North African fleets.[11]

Then, in the autumn of 1609, the expulsion of the Moriscos from Spain began. More than a quarter of a million Moriscos were expelled; most of them went to North Africa.

The "Morisco Problem"

The expulsion was not an unpopular action in Spain. Many people expected it to result in greater security along the Mediterranean coasts, since it was commonly believed that the Moriscos in Spain regularly collaborated with the North African corsairs.[12] In Valencia, which had the largest concentration of Moriscos as well as, coincidentally, the greatest vulnerability to corsair attack, there was a clamor for the elimination of this "fifth column." In December 1601, the count of Benavente, viceroy of Valencia, wrote to the king concerning the presence of five Algerian galleys at Santa Pola on the Valencian coast, from where they launched coastal raids and attacks on merchant vessels. He noted that the populace was aroused to fever pitch by the presence of the galleys and the belief that the indigenous Moriscos were ready to aid them in a major attack on the Valencian coast. He expressed the fear that a general uprising, directed against the Moriscos, would occur if the government did not act quickly to remove the threat.[13]

This fear of Morisco treachery, though perhaps heightened by prejudice, was not without foundation. Diego de Haedo charged that cooperation by the Moriscos was an important element in North African attacks on Spanish villages. As an example, he cited the raid on Alicante in 1582 by the Algerian corsair Hasan Paşa, who had forewarned some of the local Moriscos of his coming. Haedo alleged that many of the Moriscos assisted the corsairs in sacking the city and then some two thousand of them embarked with their possessions in the Algerian galleys.[14] The Moriscos of Almenara were accused of collaboration with the Algerian corsairs in their attack on Chilches in September 1583, and exemplary punishment was meted out to fifteen of them, who on October 19 were quartered for having "guided the corsairs from the sea in the sack of Chilches and burned the church."[15]

Other evidence exists that lends credence to the fears and suspicions that the old Christians had of the Moriscos. During the war of Granada, rebelling Moriscos had exchanged Christian captives for Algerian arms right on the Granadine coast.

Of the eighty-five captives surveyed for 1561–1570, eighteen had been captured in this way.[16]

An element in this collaboration was the defection to North Africa, during the course of the sixteenth century, of thousands of Moriscos, many of whom joined the corsair fleets. The clandestine flight of Moriscos from Spain had taken place since the beginning of the sixteenth century and had intensified with the Germanía rebellion in Valencia in 1521. By midcentury a complex organization existed to facilitate the departure of Valencian Moriscos, as well as those of Aragón and Castile.[17]

These defectors were frequently implicated in corsair raids. For example, in April 1595, the viceroy of Valencia reported an attack on Teulada, two leagues from the sea, by Algerian corsairs who killed Antonio Vallés and captured his wife and two children, as well as four other youths. He remarked that they would not have been able to go so far inland were it not for the help of two Moriscos, personal enemies of Vallés, who had earlier fled to Algiers where they had joined the corsairs. In November 1606, the viceroy reported that a village a league inland from Altea had been attacked by eight Muslims from an Algerian frigate, all of whom were identified by witnesses as Moriscos who had gone to Algiers some years before.[18]

This history of collaboration led many Spaniards to expect the expulsion of the Moriscos to alleviate the problem of North African piracy on the coasts by eliminating the group that might be expected to assist the exiles, the Morisco friends and relatives who were left behind. But the desired effect was not achieved. Indeed, in the seventeenth century, which one historian has called the "golden age of the Barbary corsairs,"[19] pirate attacks on Spanish coasts and shipping multiplied.

A key element in this intensification was the transfer of large numbers of aggrieved Moriscos to North Africa. There, their familiarity with the Spanish coasts and their ability to pass as Spaniards, their desire for revenge and to demonstrate to their coreligionists that they were good Muslims, and the ideological base that the expulsion provided for attacks on Spain combined to make them a greater threat than when they had lived under Spanish jurisdiction.

The Spanish government had not intended to send large numbers of Moriscos to Muslim lands. But many of those whose original destinations were other Christian states either overpowered or bribed the captains and crews of the vessels transporting them and persuaded them to go instead to North Africa. Others arrived at their original destinations and then reembarked for the Maghrib. The files of the Council of State for this period are filled with communiqués from the governors of Spain's North African presidios expressing alarm over the large numbers of Moriscos arriving in North Africa. On March 26, 1611, the council took note of these developments and expressed the hope that the intensification of corsair activities that was bound to occur would not force them to increase the size of the fleet charged with the defense of the Spanish coasts.[20] The council's worst fears were realized.

The Heyday of the Corsairs

The survey of captives indicates a change, almost on the heels of the Morisco expulsion, in the pattern of anti-Spanish activity by the corsairs. The new developments were of two kinds. One was a greater concentration of pirate attacks on the Spanish coasts. Whereas 31.9 percent of those in the survey for 1570–1609 had been seized on the coasts, the percentage of such captives jumped to 54.2 percent in the next decade and ranged between 40 and 43 percent for the balance of the first half of the century (see table 2).

An even more striking phenomenon was the large-scale movement by the corsairs into the Atlantic. The peak period for corsair activity against Spain in the Atlantic was the three decades following the expulsion, 1610–1639, when more than a quarter of those surveyed were captured there. This represents a startling and dramatic increase over the preceding four decades, when, as noted, this region yielded fewer than 3 percent of the captives. During the second half of the seventeenth century, between 16 and 23 percent of all Spanish captives surveyed were seized in the Atlantic (see table 3). Clearly, by the early seventeenth century North African piracy had

Table 2. Survey of Captives Seized on Spain's Coasts, 1570–1769

Years	Percentage Captured on Mediterranean Coasts	Percentage Captured on Atlantic Coasts	Total Percentage of Captives from Coastal Regions[a]
1570–1609	31.0	0.9	31.9
1610–1619	37.2	17.0	54.2
1620–1629	21.3	18.5	39.8
1630–1639	22.1	21.5	43.6
1640–1649	31.2	10.9	42.1
1650–1659	22.3	6.6	28.9
1660–1669	26.5	9.5	36.0
1670–1679	30.7	8.1	38.8
1680–1689	24.1	6.4	30.5
1690–1699	14.9	10.4	25.3
1700–1709	7.2	2.5	9.7
1710–1719	26.9	4.9	31.8
1720–1729	38.9	7.9	46.8
1730–1749[b]	. . .	. . .	. . .
1750–1759	48.4	9.8	58.2
1760–1769	55.9	7.6	63.5

[a]This figure includes only those captured on the coasts of the peninsula, not those taken in the Mediterranean or Atlantic islands.
[b]Insufficient data to analyze.

ceased to be an almost exclusively Mediterranean institution and had become a serious threat in the Atlantic as well.

Carrera de las Indias

The intensification of corsairing in the Atlantic was felt even by the Indies fleet. Reference has already been made to the absence from the survey in the sixteenth century of captives from the *carrera*. Such individuals do begin to appear in the statistics from the second decade of the seventeenth century. Of those captured between 1610 and 1619, 6.2 percent were from the carrera. This was only the beginning of a trend toward an increasingly larger percentage of captives from the fleet. During 1620–1629, 14.4 percent, and from 1630–1639, 9.6 percent of the captives surveyed came from the carrera. After that, as with all captives from the Atlantic, the percent-

Table 3. Captives Seized in Atlantic in Seventeenth Century[a]

Years	Total Surveyed	Number Captured in Atlantic	Percentage of Total
1610–1619	400	109	27.2
1620–1629	416	110	26.4
1630–1639	753	198	26.2
1640–1649	751	143	19.0
1650–1659	840	159	18.9
1660–1669	1,146	203	17.7
1670–1679	765	126	16.4
1680–1689	373	70	18.7
1690–1699	288	66	22.9

[a]Includes those captured in northwestern Spain, along the Portuguese coast, in the Canaries, traveling between Spain and the Canaries, and from the Indies fleet.

Table 4. Military and Indies Fleet Captives

Years	Percentage of Military Captives	Percentage of Captives from Indies Fleet	Total Percentage of Captives from Preferred Groups
1570–1609	24.1	0	24.1
1610–1619	15.7	6.2	21.9
1620–1629	21.3	14.4	35.7
1630–1639	19.2	9.6	28.8
1640–1649	16.9	3.9	20.8
1650–1659	15.1	5.5	20.6
1660–1669	15.0	20.9	35.9
1670–1679	10.5	6.4	16.9
1680–1689	4.8	1.3	6.1
1690–1699	5.9	5.5	11.4

age of those from the Indies fleet declined—between 1640 and 1659 they represented 4.8 percent of the total surveyed. In the decade 1660–1669 the proportion rose, due to several important seizures of carrera vessels, but thereafter it dropped considerably (see table 4). Nearly all the vessels were captured at the eastern end of the route.

It should be noted that the numerous captives from the Indies fleet were not victims of occasional, isolated incidents in which large numbers of people were captured at one time, but of repeated assaults. Groups of captives from the carrera appear in the statistics for fifty-one of the seventy years between 1610 and 1680. This means that at least one vessel from the fleet was captured in each of those years. Captives from the carrera appear in every year between 1653 and 1677.

While it is true that most of the vessels captured were escort or dispatch boats, and the New World treasure was never taken by the North Africans, the frequent seizures indicate that the fleet was now more vulnerable to attack and the treasure in greater danger than in the past. Furthermore, many prominent people traveled to and from the Indies with the fleet, and some of them were captured. The captain of one of the vessels in the carrera, Juan de Villalobos, had his boat captured twice, in 1663 and 1667. Both times he was carrying a number of high-ranking passengers and their families, as well as private treasure.[21]

Several explanations may be offered for the increase in assaults on the Indies fleet. The general movement into the Atlantic by the North African corsairs has already been mentioned and will be discussed at greater length. The mere presence of larger numbers of corsairs in this region made attacks on the fleet more likely. At the same time, the increase in Spanish shipping in the seventeenth century certainly made it more attractive to the corsairs. Corsair assaults on the fleet may also have been encouraged by the fact that it was now easier prey than in the sixteenth century. The carrera sailed in convoy, as it always had, and was protected by an *armada de guardia* (a naval escort). Although the records of the *consulado* of Seville, which was responsible for the upkeep of the guardia, indicate increasingly heavy defense costs, in fact effective defense of the fleet was weakened in the seventeenth century due to the use of the escort boats as merchant vessels.[22]

Atlantic Coasts

Action against Spain in the Atlantic was not limited to attacks on the Indies fleet. Northwestern Spain, which had yielded only a tiny percentage of the captives in the sixteenth century, was now the scene of regular corsair aggression, and fishing and commerce in this region, as well as along the Portuguese coast, became very hazardous. Approximately 20 percent of those in the survey for 1610–1639 were captured on the coasts of northwestern Spain or Portugal. Thereafter, the percentage of captives from this region declined somewhat, ranging from about 7 to 11 percent for the remainder of the century (see table 2).

Documentary sources buttress the statistical evidence of an increasing incidence of North African corsair attacks in north-western Spain. An examination of the correspondence of the governors of Galicia with various local military officials, from the mid-sixteenth century through the fourth decade of the seventeenth, reveals no mention of what are referred to as "Turkish" corsairs until 1617. Earlier letters had dealt only with the threat posed by Protestant pirates. Two reports on the state of defense of Galicia, one dated 1589 and the other 1604, discuss defensive measures to be taken against the threat of attack by English privateers; no mention is made in either report of Muslim corsairs.[23]

The first reference to North African corsairs appears on May 8, 1617, when the marqués de Cerralvo, governor of Galicia, wrote concerning the appearance of "Turkish" pirates in the waters off Galicia and the threat that they would disembark at some point along the coast. Although they did not attack at that time, they did seize a number of fishermen in the area. On December 8 of that year, North African corsair vessels were once again sighted off southern Galicia. The following day they attacked and burned the village of Cangas, on the Ría de Vigo, killing or capturing large numbers of people. Individuals abducted during that raid represent 13 percent of the captives in the survey for that year. Following the assault on Cangas, the corsairs remained in the region, making hit-and-run raids on the coasts and attacking those fishermen with the temerity to venture out of port; they finally pulled up their sails and left the area two weeks after the incident at Cangas.[24]

Reports of the North African danger to this area continued to appear during the next decade. On April 20, 1624, the monks of the monastery of Nuestra Señora de Oya, near the Portuguese border, helped to repel an attack by five "Turkish" ships.[25] On July 9, 1630, Pedro de Villatoro reported the presence on an island in the Ría de Arosa of three vessels of Muslim corsairs who, that morning, had captured "a large number of people."[26] In December 1632, the governor of Galicia, Pedro de Toledo, wrote to Lope de Mendoza warning him to "take particular care that the fishermen who go out to sea carry arms to defend themselves against the Turkish boats roaming up and down these coasts."[27]

Most of those captured in northwestern Spain were residents of the region and the Galician fishing industry suffered from this corsair activity. The Mercedarian friar Isidro de Valcazar wrote in the early seventeenth century that the Muslims took captives from all coasts of Spain, including Portugal, Galicia, and Asturias. "The fishermen, whose living is in the sea, are not able to enjoy it without placing themselves in manifest danger."[28] Information on the circumstances under which they were captured is provided for 65.7 percent of those from the northwest in the seventeenth century; 80 percent of these were identified as having been seized while fishing in coastal waters.

In view of the importance of fishing and waterborne commerce to the life and economy of northwestern Spain, this piracy and its ever-present danger must have had severe economic and psychological repercussions. Antonio Domínguez Ortiz notes that the greater part of fish consumed in Spain in the seventeenth century was imported, a direct result, he suggests, of the inhibiting effect of corsairing on the fishing industry.[29]

Attacks on land were also a problem in the northwest. At least 10 percent of the captives surveyed who had been seized in this area were captured on land. The assault on the village of Cangas in December 1617 has already been discussed. In 1621 the village of Portonovo was sacked and numerous captives were taken by an estimated one thousand North African corsairs who arrived in fifteen vessels.[30] The following year the villages of Maspica and Camariñas in Galicia were raided and sacked.[31] In 1629, eight-year-old Juan de Noguera was one of a group of boys captured in Cangas while chasing rabbits.[32] An infant girl, Miguela Carnossa, was seized in 1640 during the sack of Talón, in which her mother was killed.[33] In 1642 Catalina Pérez of Fisterna was abducted by Algerian corsairs as she slept in her bed.[34] These are just some of the victims of raids on villages in northwestern Spain that occurred in the seventeenth century.

The extensive corsair activity in the northwest emphasizes the degree to which North African piracy affected residents of all the Spanish coasts. This piracy has traditionally been viewed as a Mediterranean phenomenon, but, as we have seen, in the seventeenth century it became a severe problem for Spain's Atlantic coasts as well. Indeed, the situation in the northwest was so grave that in early 1667 officials of the Basque province of Guipúzcoa wrote to the crown complaining that they were unable to meet their quota for the royal levy of mariners because so many of their seamen were prisoners of the North African corsairs.[35]

Canary Islands

It was inevitable that the move into the Atlantic by the corsairs would also affect the Canary Islands. It is difficult to deal with the question of captives from the Canaries; we know that the corsairs were very active in this region in the seventeenth century and yet, because the redemptors gave priority to the rescue of those from the mainland, the survey shows a much lower rate of captives seized in the islands than one would expect.[36] But the survey does indicate that the proportion of captives taken from the Canaries increased from the early seventeenth century. While only a handful of people were identified as having been captured there in the sixteenth century, 6.2 percent of the captives in 1610–1619 were seized in this region. Among them were twenty-one people captured when Algerian pirates attacked the city of Lanzarote in 1618. The percentage of captives from the islands dropped off during the rest of the first half of the century, but rose again in the second. Between 1640 and 1699, 6 percent of those surveyed had been seized in the Canaries. It is likely that their proportion of the actual Spanish captive population was somewhat higher than the percentage of those rescued. The intensification of corsair activity in the Canaries is probably related to the increased pressure that the corsairs placed on the Indies fleet, since the islands were a stopping place for traffic coming from the New World. Another source of large numbers of captives in the Atlantic was the route between Spain and the Canaries.

Mediterranean Coasts

At the same time as corsairing escalated in the Atlantic, it continued unabated on Spain's Mediterranean coasts. During the years from 1570 to 1609, 25 percent of the captives in the survey had been taken on the Andalusian and Levantine coasts of Spain. In 1610–1619, the percentage of those from these regions climbed to 31.5 percent. From 1620 to 1629 it declined to about 20 percent, and remained at between 20 and 25 percent for most of the remainder of the century.

Thus, during the ten-year period following the Morisco expulsion, the percentage of captives from southern and southeastern Spain increased by about one-fourth over the previous forty years. Thereafter, it declined and then stabilized. It should be noted that these figures do not include Catalonia, which actually experienced a very slight drop in the percentage of captives represented in the survey.

In this area, too, attacks on land were a serious problem. The redemption lists are studded with the names of agricultural workers and livestock tenders who were captured near the Mediterranean coast. In September 1655, nine young female agricultural workers were the victims of corsairs who landed and disembarked after nightfall, seized the women, breaking down the door of the shelter in which they slept, and carried them off in their nightclothes.[37] In 1662 Joseph Sánchez of Vera and his two young sons were abducted from their own garden.[38] In 1670, one of the many attacks on Almería in the seventeenth century yielded a large number of captives from a farm in that village. Although the total is not known, the names of sixteen of these captives appear in the redemption records.[39] In July 1689, three women were seized by Algerian corsairs while gathering esparto grass in one of the coves of Los Alumbres de Cartagena.[40] Travel along the roads of the region was also risky. In 1610 Juan Rodríguez of Granada was captured while traveling by land from Almería to Cartagena.[41] In 1655 Father Alonso Verdugo of Valencia was on the road to Alicante, where he was to perform religious services, when he was taken captive.[42] Similar examples abound. Indeed, even residents of localities that were presumably well defended were not immune. In 1608 Estevan Renia was captured by Algerian corsairs as he fished on the beach at Barcelona.[43]

At times the corsairs abducted the populations of entire villages, especially in Valencia. At the beginning of August 1637, the viceroy of Valencia received word of the arrival at the island of Formentera in the Balearics of seven Algerian galleys that planned to land from seven hundred to eight hundred men at selected spots along the Valencian coast, including Calpe, Benisa, and Teulada. The warning came too late to save Calpe, since simultaneously with this message the viceroy learned that on August 3 it had been invaded and sacked by corsairs from this fleet, who captured or killed everyone found in the village. Most of the men of Calpe were working in the fields when the attack came, so nearly all of the 315 captives were women and children. The other villages marked for attack were able to repel the corsairs, who did not leave the area, but simply dropped anchor at Moraira, and continued to threaten the region.[44]

The corsairs did not confine their activities to the seacoast. In 1609, fourteen-year-old Diego Rodríguez was captured in Mijas, several kilometers inland, between Málaga and Marbella.[45] In 1613, Juan González was carried off while tending cattle in Casabermeja, a village about 30 kilometers inland from Málaga, along the Guadalmedina River.[46] A communiqué of July 11, 1640, to military commanders on the coast of Andalusia reported that at about 8:00 A.M. on the morning of July 10, large numbers of corsairs had disembarked on the coast of Granada and then traveled several kilometers inland to sack the village of Gualchos in the Alpujarras, killing or capturing many of the inhabitants. After the attack on Gualchos, the fleet proceeded in a westerly direction, threatening the other populated settlements along the coast.[47] Although the document does not indicate the total number of captives seized in Gualchos, the names of twenty-one of them were found in the redemption books examined.[48]

Thus, the evidence indicates that corsair activity along Spain's coasts not only increased in the seventeenth century but also encompassed a broader area. Nearly all those in the survey who were captured between 1570 and 1609 had come from the Mediterranean region. But after 1610, while the percentage of captives from Mediterranean Spain held firm, substantial numbers began to appear who had been taken prisoner on the Atlantic coasts. Consequently, the total percentage of those surveyed who were seized from Spain's coastal regions was significantly higher during the seventeenth century than it had been in the sixteenth. Indeed, from 1610 to 1689 the proportion captured on the coasts ranged from about 30 percent to more than 54 percent of the total surveyed. It should be kept in mind that they undoubtedly accounted for an even higher proportion of the actual Spanish captive population.

It might be possible to attribute part of the increase in the percentage from coastal regions to the fact that there were probably fewer military captives in the seventeenth century than in the sixteenth. It has already been noted that this group received preference in the redemptions. Most military captives rescued in the sixteenth century had been taken prisoner during major engagements in North Africa, such as the struggle for Tunis. Encounters of this sort were far less frequent in the seventeenth century, when most of those captured in North Africa were the victims of minor skirmishes or forays made by Muslim raiders to the environs of the Spanish presidios for the specific purpose of obtaining captives. Thus, some of the increase in the ratio of captives from the coastal areas could be due to the fact that, with a smaller percentage of military captives in the total population, the redemptionists were able to ransom a larger proportion of those abducted from the coasts, who were usually civilians. But the survey indicates that this was not the case; the decline in military captives was offset by the increase in captives from the carrera de las Indias, the other group to which priority was given in the redemption. Comparing the combined percentages of military captives and those from the Indies fleet in the seventeenth century with that of military captives in the survey for the sixteenth, it is clear that the preferred category remained fairly stable until the last third of the seventeenth century (see table 4).

For the most part, then, the increase in the proportion of captives seized on the coasts can be attributed to the fact that the undeclared war that the North African Muslims continued to wage against Spain in the seventeenth century was, to a greater degree than ever before, fought on the Spanish coasts.

The Moriscos in North Africa

The role played by the expelled Moriscos in North African corsairing varied from region to region. The great majority of the expellees, to be sure, were peasants, artisans, and small businessmen. Their activities in North Africa are best documented for Tunisia, to which an estimated eighty thousand Moriscos immigrated. The Tunisian government encouraged this immigration and even helped settle the Moriscos on agricultural lands, especially in the north, where they made important contributions to rural development. The influence of the Moriscos was also felt in Tunisian industry and commerce.[49]

Much less is known about the approximately sixty thousand expellees who went to Algiers where, in contrast to Tunisia, they encountered a cool welcome because of cultural differences and suspicions about their non-Muslim ways.[50] But the activities of most of them in Algiers were probably similar to those in Tunisia—they were engaged in agriculture, artisan industry, and commerce, just as they had been in Spain. For example, as in Spain, the silk industry in Algiers was concentrated in the hands of the Moriscos.[51]

These were the occupations of most Moriscos, but not all. Throughout the sixteenth century there had also been a tradition of banditry among a segment of Spain's Morisco population, and these bandits had often acted in concert with, or even as agents of, the North African corsairs.[52] In view of this, of the high profits from corsairing, and of the desire for revenge against Spain, it is not surprising that the corsairs should have found eager recruits for their crews among the new immigrants.

A few Moriscos even had their own vessels. In 1618, a Spanish patrol boat captured Julián Pérez, an expellee from Morón de la Frontera, whose exploits that spring had plagued the Valencian and Andalusian coasts. According to the report of his capture, Pérez had risen from poverty to become a prominent cloth merchant in Spain, and at the time of the expulsion he was able to take much of his wealth with him. In Algiers he became active in the trade in Christian slaves and as a moneylender to high officials, and was eventually given permission to arm two large corsair vessels, of which he was named captain.[53]

In the same year, a Spanish fleet sent to patrol the Valencian coast because of the increase in corsair activity there found large numbers of Moriscos in the vessels it captured. The captain of one, Ali Zayde, was an expellee from Zaragoza.[54] Another Morisco who became a corsair in Algiers was Blanquillo Morisco, who owned a brigantine manned by about two dozen other expellees.[55] The account of their activities, which reports that they always traveled dressed as Spaniards and spoke excellent Castilian, and so were able to penetrate well inland, underscores the danger that these individuals presented to Spanish coastal regions.

Most Moriscos lacked either the means or the military background to rise high in the corsair ranks. Their important contribution, because of their unique knowledge of the Spanish coasts and their ability to pass as Spaniards, was as spies or guides. They appear in this capacity in a communication from the viceroy of Mallorca to the Spanish crown at the end of May 1610, which reported on news from Algiers of the departure on a corsair expedition of a fleet of twelve large ships that carried "many Moriscos," some going as soldiers and others to guide the corsairs in the coastal villages.[56] In 1619 the English ambassador to Spain wrote that no nation was as annoyed and infested by pirates as Spain, where the expelled Moriscos served as guides to "the Turks and Moors to do mischief on the coastal towns."[57]

These activities suggest a relationship between the expulsion and the rise in the proportion of captives from Spain's southern and southeastern coasts during the following decade. There was undoubtedly a strong desire for vengeance among these exiles as well as a wish to prove themselves to their fellow Muslims.[58] Furthermore, the expulsion itself fed the hatred that the Algerians already felt for Spain and provided ideological justification for corsairing. Finally, the coasts of southern and southeastern Spain were familiar to the Moriscos and it was there that they could be most effective.

The Morisco role in corsair activity in Morocco is even clearer. The movement of Muslim corsairs into the Atlantic was facilitated by the establishment, on the Atlantic coast of Morocco, of two communities of exiled Moriscos, who not only devoted themselves to piracy, but also extended a warm welcome to northern European and Algerian corsairs, providing them with a safe Atlantic port where they could seek shelter, outfit their boats, find financing and men for their expeditions, and sell their booty.

Some forty thousand Moriscos were warmly received in Tetuán by a population that was composed primarily of earlier Muslim and Morisco émigrés from Andalusia. Here some Moriscos became prominent in corsair activities, others as owners of Christian slaves. In contrast, Salé, on the Atlantic side of Morocco, declined to admit twelve hundred expellees from the Extremaduran village of Hornachos in 1610. When the old community of Salé, repelled by their non-Muslim ways, rejected them, the Hornacheros moved to the south bank of the Bou Regreg estuary, where they erected a citadel that became known as the Casbah of Salé.

The Hornacheros had a reputation as thieves and brigands, who while still in Spain allegedly bribed agents of the Spanish crown to permit them to carry arms. According to contemporary sources, in spite of the reservations of the people of Salé (the Slawis), who called them the "Christians of Castile," they were sincere Muslims who had retained not only their Islamic faith but the Arabic language as well.[59] The community that they established was prosperous, since its members had succeeded in bringing all their belongings with them from Spain.

So the Moriscos who settled at the Casbah possessed both wealth and a bandit tradition. They also had cohesion, a firm attachment to Islam, and a desire both for revenge against Spain and to prove to the Slawis that their suspicions about their faith were incorrect. Once having established themselves at the Casbah, they encouraged other Morisco refugees to settle nearby, in the area that became the modern city of Rabat. There the group known as the Andalusians created a community that was separate from and often feuding with the Hornachero settlement of the Casbah.

Thus, there were three separate states in the Bou Regreg estuary, all of which were quasi-republics in the face of the political turmoil and civil wars in Morocco at that time. Although Europeans of the period referred to all of them collectively as Salé, it is important to note that the famous "Sallee Rovers" of the seventeenth century were not from Salé at all but from the newly established Morisco settlement on the opposite bank of the Bou Regreg, referred to hereafter as Rabat-Salé.

The Moriscos of Rabat-Salé were engaged almost exclusively in piracy and related activities; from early in the seventeenth century this was the most important source of wealth for the region. The Hornacheros furnished the initial capital for the establishment of the corsair fleet, which by the third decade of the seventeenth century numbered some thirty to forty vessels of twenty cannons each. In the mid-1630s the size of the fleet was estimated at forty to fifty vessels. The captains themselves provided a large share of the financing for their cruises, although this was a popular form of investment for others as well. Indeed, the formerly aloof Slawis of the right bank participated in corsair activity both as investors and crew members. Furthermore, a merchant community that dealt in corsair booty grew up in Rabat-Salé.[60]

The creation of this corsair community on the Atlantic coast of Morocco was a direct result of the expulsion of the Moriscos from Spain. While shipbuilding and piracy had existed in old Salé since the thirteenth century, the development of a fleet of corsairs who "could terrorize the high seas and the coasts of Europe did not begin until the arrival of the Hornacheros and Moriscos on the left bank of the Bou Regreg."[61]

Various factors contributed to the success of the new corsair capital. Its geographical situation was vital. The entrance to the Bou Regreg was guarded by a sand bar that permitted entry only to smaller vessels and provided a sheltered harbor from which access to Spain's Atlantic coast and shipping lanes was relatively simple. European corsairs were an invaluable source of technical skills. In 1603 James I of England had expelled the English and Dutch corsairs from English ports. Many of them transferred their operations to La Mamora, on the Moroccan coast, but they were forced to leave in 1614, when it was occupied by Spain. At that time, they were welcomed into the Bou Regreg community and incorporated into the corsair fleet. In 1624 a Dutch renegade was named captain of that fleet.[62]

In addition, corsairs from Algiers and other parts of the eastern Maghrib began to frequent the Bou Regreg region, stopping there to replenish their supplies, refit their vessels, and sell their booty. In the redemptions carried out by the Spanish orders in the earlier decades of the seventeenth century, many captives were listed as having been seized by Algerian pirates and then taken to Salé to be sold. The Algerians came and went freely with no obligation other than the payment of a tax on the booty they sold. These taxes, which in 1622 were levied at a rate of 15 percent, were an important source of income for the state.[63] Some of the Algerian corsairs even transferred their operations entirely to Rabat-Salé, where they became an integral element in the corsair community, providing not only additional manpower but also generations of experience.

Thus, the importance of the corsair settlement at Rabat-Salé lay not merely in the activities of the Morisco exiles, but also in the opportunities they provided for the increasingly aggressive corsairs of the eastern Maghrib and northern Europe by creating a safe base from which they could operate in the Atlantic. At the same time, it was the presence of these experienced corsairs from other regions that assured the prosperity of the new settlements.

Spain was the principal target of the corsairs of Rabat-Salé. Although their expeditions sometimes took them as far north as the English Channel and perhaps even Iceland, their sphere of operations was generally within 500 miles of the Bou Regreg estuary, and included the Iberian coasts and the Atlantic islands.[64] In September 1635, two fleets, totaling twenty-two ships, sailed from Rabat-Salé; one headed for the Canary Islands to lie in wait for the returning Indies fleet, while the other went toward the Spanish coast.[65] The degree to which the activities of these corsairs were concentrated on the Atlantic coasts of Spain is suggested by a list of captives ransomed from the Casbah by the Trinitarians in 1632. Of fifty-three captives, thirty had been seized on the coasts of Galicia. It is worth noting that twenty-five of them were fishermen.[66]

Thus, while the expulsion of the Moriscos may have eliminated from Spain a potential "fifth column," it also contributed to the augmentation of North African piracy against Spanish coasts and shipping that presented a far greater danger than had the presence of the Moriscos in Spain. The expulsion provided for the corsairs crew members with a desire for revenge as well as an intimate and invaluable knowledge of the Spanish coasts, it strengthened the ideological base for corsairing, and it led to the creation by expelled Moriscos of the settlement at Rabat-Salé, which not only devoted itself to corsairing and related activities, but also eased the movement of the anti-Spanish corsairs of the Mediterranean into the Atlantic.

The Decline of the Corsairs

Political changes in North Africa in the seventeenth century and a powerful effort against the corsairs by the European sea powers brought about a decline in North African corsairing from the last third of the seventeenth century.

In Morocco, the autocratic sultan, Mawlay Ismāᶜēl, met with considerable success in restricting the activities of the corsairs of that region. Mawlay Ismāᶜēl attempted to proscribe corsair activity because he regarded it as incompatible with the genuine economic development of Morocco and the extension of its legitimate commercial activities that were part of his program.[67] An added factor may have been his wish to restrain the corsairs, the element of Moroccan society that was most independent and least susceptible to control by a centralizing monarch.

In contrast to Morocco, the political decay that began in Algiers at the end of the sixteenth century continued through the seventeenth and even the eighteenth centuries, a time that was marked by disorder, abdications, and assassinations. During the course of the seventeenth century, the authority of the Porte-appointed paşa gradually deteriorated, and the government of the state came entirely into the hands of the ağa, who was aided by the divan. In 1671, the last of the ruling ağas was assassinated by the reis, who replaced him with a ruler of their own choosing, the *dey* (governor). In 1710, the dey took the title of paşa as well, and assumed autocratic rule. This change, however, did not make the Algiers of the eighteenth century more orderly than that of the seventeenth.

It is difficult to estimate the extent, if any, to which this political disorder affected the Algerian corsairs. Certainly, it did not retard their activities during the first half of the seventeenth century. This was the great age of the corsairs, when their status in Algerian government and society was commensurate with the important role that corsairing played in the economy. But in the long run, the chaos may have exacted its toll. From the last third of the seventeenth century, the size of the corsair fleet and the extent of corsair activity declined, due primarily to Algiers' vulnerability to action taken against it by the British, Dutch, and French navies. This included the destruction of seven of its best ships by a British fleet in 1671, the sinking by Dutch warships of eighteen corsair vessels in its harbor in 1673, and the bombardment of the city of Algiers in 1683 by the French, in which the powder works were blown up and large numbers of people were killed.[68] The primary effect of this offensive was to force Algiers into treaties which protected the commerce of these powerful maritime states against corsair assaults.

Spain benefited little from these developments. The Barbary pirates continued their assaults on Spanish coasts and shipping, though on a smaller scale than before, throughout most of the eighteenth century. Indeed, the situation was so serious that in 1724 the Spanish crown, foregoing its usual fifth, granted to privateers from Spain's Mediterranean regions full rights to any corsairs they captured, in order to encourage those who were interested in "cleaning up the coasts." Two years later, it authorized all boat owners to arm their vessels for corsairing against the North Africans.[69] These measures did not end the danger; in 1734, the *regidores* (city councilors) of Blanes in Catalonia reported that the coastline was "infested with Moors" and that seven fishermen had recently been seized very close to their village.[70]

The quantitative survey reinforces the impression of a continuing North African offensive against Spain's coasts in the eighteenth century. The statistics for the first decade of the century are dominated by military captives, who were taken prisoner when Spain lost Orán to Algiers in 1709. The reason for this is that the ransoming expeditions to North Africa in the years following the Spanish defeat were made for the specific purpose of rescuing soldiers who had been seized during this conflict, to the almost complete exclusion of other captives, except for those from the carrera de las Indias. Of the 847 individuals in the survey who were captured between 1700 and 1709, 54.7 percent had been taken prisoner at Orán. In this same period, the percentage of captives from the Indies fleet rose to almost 10 percent of the total. This rise was only temporary and may have been due to the same factors that contributed to the defeat at Orán—Spain's complete preoccupation with the war at home, the War of the Spanish Succession. During these years, captives from coastal regions represented only 9.7 percent of those surveyed.

In the following decade the proportion of captives seized on the Spanish coasts rose to 31.8 percent, while they accounted for 46.8 percent of those captured in the 1720s. It is not possible to observe the trends from 1730 to 1749, because of the absence of sufficient data for those years, but during the last two decades surveyed, 1750–1769, captives abducted on the coasts of Spain constituted 63.5 percent of the total. Only 7 percent had been captured in North Africa, while 21 percent were taken at sea in the Mediterranean. These figures reflect not only corsair attacks on the Mediterranean coasts but also continued activity in northwestern Spain, which accounted for 7.7 percent of all captives surveyed in the eighteenth century. It is clear then that during most of the eighteenth century, when North African piracy was ostensively in decline, the overwhelming majority of Spanish captives in North Africa had been victims of piracy, and the Spanish coasts were the source of more than half the total.

In the final analysis, for the better part of two centuries the problem of captives in North Africa was not one of prisoners of war in the traditional sense—that is, fighting men seized during military engagements—but rather of those who lived or worked on the Spanish coasts. Throughout nearly all of the age under study, these captives were the largest single group in the Spanish captive population, and often constituted a majority of that population. Most of those captured on the coasts were civilians who were seized while engaged in commonplace, everyday activities.

The problem of defending against attacks on the coasts was one that vexed both the crown and the affected localities. In the seventeenth century, critics of the redemption frequently proposed that the money spent to ransom captives would be better utilized for an armada that would effectively guard the coasts of Spain and end corsair activity there. Many of them pointed out that the certainty that ransoms would be paid stimulated, rather than discouraged, corsair aggression. The redemptionist friars objected, arguing that even in the unlikely event that the coasts were to cease to be a source of captives, Spaniards would still be captured at sea or in North Africa itself.[71]

The critics were undoubtedly correct. As we shall see in later chapters, the expansion in corsairing was accompanied by an augmentation of the activities of the friars, both in ransoming and providing a variety of services that were intended to ease the plight of those captives who were left behind. This certainly encouraged the Muslims in their exploits, by ensuring that the taking of Spanish captives would be profitable.

Although it is doubtful that serious consideration was given to terminating the redemption at this time, the fact that critics urged the shifting of resources to coastal defenses indicates that in the seventeenth century the seizure of captives from the coasts was regarded as the most serious aspect of the problem of Spanish captives in North Africa. That it continued to be in the eighteenth century is not only shown by the statistical evidence, but is underscored by a request made in 1740 by the crown to the captains-general of the coastal provinces for suggestions for a "radical remedy" to the problem of Muslim corsairs on the coasts of Spain.[72]

Chapter 2
The Response to the Challenge

Various measures were taken to prevent pirate attacks on the coastal villages of Spain and to protect coastal shipping. These were frequently inadequate, often due to the reluctance of the crown, which was badly overextended, the localities, or the local noblemen to provide the necessary financing and manpower. Indeed, it is by no means clear, nor was it at the time, where responsibility for defense lay.

Areas where the crown had established fortresses were defended by these. But the protection of the cities and villages along the coast was often the responsibility of local militias.[1] A common measure, the remnants of which can still be seen along the Spanish coasts today, was the erection of watchtowers and fortifications, both for observation and defense. For example, in response to major corsair attacks in 1543, fortifications were erected by the Catalán villages of Rosas and Palamós.[2] In 1577 the crown authorized the construction of defensive towers by localities all along the Mediterranean coast.[3] The lookouts in the towers were to warn of the arrival of pirates. They alerted not only their own villages, but also adjoining towns and any defense forces that might be nearby.[4] In Andalusia, the sentries usually depended on a combination of smoke signals and beacons for their warning system.[5] In the Catalán village of Bagur sirens were used. In addition, a bugler went through the village playing a warning tune called "Moors on the Coast."[6] This alarm system was successful on Holy Saturday in 1588, when five North African galleys were spied from the watchtower of Tortosa. Word was sent to the fleet of Gian Andrea Doria, which was outside Barcelona at the time and sailed down to repel the corsairs.[7]

From the late sixteenth century the crown frequently re-

33

sponded to the demands of coastal residents for protection by licensing privateers to go out in search of Muslim vessels. Perhaps the best-known privateer was Juan Felipe Romano, who not only pursued Muslim ships but also conducted raids on Algiers in order to rescue Christian captives.[8] There were others as well. On May 8, 1595, the viceroy of Valencia wrote to the king asking him to allow Bartolomé Estevan, who owned a vessel of fourteen oars, to "*andar en corso.*" At the same time, the crown authorized Estevan to travel to North Africa to negotiate the ransom of captives.[9]

In 1625 Francisco Imperial of Alicante requested permission to engage in corsairing with three large, heavily armed, seagoing ships.[10] The viceroy of Valencia, in recommending Imperial to the crown, noted that the coasts of the kingdom were so harassed by Muslim corsairs that there were daily incidents of piracy at sea and on land, and large numbers of people were being captured. Since there were no galleys in the region "or other warships that can safeguard the sea," he viewed private corsairing as an important means of combating North African piracy.[11]

In the seventeenth and eighteenth centuries, the most active Spanish privateers were the Mallorcans, who at least as early as the mid-seventeenth century regularly went out in search of Muslim corsairs.[12] The degree of their effectiveness is unknown, but they undoubtedly were of some value since in 1724, when Mallorcan corsairing had been suspended for some time due to an epidemic, the administrator of the Trinitarian hospital in Algiers wrote of the extraordinarily large numbers of captives who had recently been seized on the Spanish coasts. He attributed the increase in captives from these areas to the ban on corsairing by the Mallorcans. In the past, he said, they had been able either to drive some of the North Africans out of Spanish waters or even to capture them.[13] A less formal type of citizen participation in the defense of the coasts was encouraged by the crown, which frequently conceded to residents of Valencia who captured Muslims the entire value of the capture. In the sixteenth century, if the prize was a fugitive Morisco, the captor was granted, in addition, all money and goods that the runaway had left in Spain.[14]

In general the efficacy of coastal defense was limited. Complaints about the failure to safeguard the coastline were frequent in the Cortes of the period. In 1551 the *procuradores* noted that Muslim raiders had done great damage to Cartagena and that the reason for this was that the coast was unprotected.[15] They were concerned too about the effect that this piracy had on Spain's economy. They complained that commerce in the Mediterranean had virtually ceased because of the activities of the Muslim corsairs, who had also caused a great deal of destruction on the coasts of Spain. Pride and honor were involved, as well. It was a disgrace, they said, that a single frontier region such as Algiers could cause such damage and offense to the entire Spanish kingdom. It was suggested that since the king paid so much money each year to maintain galleys and had so many important fleets, he assign some of them exclusively to the defense of the Spanish coasts, from Perpignan to the Guadalquivir River.[16] Another petition in the same Cortes asked that fortifications along the Mediterranean coast be improved, especially in the important cities of Cádiz, Gibraltar, and Cartagena.[17]

In 1560 the procuradores objected to the use of the Spanish fleet in the attempt to conquer Tripoli and proposed that, in view of the damage that Muslim corsairs did to the agriculture and commerce of Spain, the armada be occupied solely in defending its Mediterranean coast.[18] They failed to recognize that the conquest of Tripoli, a corsair center, would have brought greater security to the coast than a naval patrol.

In 1566 they charged that "the galleys spend the spring in Italy and other parts, and the coasts of these kingdoms remain unguarded." Coastal defense was so poor, they added, that even a few Muslim vessels could do a great deal of damage and carry away large numbers of captives. The petitioners regarded the situation as scandalous. "It is not right," they remarked, "that the greatest monarch of the world should rule a land that is so insecure and poorly defended."[19]

More important than the lack of coastal patrols by the galleys, which were of questionable value in any case,[20] was the state of land-based defenses. Officials of the coastal regions regularly complained about these. In 1556, the *corregidor* (royal official of the town) and *alcalde* (municipal justice) of Málaga wrote to the crown concerning the poor condition of the fortresses of that important city, which suffered from severe shortages of arms and ammunition as well as coastal guards and defensive forces.[21] Two years later the situation had apparently not improved. In a letter of June 23, 1558, the corregidor, Francisco de Molina, reiterated the earlier complaints about shortages of men and ammunition, and added that many of the watchtowers had collapsed or were in an advanced state of deterioration. He noted that the circumstances were particularly acute at that moment, since he had received reports that twenty corsair galleys had left Algiers for the coast of Andalusia.[22]

Also in 1558, a series of communications from the count of Tendilla indicated that such conditions were not confined to Málaga, but existed on the entire littoral of the kingdom of Granada. In a report on the defensive state of key spots along the long coastline, from Mojácar at the eastern end to Fuengirola in the west, he presented a picture of defenses that, with few exceptions, were in an advanced state of decay—undermanned, poorly munitioned, and virtually indefensible in the event of an attack by a powerful fleet. He noted that he had frequently advised the crown of the deteriorating state of the towers and had requested authorization to raise money for their repair from the cities of the kingdom, but no action had been taken.

As for the shortage of coastal guards, the count of Tendilla found it impossible to recruit individuals for those posts because the salary fixed by the crown was only 25 or 30 maravedís per day, a rate that had been established sixty years earlier. Since prices had tripled in that time, and the job was a taxing and very dangerous one, it was not possible to find people willing to serve for such low wages. Those who were willing were unsuitable for the positions.[23] Finally, the defensive forces of the region were inadequate. In September he wrote that the pay of the 350 soldiers who were normally stationed on the coast of Granada was two years behind, and for that reason many of them had left for Orán to take part in the count of Alcaudete's ill-fated expedition against Mostaganem. He noted that those who had departed were the best men, and the ones most familiar with the coast; few of those who remained were of this quality.[24]

In spite of the count of Tendilla's repeated pleas for assistance, the situation in Granada was unchanged when the Morisco rebellion erupted in 1569. Indeed, their awareness of this military weakness may have encouraged the Moriscos to revolt.[25] Nor was there an improvement in forces after the rebellion had been suppressed. Late in 1571 the duke of Arcos wrote to the king that the companies of coastal guards in Granada were less than half up to muster, and were especially short of cavalry. According to the captains with whom he had spoken, the reason was that the men had not been paid in two or, in some cases, three years. He reported further that the watchtowers of Motril and other parts of the coast were without sentries, because the pay had not been raised since the early part of the century and was too low in view of the risks involved.[26] The danger of the work becomes apparent when one examines the redemption books and encounters many individuals who were seized while guarding the coasts. One of these was a sentry named Bartolomé Claro of Almuñécar, who was captured as he was hurrying to warn the people of his village that five Algerian boats had just landed on the coast. He spent twenty-three years in captivity.[27]

Supplies of munitions were also inadequate. In 1571 Sancho de Leyva, captain-general of the Galleys of Spain, wrote to the king concerning the lack of provisions in the presidios of Andalusia. The shortages, he said, were due to the failure of the quartermaster to fulfill his obligations.[28] An inventory of the armaments in the nine presidios of Barcelona in 1571 contains the note that "most of the arms contained in this report are of no value because they are old and broken."[29]

In 1562, when fear of Muslim attack was particularly intense, Philip II attempted to remedy this situation in Valencia by dispatching the engineer Gian Baptista Antonelli to make an inspection tour of the ports, towers, and fortifications of the kingdom and to make recommendations and provide cost estimates for their repair. The viceroy was directed to take immediate steps to raise the money from the localities involved in order to carry out Antonelli's recommendations.[30]

In Antonelli's final report, submitted in 1569, he pointed out what would be immediately apparent to a traveler even today: that the coast was a corsair's paradise, since it was studded with coves where small vessels could easily land at night and be concealed. It also had numerous sources of fresh water, which made it doubly attractive to corsair vessels. He recommended the construction of towers equipped with artillery at all coves and sources of fresh water. His advocacy of towers as an effective means of coastal defense was based on two factors: they would eliminate the corsairs' hiding places and force them out on the open sea, where they could be easily sighted, and they could warn ships at sea of the corsairs' presence. Furthermore, the eradication of their hiding places would end the easy communication that the corsairs had with the Moriscos. Antonelli proposed, in addition, that a fortress be erected on Santa Pola, on the Valencian coast, which was a favorite haunt of the Muslim corsairs. He concluded by pointing out that the investment in the construction of new towers and the repair of old ones, as recommended, would result in a well-guarded coastline, which could then be defended by only two cavalry companies. He noted that the cost of these companies (12,000 ducats) would equal that of the salaries for two galleys, which were clearly not sufficient to guard the long coastline. Antonelli advocated this method of defense for the entire Spanish coast and the Mediterranean islands and estimated that the expense of providing it would be equivalent to the cost of only ten galleys.[31]

In 1570 Antonelli reported on a survey he had made of the Murcian coast. His observations and recommendations concerning this region were essentially similar to those for Valencia.[32]

The documents do not reveal the extent to which Antonelli's recommendations were carried out, but in 1601 the kingdom of Valencia was terrorized by five Algerian galleys that for several months used Santa Pola with impunity as a base from which to attack shipping and the Valencian coast. There was no manned fortress there at that time and it is doubtful that one ever was erected.

The incident at Santa Pola demonstrates vividly that, despite frequent demands in the Cortes for greater protection of the coasts by galley fleets, the galleys were often useless for coastal defense. The plea of the count of Benavente, viceroy of Valencia, for six to eight "well-armed galleys" to come to the rescue had to be turned down by the Council of State on the grounds that the Galleys of Spain, the only ones that could help, were already in their winter port and could not be brought out again quickly enough to be of any value. The date of Benavente's first appeal was November 22, and at that time the council advised him that eight galleys would be made available at the beginning of March.[33] In fact, they were probably already scheduled to be put into commission at that time, since March was the start of the traditional campaigning season.

The problem, however, was not simply one of galleys and fortifications. Undoubtedly, the most effective means of controlling corsair assaults on the coasts would have been to strike a blow against the pirate bases, the only role for which Spain's galley squadrons were tactically well suited. This was the policy that both Ferdinand the Catholic and Charles V had pursued and then abandoned in order to direct their energies and resources toward Europe. It was taken up again by Philip II, but only briefly and with limited results. In 1564 Spain sent a fleet to the river of Tetuán, in order to block the passage of corsair vessels from that region. The effort was successful, but its effect was only temporary. The campaign by the Holy League that culminated in the Battle of Lepanto was also viewed as a means of dealing with Muslim corsairing, but, as we have seen, its consequences too were short-lived.

There is no evidence of any comprehensive, long-range program on the part of the crown to bolster coastal defenses or to take the offensive against the corsairs. The archives are replete with documentation of missions such as Antonelli's to Valencia and Murcia, but there is no indication that the recommendations of the surveyors were ever carried out to more than a limited degree.

An example of the difficulties involved in implementing programs for defense is provided by the mission of Luis Bravo de Laguna. In 1577, Philip II sent Bravo, a military engineer, on a tour of western Andalusia in order to study the condition of its coastal defenses and to make proposals for their improvement. He reported that the region inspected was poorly protected, particularly in view of the constant danger of Muslim corsair raids to which it was exposed. In some places there were no fortifications at all; in many regions where fortifications nominally existed, in reality they were all but dismantled, and most defensive sites that were still standing were poorly manned and short of artillery. In some areas where defensive works were underway, the work proceeded slowly and carelessly. Furthermore, there were numerous strategic places where corsairs were likely to strike that did not contain even rudimentary defenses.[34]

A good example was the city of Gibraltar, which in 1540 had been so poorly protected that an Algerian corsair fleet was able, with little difficulty, to land there and disembark some nine hundred men, who sacked the city and took numerous captives. More than a third of a century later, Gibraltar's fortifications and armaments remained inadequate. Bravo described similar conditions for other localities along the coast. Particularly vulnerable was the area known as the Arenas Gordas in the Bay of Cádiz, which he characterized as so dangerous that "anyone who could not travel through the region armed with arcabuses and protected by cavalry ought not do so at all."[35] The danger of being taken captive that was always present in this region was underscored for the engineer by a close call that he himself experienced. While surveying the Arenas Gordas area, he witnessed the seizure of four caravels by Muslim galliots and barely escaped being captured himself when he was nearly trapped on a promontory jutting out to sea.

Bravo recommended the construction or repair of many of the fortifications in the western Andalusia region, but by 1608 only a fraction had been completed. Others had been started, but the work abandoned while the crown and the local lords engaged in a long legal struggle over the financial responsibility for the construction and maintenance of the new defenses.[36] Indeed, the story of the attempt to improve defenses along this coast is one of almost complete paralysis of the royal government machinery as a result of this protracted lawsuit and the opposition and resistance of the high nobility of the region.

In Valencia, too, there were numerous arguments between officials of the crown and the local governments over responsibility for costs. Even in the face of an upsurge in Algerian corsairing on the Valencian coast in 1582, the Cortes vigorously protested, as a violation of the *fueros* (legal codes), the viceroy's actions in exacting 100,000 libras from the *Diputación* for fortifications and directing the quartering in certain districts of eighteen infantry companies intended to provide defense against the corsairs. In 1585, when Philip II visited Valencia, the Cortes tried to persuade him to restore the 100,000 libras and reimburse the localities for the cost of quartering the infantry. On the other hand, the estates were willing to bear a portion of the burden. In 1564, for example, the Cortes of Valencia agreed to a new tax on the export of silk in order to raise 12,000 libras a year for the support of the coastal guard and upkeep of the towers. During the years following Lepanto, the sense of danger was so acute in Valencia that the viceroy, the marqués de Mondéjar, had little difficulty persuading the Cortes to contribute 100,000 libras for fortifications. In 1585 the Cortes did agree, in spite of their protests against the measures of 1582, to an increase in the silk export tax for the purpose of coastal defense. But when the financing of the improvements proposed by Gian Baptista Antonelli had fallen on the cities and villages of the Valencian littoral, they had vigorously opposed the project in the Valencian Cortes of 1564, complaining that they could not afford the cost.[37] Decades later, in April 1637, when the coasts of the kingdom were dangerously exposed to attack, the Diputación maintained the position that defense was the crown's responsibility, and not theirs.[38]

The limited coastal defense system of the sixteenth century seems to have decayed even further in the seventeenth, when communications concerning the disrepair of the fortifications,

the lack of men to defend the coasts, the shortages of munitions, and the question of who would pay the costs became
even more insistent. In 1635, the marqués de los Vélez, then
viceroy of Valencia, wrote that the entire coast of the kingdom
was almost completely defenseless. He noted that the tower
of Castellón de la Plana had collapsed and that many others
were in such poor condition that they were of no value in the
event of an invasion. He added that even the towers that still
stood were worth little; their weapons were broken and many
towers were even unmanned. The coastal guard was severely
understaffed since many of the soldiers, who had not been
paid for eight years, had deserted.[39] Thirty years later another
viceroy wrote that the entire coast, including the ports, was
completely open to attack. The local officials would do no more
to remedy the situation than to provide sentries for the watchtowers; they insisted that the coastal patrol and defense of the
realm were the crown's obligations.[40] In 1695 the *Junta Municipal* of Orihuela wrote to the crown that its old tower had
deteriorated so badly that it was of no value for defense. The
junta pointed out that the tower was in the area of the salt
pans, which were part of the royal regalia, and since its chief
purpose was to protect those panning salt, the crown ought to
pay for the construction of a new tower and the installation in
it of a cannon.[41]

Similar conditions existed in Andalusia. In 1628 the king
advised the duke of Medina Sidonia of the sighting of a fleet
of forty-five Algerian corsair vessels that appeared to be head-
ing toward the Andalusian coast, and directed him to take the
necessary precautions. The duke replied that it would be difficult to defend the region, since the armada was at sea and
the presidio of Cádiz had only eighty-five soldiers. Other cities, he added, were also short of men. The duke emphasized
especially the vulnerability of Cádiz, which even in the sixteenth century had been regarded as not only difficult to defend because of its site, but also poorly fortified and protected.[42] Indeed, according to one historian, Cádiz was so
threatened by and exposed to corsair attack that on several
occasions consideration was given to transferring its commercial and business activities to a more secure spot.[43]

Defenses were poor in Galicia, too. In May 1617, when Muslim corsairs were sighted in Galician waters, the marqués de Cerralvo wrote to the king that if the corsairs had attacked the coast none of the villages would have been able to defend themselves because of a lack of munitions.[44] On November 15 of the same year, Alvaro de Mendoza, military commander of the Ría de Arosa district, wrote to the marqués concerning the great danger of North African corsair attack to many of the villages in his district. He pointed out that of the nine ports, three were entirely exposed, and the others were also highly vulnerable. The threat lay not only in their positions but also in their shortage of defensive forces and munitions. Mendoza noted that since there were few soldiers in the region, in order to help one village under invasion he would have to bring men from another, thus leaving it open to attack.[45]

Mendoza's warnings were borne out a month later, when he was unable to defend Cangas against Muslim corsairs. In the wake of the attack, he wrote to the marqués that he had been able to do little because of the terrible state of the defensive forces, who were not only ill clad, ill fed, and undermanned, but also poorly armed. He advised the marqués that the Muslims who had sacked Cangas were still in the region, but that he could provide no defense against them because of the lack of powder and munitions.[46]

In 1620 the marqués wrote to several high-ranking Galician churchmen concerning the danger to which the region was exposed because of the "freedom with which Muslim corsair boats travel along the coast." He pointed out that there were no Spanish warships in the area to help drive them away and suggested that since a captured Christian represented a potentially lost soul, the Galician church ought to finance the construction of six large vessels to defend the region.[47]

The Presidios

Another attempt to check the corsair threat was the erection and maintenance of a string of fortifications and presidios along the North African coast. Although this policy was initiated during the reign of Ferdinand the Catholic, the "age of the

presidios" began in earnest only in the second half of the sixteenth century, when Philip II adopted a policy of "prudence
and calculation rather than adventure," one that, save for a few
isolated though memorable expeditions, emphasized defense
rather than offense. From this time on, efforts to eliminate the
corsair danger were concentrated on the reinforcement and
extension of the presidio system.[48]

The presidios were an inadequate response to the corsair
challenge. Not only did they fail to achieve their goal of stopping the Muslim corsairs, but they created many new problems as well. Their cost in money and men was inordinately
high. In the mid-1560s salaries alone for the string of presidios
from El Peñón de Vélez to La Goletta totaled 209,000 ducats
a year. To this must be added the expenses of supply and
upkeep of the fortifications. This compares with an estimated
7,000 ducats for the maintenance of a galley and 36,000 ducats
for the guard on the coasts of the Balearic Islands or from
Cartagena to Cádiz. As we have seen, Gian Baptista Antonelli
estimated that 12,000 ducats for two companies would be adequate to defend the coasts of Valencia. Furthermore, the presidios immobilized large numbers of men, who could not be
summoned quickly for other service.[49]

The North African presidios were not only expensive to
maintain, but difficult to supply as well. Because they were
Spanish islands in an Islamic sea, they had to depend almost
entirely on the import of provisions, including food, from Spain.
But the supplies often did not arrive; in that event the men
went hungry. Even Orán, the one presidio that was able to
obtain food from friendly Muslims, the so-called *moros de paz*,
in the surrounding countryside, often suffered severe deficiencies. From the early years of the seventeenth century the
governors of Orán frequently complained to the crown about
the miserable conditions under which their men lived. These
included inadequate food and clothing and a heavy burden of
work because the presidio was short of manpower.[50]

The situation throughout the entire North African presidio
system seems to have become critical in the early decades of
the seventeenth century, when notices of serious shortages

arrived regularly in Madrid. In May 1600 the general of Tangiers wrote that more than two months had passed since wheat, biscuit, or other provisions had been distributed to the soldiers. In addition, the garrison was dangerously short of arms with which to defend itself in the event of an attack.[51] The duke of Medina Sidonia, who as captain-general of Andalusia was responsible for supplying the Moroccan presidios, noted that he had ordered supplies to be sent from Portugal, but since the suppliers had not been paid in the past he could find no one who would fill the order. In March 1610 the general of the presidio at Larache wrote that his supplies of biscuit would last only four or five more days. He added that the hospitals were filled with the sick and the number of soldiers available for service was shrinking daily.[52] In January 1613 Medina Sidonia passed on to the Council of State a report from the general of Tangiers that he had only enough wheat left for four more days and one from the general of Mazagán that his men were eating horses and dogs. The duke noted that he had sent 1,000 *fanegas* of wheat from his own stocks. He added that although he had advised Lisbon of the pressing need, nothing had been sent from there.[53]

Although the difficulties in supplying the presidios were partly attributable to maladministration, there were other problems as well. Supply ships traveling between Spain and North Africa were frequently captured by corsairs. Furthermore, food shortages in Spain often made it difficult, if not impossible, to provision the presidios. The letters of the duke of Medina Sidonia contain numerous references to this problem.

The dearth of food and supplies, which made famine a constant threat, contributed to the low morale of the men at the presidios. But these were not the only causes of dissatisfaction. The men in the presidios were poorly paid—their salaries were lower than those in Italy—and the pay arrived irregularly. In November 1606 the count of Aguilar, governor-general of Orán, wrote that his men had not been paid for some time and were nearly impoverished. The Council of State directed that they be paid at once, "in view of what might happen if they were not." In March 1612, Aguilar again wrote that the men had not been paid. They were so financially pressed, he said, that he feared many of them, in order to escape their debts, would take the drastic step of deserting to the Muslims.[54] The early-seventeenth-century Mercedarian, Friar Isidro de Valcazar, blamed the poor morale in the presidios on the harsh conditions of life there, the low pay, the cruelty of the Spanish commanders, and the usual permanence of an assignment to a North African presidio. As Braudel notes, it was tantamount to deportation.[55]

In view of these circumstances, for many soldiers there appeared to be little difference between life in the North African presidios and life as a slave in a Muslim state. It is not surprising, therefore, that large numbers of men fled from the presidios and allowed themselves to be captured by the Muslims. The gravity of the problem was noted before the Council of State in 1611, when the archbishop of Toledo reported that many soldiers from Orán, which was under his ecclesiastical jurisdiction, were fleeing to the Muslims, "driven by hunger and lack of clothing and the impossibility and hopelessness of ever being able to return to Spain."[56] The council recommended that soldiers be kept in North Africa for only limited time periods and that those with the longest tenure be sent elsewhere. There is no indication of whether any attempt was made to carry out the recommendation; if so, it did not solve the problem, since Friar Valcazar wrote that in the redemption he made in Morocco in 1615 he had seen more than 150 deserters, who were known to the Muslims and the redemptors as *bienvenidos*.[57] In 1619 the duke of Maqueda, governor of Orán, submitted to the Council of State a list of 424 men who were known or believed to have gone over to the Muslims during the period from August 1608 to September 1619. He blamed the desertions on the miserable conditions under which the soldiers lived in Orán, as a result of which "they seem more demons than men."[58]

Desertions to the Muslims continued to plague the presidios in the eighteenth century. During the eight-and-one-half-year period from 1742 through mid-1750, the combined total of deserters to the Muslims from Orán and Ceuta was 763.[59]

The deserters appear to have been motivated by the belief

that life under the North Africans would be no worse than it was in the Spanish presidios and by the hope that the redemptionist friars would not recognize them as deserters and would ransom and return them to Spain. The reception that these men received from the Muslims did not live up to their expectations. Few private slave owners would buy them, since they had no ransom value unless the redemptionists could be deceived about their identity. Therefore, nearly all of them became slaves of the state and were used primarily for the most onerous tasks—rowing in the galleys and public works projects. Furthermore, they were not generally permitted, while still enslaved, to convert to Islam, since they were not regarded as trustworthy. As one eighteenth-century Mercedarian remarked, the Algerians "esteem ten pesos more than ten renegades of this sort."[60]

In spite of the efforts to identify deserters, the redemptionists often did inadvertently rescue them. Some of those ransomed realized that they might have to face desertion charges on their return to Spain and apostatized after the ransom had been paid in order to live as free men in North Africa. But many others took the chance that their identities would remain secret and returned home.

Forty of the captives rescued from Algiers by the Mercedarians in late 1751 were detained by the authorities as suspected deserters after they arrived in Spain. All were returned to Orán to face trial. The following May the governor-general of Orán reported to Madrid that, in an attempt to stem "this serious epidemic," severe punishments had been meted out to those who were convicted of desertion. Three were hung, to serve as "mute preachers against this scandal." The governor expressed the belief that the exemplary punishments had been efficacious, since the desertion rate had dropped from ten per month to only three in the two months prior to his letter.[61] Whatever the reason, the number of deserters from Orán and Ceuta did decline during the next few years. From April 1753 to February 1755, only thirty-seven men deserted from the two presidios. During the same time period there were thirty-nine deserters from the presidio at Melilla.[62]

Deserters were not the only captives to come from the presidios. The were many legitimate captives as well, since any foray outside the walls of the garrisons held the danger of seizure by Muslims lying in wait. Twelve percent of all those surveyed were seized in North Africa. While a number were taken in actual military engagements, most were captured in the environs of the presidios while collecting firewood or other necessities. In 1680, for example, a group of soldiers and officers was captured in the fields outside the walls of Ceuta, where some had been gathering firewood and others were allowing their horses to forage. Among those seized were five of the "principal *caballeros*" of Ceuta, including Don Antonio Correa, who was a slave of the Moroccan emperor in Meknès for eight years until he was ransomed for 300 pesos and two Muslim slaves in Spain.[63] Numerous other examples of captives seized in similar circumstances can be found in the redemption books and the records of the Council of the Cruzada.[64] Thus, the presidios actually exacerbated the problem for which they were meant to provide a solution—that of large numbers of Spaniards being taken captive by North African Muslims.

Although the presidios contributed to the Spanish captive population, the most prominent members of this group throughout the early modern age, as we have seen, were those captured along Spain's coasts. There can be little doubt that the offensive of the North African corsairs helped shape certain characteristics of those coastal regions. It contributed to the gradual abandonment of portions of the coast, a phenomenon that was noted even in the early sixteenth century. In 1508, in an effort to repopulate the coast of Granada after the dispersal of the Moriscos, Ferdinand the Catholic granted the village of Almayate to the count of Tendilla, with the special privilege of permitting Moriscos as well as old Christians to settle there. However, Muslim attacks on the area were so frequent that settlers found it too risky to live there, and the village remained sparsely populated. Tendilla finally tried to sell the property, but even though he advertised its income at twice the actual value he was still unable to dispose of it.[65]

Within a century, long stretches of coastline had been abandoned. Indeed, the only inhabited areas on the Mediterranean coast were those that had strong walls and were considered well fortified. Significant portions of the coast of Granada were deserted. By the late sixteenth century the entire Murcian coast, except for Mazarrón and Cartagena, was unpopulated. Empty stretches were common in Valencia as well.[66]

The impact of the conflict on coastal regions was by no means limited to the least secure areas. The economy of the populated sections of the coastline, especially the sector that depended on the sea, was seriously affected. Fishermen, as we have seen, were always prominent among the captives. In the summer of 1581, Algerian corsairs seized thirty-two fishermen off the coast of Benidorm. In 1585 the councilors of Barcelona noted that a fleet of North African corsairs had spent the summer cruising in the vicinity of the fishing grounds.[67] Fishing in the Mediterranean was always dangerous; in the seventeenth century it became unsafe in the Atlantic as well. It was not uncommon for fishermen to go to sea armed—but how many stopped going at all?

Commerce and communications also suffered. It is unlikely that the danger reduced long-distance trade appreciably, but it did make it more costly. The effects of corsair activity on local coastal trade, however, may have been more severe. Because land communications were poor, in many instances the only way to travel from one coastal village to another was by sea. Although vessels engaged in this traffic remained as close to the coast as possible and often traveled in convoys for protection, coastal trade was still an important source of captives. Most of the seizures were of small boats carrying goods and passengers to neighboring villages. It is not possible to say to what extent, if any, the threat of capture retarded this coastal trade, but it certainly made it less profitable, both because of losses and the added cost of defense.

The constant burden of defense had a heavy economic impact on coastal regions. For example, from the early seventeenth century, taxes for the purpose of defense against North African corsairing were levied on such items as fish, meat, cattle, and silk in all communities on or near the Mediterranean coast.[68] When, as was often the case, defense was inadequate, coastal communities were faced with the task of raising funds for the ransom of their citizens who were captured by the corsairs.

Defense against North African corsairs was a continuing preoccupation of those who dwelt on the Spanish coasts. The affected communities had to maintain a constant state of preparedness against corsair attacks which, whether they occurred or not, were always expected because they were so commonplace. Reports arrived regularly in coastal regions about the movements of corsair fleets. Even after corsairs had raided a locality and departed, the inhabitants could not lower their guard, since the assailants would frequently return to the same location a few nights later. Thus, constant vigilance was necessary. Every time a warning was received, the coastal localities had to make preparations to defend themselves. These sometimes included the temporary abandonment of villages after word arrived that corsairs were in the area. This occurred in October 1543, when the residents of Villajoyosa in Valencia, hearing that the corsairs were coming, took their belongings and left. The corsairs sacked the deserted village for three days, taking what they could and destroying what they could not take.[69]

It would be a mistake to underestimate the difficulty of defending the long, cove-studded Spanish coastline, especially against the many smaller corsair vessels that went to sea in all seasons. The problem was intensified, however, by the inadequacy of the coastal defense system. Various factors contributed to its deficiencies, but the most telling was undoubtedly the staggering cost, both human and fiscal, of Spain's extensive military commitments. The documents of the mid-sixteenth century present a picture of a monarchy pressed on all sides by the demands of both defense and offense. The situation became yet more complex in the seventeenth century, when the upsurge in Muslim piracy called for increased vigilance on the coasts at the same time as the conflict in Europe and the deepening crisis at home made ever-greater demands on Spain's shrinking resources. The gravity of the problem is suggested by the letter that the marqués de Cerralvo wrote to the ecclesiastics of Galicia in 1620, asking them to contribute to the building of a fleet to defend the region. He explained that there were no defensive vessels along the Galician coast because they were all with the Armada of the Ocean Sea, which was occupied in "assuring the vessels coming from the Indies, guarding the Strait of Gibraltar, and other things that cannot be done without, and there are simply not sufficient forces to divide them."[70] On April 8, 1641, the duke of Medina Sidonia wrote that it was not possible to defend against the Muslim galleys that had been sighted off the coast of Cartaya, because all the troops, arms, and galleys had been sent to Portugal to quell the revolt there.[71]

The subjugation of the North African corsairs stood low in the state's priorities. A decision had been made quite early that North Africa was not to be a major focus of Spain's foreign policy and military efforts. The crown's interest in that region in the sixteenth century was primarily due to its connection with the greater struggle in the Mediterranean and to a desire to halt Ottoman expansion; after the 1580 truce, that interest waned. The corsairs may have terrified most Spaniards, but to the crown they were little more than a nuisance. Their attacks were a threat to the security of individuals and local communities, never to the security of the state. So other struggles took precedence over this one.

The low priority given this problem may also have reflected the crown's geographical orientation. The principal victims of the corsairs were the inhabitants of coastal regions—the periphery and not the center.

In the final analysis, the problem of the captives and the corsairs was more social than military or political. Although the crown did make some effort to control corsair activity, that effort was limited both by a lack of resources and by the monarchy's own interests.

PART 2

CAPTIVITY

Chapter 3
Life in Captivity

In his report on coastal fortifications in Murcia, Gian Baptista Antonelli remarked that while all the coasts of Spain were vulnerable to attack by a powerful armada, it was dread not of an armada that led to the abandonment of coastal regions, but rather of Muslim corsairs in small boats, because "they come onto land, where they capture Christians."[1] Antonelli had perceptively recognized that what terrorized coastal residents was not so much the violence of an attack itself as the possibility of being seized by the corsairs.

Although the prospect of being captured and enslaved is never a pleasant one, the fear that Spaniards felt in the case of the North Africans was intensified by popular conceptions of the ferocity of the corsairs and of the horrors awaiting them in North Africa. The notion of contemporary Spaniards and, indeed, of most Europeans was that those who fell into the hands of the so-called Barbary pirates could expect a life of hard labor and cruel treatment, far crueler than that meted out to prisoners and captives in Christian societies or, for that matter, in any society in the past. Furthermore, for women and young children there would be sexual abuse, and for all captives constant pressure to apostatize and become Muslims. This view was strongly influenced by the polemical writings of the religious redemptionists and was reinforced by the literature of the period.[2] These impressions may also have been encouraged by official government policy, in an attempt to limit contact with the Muslims.[3]

But the North Africans regarded their Christian prisoners as the most valuable type of corsair booty. Captives were prized both as slave labor and for their potential ransoms, and a conscious effort was made to keep them alive and healthy. For this reason, while instances of cruelty undoubtedly did occur, in general the treatment of captives in North Africa was at least consistent with the standards of the age.

The Distribution of Captives

The disposition of Christian captives once they arrived in North Africa depended on the circumstances under which they had been taken prisoner. All those seized in military encounters became the property of the state. Many of these were retained in the ruler's service or allocated to high officials or government departments.[4] Individuals who had been captured by corsairs belonged to their captain and the partners who had participated in financing the expedition. Under certain circumstances, captives might be claimed by crew members of the corsair vessel.[5]

The ruler of the place of embarkation, who sometimes helped the corsairs equip their galleys and frequently provided slaves for the oars, was entitled to about one-seventh of all the booty, including the captives. He had the right to choose those who were most likely to command a high rescue price.[6] This occurred in the case of Friar Jerónimo Gracián, a former confessor of Saint Teresa of Ávila, who was captured in 1592 by corsairs of Tunis. He expected to be offered for rescue quickly, because the captain of the galley that had seized him was in need of money. But the captain became convinced that Gracián was an archbishop, that he had gone to Rome to become a cardinal, that he had an annual income of between 10,000 and 20,000 ducats, and that he ws a relative of the king of Spain. He boasted publicly that he expected his prisoner to command a very handsome rescue price. When the governor of Tunis heard about this supposedly valuable captive, he promptly claimed Gracián for himself.[7]

After the ruler had received his share, most of the remaining captives were taken to the marketplace to be sold. All of the North African coastal cities had an active and profitable trade in captured Christians. In Algiers they were sold at auction in a market known as the *zoco*, where the principal shops of the city were located. They were displayed at the zoco for three days before they were actually offered for sale.[8]

Diego Galán, a native of Toledo, fourteen years of age when captured in 1589 while traveling from Málaga to Orán, where he was going to serve in the army, described the slave market in his memoirs. He compared the sale of captives at the market to the sale of animals, and noted that while he was being displayed in the market, "some came to look at me and to ask if I had any illnesses, and made me walk back and forth to see if I was lame, or crippled in any way, touching my arms and looking at my teeth."[9] In Cervantes' *El trato de Argel*, the mouth of a young captive was examined by a prospective purchaser to be sure he was healthy.[10] It was not unusual for a potential buyer to demand that a captive disrobe, to see whether he had hidden defects.[11] The entire procedure could be quite humiliating, but had to be endured by the captive.

The prices paid for the captives varied, depending on age, sex, and the prospective purchaser's expectations concerning their social status and possibilities for redemption. Spaniards were considered the most valuable slaves and commanded the highest prices, because they were regarded as the best workers and because the likelihood of rescue was greater than for captives of other nationalities. For this reason, prisoners frequently were required to tell potential buyers that they were Spanish, even when they were not. A skilled craftsman of any nationality, particularly one experienced in shipbuilding, was extremely valuable. These often commanded four or five times the price of ordinary captives in the slave market.[12]

At the conclusion of the sale, the governor had the right to purchase any of the captives for the highest price bid. If a reasonable sum had been offered for an individual whom the governor desired, he would buy the captive instead. Diego Galán became a slave of the governor of Algiers in this way. After three days of being displayed in the zoco, Galán was approached by a renegade Christian from Toledo who, on learning that the young man was a native of his own city, at once agreed to buy him for 150 ducats.[13] When the sale was over, the captives were taken before the governor, who selected Galán and four other youngsters, all Andalusians.[14]

Often entire families were captured, and although one buyer would sometimes purchase them all, in many cases families were separated. The Spaniards were particularly concerned about the separation of young children from their parents, since they believed it would be easier for the Muslims to convert the children if their parents were not with them to remind them to remain good Christians. In *El trato de Argel*, an entire family was exhibited for sale at the slave market. Their two young sons were sold separately from the parents, who were helpless to do anything other than implore them to remain true to the faith.[15] In Cervantes' other dramatization of captivity in Algiers, *Los baños de Argel*, two boys, one so young that his father carried him in his arms, were separated from their family. After the sale, one of the Algerian officials predicted that they would shortly be in the service of Muḥammad.[16]

As a rule, the possibility that an effort would be made to convert captives was more a fear on the part of the Spaniards than a reality (see chapter 4). However, the Muslims were sometimes interested in the conversion of young boys because they were regarded as candidates for the janissary corps.

In any case, the lists of rescued captives do include many families that remained together during their captivity. In 1618, Ana Canbil of Jerez de la Frontera and her year-old son, Juan, were rescued from Hamet Benamar of Algiers, who was identified in the documents as a Morisco. They had been captured almost a year earlier.[17] In 1670, the Trinitarians rescued from the governor of Algiers Bernabe Sapena of Almería, his wife, Ana Hernández, and their three children, Joseph, age seven, Andrea, age three, and Luis, who had been born a month before the redemption, while his parents were still slaves. The family had been captured about four months earlier, along with a number of other people, from a farm in Almería.[18] In the same redemption, several other families abducted during the raid on Almería were also rescued. Among them were Antonia de Morales and her two children, Gabriel de Casas, age four, and Antonio de Casas, age one and one-half, and Teresa Nuñez and her son, Bernardo Francisco, age two and one-half.[19] Families that remained together also appear on the lists of redemptions made in the kingdom of Morocco.

Although most captives were slaves of the North African

states or the corsairs, there were many private slaveowners as well. Prominent among the private owners in the sixteenth and early seventeenth centuries were Moriscos who had fled or been expelled from Spain. The redemption lists reveal large numbers of Morisco slaveowners, particularly during the generation or so following the expulsion of the Moriscos in 1609. Indeed, in the Mercedarian redemption in Tetuán and Salé in 1625, almost all of the owners were identified as Moriscos, and some of them owned large numbers of slaves.[20] Jews also appear frequently in the rescue books as owners of Christian slaves.

Thus, a Spanish captive might be a slave of the state or of its ruler, of a galley captain, or of a private individual, possibly a Morisco or Jew with antecedents in Spain. How he lived and how he was treated during his captivity depended primarily on who his master was and the purpose for which he had been bought.

Living Conditions

During most of the first half of the sixteenth century, there were no government prisons for captives in Algiers. They were able to wander freely about the city, "and there was no place closed to them."[21] As Gómez de Losada, writing in the seventeenth century, remarked, at that time they could have been a powerful force for any rebel leader who wanted to make use of them.[22] By the second half of the sixteenth century, however, almost all captives, those belonging to the state as well as to private individuals, were kept in prisons known as *baños*.[23] It was not uncommon for several private slaveowners to house their captives together in one baño, and there were small baños in private homes as well. "There is no house in Algiers in which they do not have these cruel prisons. Some houses, especially of those who engage in the buying and selling of captives, have 200 or even 300 slaves."[24]

In the seventeenth century there were eight large baños in Algiers. By the second half of the eighteenth century only three of these remained, demonstrating the decline in successful corsair activity and, as a result, in the number of Christian captives in Algiers.[25] The largest of these was the *baño grande del rey*, a prison where the slaves belonging to the governor of Algiers were housed. Because the governor usually owned the most valuable slaves, many important persons resided in this baño. Private owners also kept their captives there, particularly when they were waiting to be rescued, "because there they kept them fairly healthy and secure until the rescue came."[26] For this privilege, private owners paid a small fee to the *guardianes* (wardens) of the baño. In the sixteenth and seventeenth centuries there were usually between fifteen hundred and three thousand captives in this baño, but by the mid-eighteenth century it housed no more than one thousand.[27] The other government prison was the *baño de la bastarda*,[28] which was somewhat smaller than the baño grande. It held only about five hundred captives, the *cristianos del común* or of the *deylik*, who were slaves of the Algerian state. These slaves were used primarily on public works projects, such as the repair of the port of Algiers, although they were sometimes sent to row in the galleys.[29] The other baños were those of private individuals, usually the reis of the galleys, who owned large numbers of slaves.

The baños in Algiers were like large corrals, surrounded by small rooms or cells, which contained various appurtenances of prisons, such as chains and shackles. The baño grande was built on two levels; the lower one contained a church in which Roman Catholic religious services were held all year round. In the seventeenth century, after the foundation of the Trinitarian hospitals in the baños of Algiers, this baño housed the largest hospital and pharmacy as well. In the middle of the baño was a cistern of pure water.

An institution common to the prisons for Christian slaves throughout North Africa was the tavern, where they could purchase wine and brandy. In spite of Islamic restrictions on the consumption of alcoholic beverages, the Muslims were regular patrons of these taverns, which were run by captives, who paid a percentage of their profits to the state. These establishments were social centers and a great source of pleasure for the captives, providing a place where they might meet and relax in the evening after a day at hard labor.[30]

The slaves in the baño grande usually had to remain inside the baño at all times, except when they were taken out to work. Because they usually had the highest potential ransom prices, close watch was kept on them. But the slaves in the baño de la bastarda, who were less likely to be rescued, had more freedom. They were able to go out and stroll about "wherever they pleased," without being bothered by their overseers.[31] The atmosphere of all the larger baños was generally quite open, with both North Africans and slaves who were not residents free to come and go as they pleased during the day. At nightfall, however, a signal was given for outsiders to leave. Anyone who did not go at once had to spend the night, for once the gates were closed, they were never opened before daybreak.[32]

The principal overseer of each baño was known as the *guardián baji*, and under him were a number of assistants. The guards in the baño de la bastarda were all janissaries under the direction of their ağa. In addition to guarding the captives in prison, the guards escorted them when they went out to work, or when they had been rescued and were to be turned over to the redemptionist friars. In the latter case, each captive had to have a permit or license, for which the friars paid the guardián baji 6 reales.[33]

Slaves of private individuals were housed under varying conditions, depending on the master. Some private owners kept their captives fettered in dungeons; others regarded them as members of their households whose living arrangements corresponded to their status in the house. Francisco Jiménez de Santa Catalina, a Trinitarian friar who served at his order's hospital in Algiers from 1717–1721, tells of a female Spanish renegade, a native of Alicante known as Lila Fatima, who was the widow of an assassinated Algerian governor. He says that at all times she kept her captives in a dungeon, "in the worst fetters in all of Algiers." She would not permit them to go to the hospital to be cured if they were ill. Nor would she allow a priest to administer the sacraments if one were dying.[34] But a Spanish captive writing from Algiers in the late eighteenth century noted that many privately owned Christian slaves were very highly regarded by their masters and lived as though they were free.[35] Many household slaves did have considerable freedom of movement and were able to participate fully in the religious and social life of the large baños.

In Meknès, from the time of Mawlay Ismāᶜēl, the Moroccan sultan housed his unmarried captives in a quarter called the *sagena*, which had the formality, if not the trappings, of a prison. The sagena was a large square, surrounded by very high walls. A fortified tower marked each of the four corners, and the entrance was protected by a grilled iron gate. Within the compound, guards were stationed in two circular iron cages. The captives' quarters were four large, barracks-type structures, which were generally very crowded. "Although they were large enough, they were very uncomfortable because of the growing number of slaves."[36] An effort was made to provide some amenities within the sagena. The center of the square contained a small, patiolike plaza with a lovely fountain. The quarter also contained a church, purportedly built by the Visigoths, which was used for religious services by the captives. It was located in a wide street which divided the compound from the outer walls of the sagena.[37]

The slaves were divided up by nationality, with each group having its own quarter. Each nation had a majordomo, who was exempt from work. This official was elected annually by a majority vote of his fellow countrymen. His principal responsibility was to distribute alms sent from their home country among his constituents. From this money, he would set aside a percentage for the care of the sick. In addition, he had the right "to castigate those of his nation when they deserved it."[38]

The sultan provided his married captives with a separate quarter, known as the *trecenal*. His reason for permitting married men to live with their families was that a man with a family was considered more likely to be conscientious about his duties. These families were not given any sustenance by the emperor, but were usually placed in positions which permitted them to provide for their own needs.[39]

Work and Treatment

Christian captives served in numerous capacities in North Africa. As we have seen, the North Africans tried to keep their slaves fit, so as not to lose their economic value. Nevertheless, the North Africans, like most societies of that day, frequently turned to the forced labor of captives for work that free men were loathe to do—such as rowing in corsair vessels, working in mines, or performing particularly arduous tasks on construction projects—and, as was common to other societies, attempted to make this labor more efficient by keeping it under the lash. But Christian captives were also employed in other kinds of work—as skilled laborers, in agriculture, in shops, as domestic servants, and, in a few cases, in government service. Almost all captives were regarded as slaves and required to work.[40]

The most onerous labor was rowing in corsair vessels. Algerian galleys had from eighteen to twenty-four banks of oars, with each oar requiring from three to five men. Smaller corsair vessels required proportionately fewer oarsmen. Brigantines, for example, had from eight to thirteen banks of oars. A corsair boat, therefore, might require as many as 240 oarsmen. Although captains of galleys usually owned large numbers of slaves, they frequently did not have enough to man the oars of their vessels. If, as was often the case, the ruler was a partner in the expedition, he would provide some of his own slaves for the oars. Captains might also hire oarsmen from merchants who kept slaves for this purpose. In the sixteenth century the merchants were paid the equivalent of 12 gold escudos per captive for a voyage. From the second half of the seventeenth century, galleys were used less frequently by the Algerians; then Christian captives performed other duties on corsair vessels. In the coastal towns and cities of Morocco, too, Christian captives served on corsair ships. They were used even during battles, when they served on the masts and yards to handle the sails and splice any riggings that might be cut.[41]

It was not unusual for oarsmen to row continuously, without rest, for very long periods. Francis Knight, an English captive in Algiers in the seventeenth century, remarked that the lack of sleep made many slaves delirious. When sleep was possible, perhaps for one out of every twelve hours, it had to be taken sitting up on the rowing bench, with no room for the slaves even to stretch their legs.[42]

Frequently the work of the rowers was made even more difficult by a diet that, at best, was inadequate. As Haedo noted, "the food . . . is no more than a bit of bread crumbs, two or three pieces of dirty and often rotten biscuit, and . . . a little watered-down vinegar."[43] He added, however, that the Muslim crew members had the same rations. "As for drink, each one has to provide for his own needs when they stop for water in some place, which must always be done quickly." The problem of obtaining fresh water was particularly acute, and galley slaves sometimes died of thirst. One captive remarked that they would "pawn their souls" for a drop of water and often had to drink the salt water from the sea.[44] Haedo cited an incident that occurred in June 1579, when thirty-two Christian oarsmen in one vessel died of thirst. Gómez de Losada related the death of about twenty rowers "in a large corsair boat" and added that for a period of eight days those who survived had nothing to drink but seawater.[45]

It should be pointed out that the conditions on corsair ships were hardly better for free Muslim seamen. Furthermore, these conditions were typical of galley life throughout the Mediterranean. A physician's report on two Spanish galleys docked in Barcelona in 1719 noted that 156 of the rowers were extremely ill and that 8 had already died as a result of exposure to a long spell of wet and cold weather. The report added that all of the rowers were considerably weakened by a combination of poor diet and exposure. As Gregorio Marañón remarked, the ones who died at the oars were probably envied by those who survived them.[46]

Not only were conditions on the galleys and other corsair vessels extremely poor and the work very arduous, but the slaves were sometimes treated very harshly. One of the reasons for this may have been to prevent them from rebelling. The possibility that galley slaves might rebel or attempt to escape was clearly a problem for the North Africans, and it required considerable vigilance. In order to prevent an escape attempt while the corsairs were disembarking with their booty, the slaves had to drop the oars, which were attached to the boat by lines, into the water as soon as they arrived in a North African port.[47]

Although escapes and rebellions by galley slaves were not common, they did occur occasionally, sometimes in concert with the authorities of Christian states. In May 1570, plans were laid for an uprising of Christian slaves in Tripoli in conjunction with a proposed Spanish invasion. Neither that revolt nor the invasion actually took place. But in May 1601, 140 Christian galley slaves revolted and killed a number of their Muslim overseers and the governor of Tripoli, Hasan Paşa, and seized his wife and children, with whom they fled in a large galley to Palermo. The leaders of and participants in the rebellion were generously rewarded by the Spanish crown.[48]

The oarsmen spent the winter on land, where their work might consist of hauling carts, selling water, chopping vines and building houses. Ali "Pichilin," admiral of Algiers and one of the great slaveowners of the seventeenth century, used his galley slaves for an ambitious building project on which they worked from the time the fleet returned for the winter until it embarked again the following May. Although the work there was also very taxing, the captives preferred it because water was plentiful and they could rest at night.[49]

The captives who worked in the mines or on public works usually labored in chain gangs, sometimes with iron collars on their necks. Their work was as arduous as that of the galley slaves; their tasks were frequently those of beasts of burden. A project that required slave labor almost continuously was the reinforcement of the mole that protected the harbor of Algiers from the wind. The captives had to break stone in the quarries about 2 leagues inland, load it onto wagons, and pull the wagons the distance to the port. Francisco Jiménez described this work: "A Moor goes with them driving and beating them if they do not pull well. Each day they are obliged to make five trips, and if they do not do it they punish them rigorously."[50] In 1736, a group of nineteen Spanish captives, who identified themselves as "officers and soldiers . . . of Your Majesty," wrote to Philip V of Spain complaining of this work. They said that in the three and one-half years they had been captives in Algiers they had never gone without "very heavy chains" and that during this time they had worked daily on the reinforcement of the mole, making four trips each day pulling the carts filled with stone from the quarry to the port.[51]

Even captives who could command good rescue prices were not always exempt from this work. Don Baltasar Hernández de Rivadeneyra, a high-ranking officer, was a captive in Algiers for more than two years until he was exchanged in 1680 for the son of the governor of the Algerian province of Tlemcen. He testified that during his captivity he had worked daily pulling a wagon loaded with stone for the mole. He added that he always wore a chain weighing about 50 pounds while he worked.[52] Captives also worked on the docks, loading and unloading heavy cargo. The strongest men were usually chosen for this work.

It was not uncommon for captives to become ill, for some even to die, as a result of the combination of overwork and generally deteriorating physical condition. One enterprise that took a heavy toll was the excavation, in the second decade of the eighteenth century, of a Roman ruin located outside the city of Algiers. The captives working on the excavation labored from morning to night. On July 4, 1719, five Christians who had been hauling rock at the ruin were brought to the Trinitarian hospital. "They said that the water at the excavation was so bad that most become ill. The overwork and poor nourishment also caused them to fall ill."[53]

By October 10, 1719, there were forty-six patients in the hospital who had been brought there from the excavation project. On October 25, one of them, Joseph Nicolás, a native of Molina in Aragón, died of an illness contracted at the site, where disease apparently was reaching nearly epidemic proportions. Jiménez remarked "that the same thing happened to others who went with him, and almost all have died."[54] Factors that contributed to the high incidence of serious illness and death were not only the hard work, but also beatings by the guards, food that was inadequate and often spoiled, and especially the long hours working under the hot Algerian sun. Because these slaves were already considerably weakened, they were highly susceptible to illness. When disease struck it could be devastating.

In Morocco, too, captive labor was utilized for public works. A slave of the sultan of Morocco in the 1670s described the work at a construction project in Fez as harder than any he had ever done. Walls of buildings were erected by filling wooden forms with a mixture of earth, lime, gravel, and water and pounding the sides of the forms with heavy rammers until the molds had set. The wood was then removed and the walls permitted to dry. No scaffolds or ladders were available and all of the materials, which were very heavy, had to be hauled up by a pulley with a small cord that burned and cut through the fingers of those who pulled at it. The men working above had to pound the wooden forms constantly, and if they stopped for even a moment the overseers would throw stones at them.[55]

The great Moroccan sultan Mawlay Ismāᶜēl was said to have employed some thirty thousand men, at least two thousand of them Christian captives, in building the city of Meknès in the last quarter of the seventeenth century.[56] The slaves who worked on this enterprise labored in teams under a black slavemaster who drove them with a lash. The tasks of the captives consisted of demolishing the old walls with heavy pickaxes and building new ones in the manner previously described. The captives who worked at the lime kilns were sometimes burned alive.[57]

As in the case of the galley slaves, such working conditions for slaves and forced laborers were not unique to North Africa at this time. A comparison may be drawn with the treatment of prisoners or slaves, many of whom were Muslim captives or Moriscos, in the mines of Almadén in Spain. The work at these mines was "so strenuous . . . that many became ill from exhaustion or were so weakened that they easily fell victim to infectious diseases." Prisoners who could not meet the work quotas were whipped, even those who were ill. A further dan-

ger to the workers in the mines was the risk of mercury poi-
soning, which often led to insanity or death.[58] Similar working
conditions prevailed for Indians and black slaves in the New
World. Thus, the circumstances of "hard laborers" in North
Africa were not peculiar to that society, but rather were characteristic of the age.

Slave labor was not confined to those occupations where the
workers were under the lash. Indeed, slaves were found in
nearly every occupation. Most women and children worked as
household slaves, either in the ruler's palace or in private homes.
The governor of Algiers always took the youngest and best
male slaves of the state to serve as pages in the palace, where
they were well fed and well treated.[59] Diego Galán performed
domestic tasks in the palace of the governor of Algiers. "I was
occupied in washing the clothes, keeping the household accounts, and doing other similar tasks."[60] Haedo says that the
Moorish women, other than Moriscas or renegades, generally
were not very good at domestic duties, "and for this reason
female Christian captives are so prized, especially those who
do handiwork."[61]

Many household slaves were given the responsibility of caring for their masters' children. "They take charge of them, and
do what mothers have to do . . . there are many in this occupation and they are exempt from serving in other positions,
especially if the children become fond of them. . . . Although
it is no small job to care for a child . . . these are the most
fortunate in captivity."[62] Germaine Mouette, a Frenchman who
was a captive in Morocco from 1670 to 1681, described his life
as a slave in the household of his first master, Muḥammad
Liebus, a Slawi whose wife and mother-in-law were Moriscas.
When Mouette first came to Liebus' home, he was put to work
grinding corn at a hand-mill in the kitchen, a common chore
for household slaves. Mouette disliked the work because it
was too strenuous, and in the hope of being relieved of it
deliberately ground the flour so coarse that it was unusable.
His mistress then placed him in charge of her young child,
who became so attached to him that he would not go to anyone
else. In this way, Mouette made his masters dependent on

him and he received privileged treatment. He was given white bread with butter and honey to eat, and the 25-pound chain he had worn was removed.[63]

Mouette was one of the more fortunate captives. Other tasks performed by household slaves of private individuals ranged from providing the necessities of the house by collecting firewood, tending livestock, working in the fields, and cultivating the gardens, to carrying water and breaking up rock to make lime. Don Miguel de Sesa, a Spanish nobleman who was a household slave in Tetuán at the end of the sixteenth century, was kept in a dungeon in his master's house throughout his captivity and made to drive a flour mill that was kept in his cell. Mouette told of seeing household slaves in Salé harnessed to carts together with work animals.[64] Thus, the treatment of household slaves varied considerably.

Slaves also worked as clerks or shop assistants. Some slaves were even permitted to set up their own businesses, from which they had to pay their masters a percentage of the profits. Among these were the tavern keepers referred to earlier, who paid part of their profits to their masters and to the officials of the baños in order to be permitted to carry on their business.[65]

Captives who had special skills, such as carpenters, blacksmiths, builders, doctors, or surgeons, were highly valued. Many Christian prisoners were master craftsmen and manufacture was often in their hands. For example, slave labor was indispensable to boat construction in Algiers, and those who were skilled in this craft were highly regarded. Although most of the labor consisted of the slaves of the ruler, some corsair captains owned captives who were skilled ships' carpenters, cannon founders, or master boatbuilders. These workers were generally treated well. When a vessel was completed, the captain would hold a celebration to which his friends would come with gifts of cloth, silks, and velvets for decorating the new boat. The master builders would take most of these gifts as payment for their work. The corsairs also saw to it that the slaves who worked on their craft were fed well.[66]

Talented slaves often had special privileges. Haedo tells of a Catalán slave of the ruler of Algiers, known as Maestro Pedro, who had been a captive for many years and had become a master of the galleys. He had his own house in Algiers, which even contained a small chapel. But his privileged position did not deter Pedro and six other masters of the galleys from seizing a boat and fleeing to Valencia in August 1582.[67] There were many surgeons among the captives since, as Jiménez wrote, "any Christian who has served even one day as a barber is accredited as a surgeon," and these too enjoyed exceptional treatment. "They put them in military dress and three-cornered hats and their patrons do not assign them to any other work but that of their profession, and they live a very good life."[68] Because of the value placed on such captives, however, their rescue prices were very high and sometimes they could not be ransomed at all.

Christian captives sometimes served in high government posts. In the early part of the eighteenth century, a Spanish slave named José Díaz was a favorite of the sultan of Morocco, who made him master of the gunpowder factories. In 1708 the sultan sent Díaz on an embassy to the king of Portugal to negotiate a treaty for a exchange and general rescue of Portuguese captives. Díaz came back with a treaty and gifts worth 240,000 escudos for his master from the king of Portugal. His future seemed very promising, but shortly after his return the treaty was renounced by the sultan, who nevertheless retained the Portuguese gifts. Díaz was accused of having failed to execute his orders faithfully and was removed not only from his ambassadorial post, but from that of master of the powderworks as well, and sent to work with the other slaves.[69] The Díaz case emphasizes how tentative and precarious were the privileges enjoyed by the more favored captives. At any time they might revert to the condition and hardships of ordinary slaves.

Wealthy captives, who could afford to bribe the guardianes of the baños, often were able to buy special privileges. In *Los baños de Argel*, the guardián baji called the captives out to work:

Guardián: . . . To work, Christians. No one remains inside, sick or healthy, . . . I want everyone to work, even priests, even noblemen.

. . . .

Slave: (assigning captives to various tasks) . . . Where will the noblemen go?
Guardián: Leave them until tomorrow, then they will be the first.
Slave: And if they pay?
Guardián: It is clear that where there is money there is rest.[70]

Gómez de Losada observed that "noblemen and those who are known to have a high rescue price" were not sent out to work because "the Turks want their money very much, and only those who are poor suffer this labor."[71]

Not all wealthy and valuable captives, however, received favored treatment. Although they were not sent out in the work gangs, those who could command high rescue prices were often kept inside the baño, in chains, at all times. The captive in *Don Quijote* was believed to be wealthy because he was a military officer, and he was expected to command a high rescue price. "They put a chain on me, more as a signal that I was for rescue than to guard me with it, and thus I passed my life in that baño, with many other noblemen and important people."[72] The reason for this was that their captors thought it would be easier to obtain high prices for important captives if they were kept in miserable surroundings.[73] Cervantes tells us that although the captives who were awaiting their rescue did not usually go out to work with the others, "if their rescue was late, they made them work and go out for firewood, which is no small job, in order to make them write for the rescue with greater urgency."[74]

Don Miguel de Sesa, who was captured near Barcelona in 1596, spent fourteen years as the slave of a Portuguese renegade named Morato, a corsair of Tetuán. The price that Morato demanded for him was so high that eight redemptions came and went before he was rescued. During his captivity, he was kept in a small dungeon in his master's house. He was not allowed to speak with or see other people, "neither Christian, Jew, nor Moor." As noted earlier, he was kept in chains at all times and was put to work driving a flour mill that his master kept in his cell. When the Mercedarians made their redemption in 1609, Don Miguel was brought before them "so weighted down with chains and misfortune and hardships that all those present were moved."[75] After several days of negotiation, Morato agreed to come down from his asking price of 680,000 maravedís, and Don Miguel was rescued for the still-exorbitant price of 561,000 maravedís.[76]

Another important captive who was kept in his cell at all times was Don Baltasar de Villalba, the governor of Almarza-quivir in Orán, who was captured when Spain lost Orán in 1709. Friar Francisco Jiménez described in his diary regular visits to the governor, who, he reported, was kept in chains and never allowed to go out of the baño.[77]

Although many captives were forced to do hard labor which caused some to become ill and some even to die, as a rule they do not seem to have been exposed to deliberate, purposeless physical brutality. In modern terms, the treatment of the captives was often exceptionally cruel. But the period under consideration here was not a humane age, and the use of physical force to increase the productivity of slaves and forced laborers was common to virtually all societies. This is not to argue that brutal treatment of captives under other circumstances did not occur in North Africa. But barbarity exists in any society in which some individuals have absolute power over others. In the case of the North Africans, then, the question is whether such treatment was usual or exceptional.

With respect to galley slaves, the allegations concerning cruelty were often correct—they were generally treated worse than other captives, particularly in Algiers. Works by Christian authors of the period are filled with tales of galley slaves who were physically abused, beaten, and mutilated. Gómez de Losada remarked that when the corsairs came back to Algiers from their raiding expeditions, there were always a number of galley slaves who returned without ears and noses.[78] Haedo speaks of similar atrocities, and says that the corsairs kept the dismembered parts as souvenirs. He cites the case of a reis who in May 1579 bit off the nose and ears of a Spanish galley slave named Cristóbal because he sang while he rowed.[79] Nor were galley slaves the only victims of brutality. Many instances can be found of slaves on land who were subjected to similar treatment.

Nonetheless, the evidence does not add up to a systematic pattern of brutality in North Africa. It should not be forgotten that many of the sources on captivity were written or inspired by religious redemptionists with a specific purpose in mind— to generate financial contributions and support for their work. Their writings, therefore, are strongly polemical—individual instances of extreme cruelty were selected for purposes of propaganda.

How captives were treated often depended on who their owners were. Many of the renegades, for example, may have been cruel to their slaves in order to prove they were good Muslims. This would help explain the excessive brutality in the galleys, where most of the corsairs were renegades. Francisco Jiménez related a conversation with a Neapolitan renegade, who told him that some renegades were so harsh with the Christians in order to prove to other Muslims that they were "Turks in their hearts. . . . It is a Turkish maxim," he added, "that a renegade can be considered a good Muslim only if he is rigorous with the Christians."[80] In contrast, the captive in Don Quijote tells of the renegade Uchali who had apostatized after being a galley slave for fourteen years and had become admiral and later governor of Algiers. "Morally he was a good man and he treated his captives, sometimes as many as 3,000, with much humanity."[81]

Other sources also provide us with a very different picture. Diego Galán, for example, was treated with great kindness by his master. Friar Jerónimo Gracián described his captivity in Tunis as a period of both spiritual happiness and physical well-being. "I have never enjoyed better health nor slept better nor eaten with greater gusto."[82] In 1692 the administrator of the Trinitarian hospital in Algiers wrote to the governor of Orán concerning the mistreatment of a captured Algerian corsair by his Mallorcan master who refused to permit him to observe his religion, gave him almost nothing to eat, and kept a chain on his neck at night. The administrator was concerned that the Algerians might retaliate against their Christian captives. "In this city," he pointed out, "they permit the slaves to go to church and to receive the sacraments; on feast days their masters send them to comply with their religious obligations. . . . They treat them uniformly well and if one complains to the governor that he has been maltreated, his master will be castigated and forced to sell him to another owner."[83] The French observer, Laugier de Tassy, wrote in 1725 that neither slaves of the Algerian government nor those of private individuals were usually exposed to the "frightful miseries of which the captives themselves wish to persuade us."[84]

Finally, many of the archival sources consulted for this work contain complete physical descriptions of rescued captives. In only a small fraction of the cases is there a clear indication of a physical impairment caused by brutality on the part of masters or overseers. Thus, while the examples of brutal treatment cited by Christian authors undoubtedly are true, they seem to represent the exception rather than the norm.

Nor would it appear that in general the Muslims treated their captives with greater cruelty than did Christians. Were the North Africans more barbarous than the French, for example, who in 1684 decreed that criminals who had been sentenced to death were to have their noses and ears cut off instead and be condemned to the galleys? This treatment caused the rowers to have such difficulty in breathing that they could not be used at the oars for long periods.[85]

Evidence for a direct comparison of the treatment of Muslim slaves in Europe with Christian slaves in North Africa is scanty because of the almost complete absence of memoirs by the former. Since the level of literacy in North Africa was generally lower than in western Europe, it was unlikely that a Muslim slave could write his memoirs. Furthermore, a Muslim captive was far less apt than a Christian to be rescued and returned to his homeland, where he might record his experiences. The examples cited earlier from European sources provide some basis for comparison. A recent study of slavery in Valencia in the sixteenth and seventeenth centuries concludes that slaves, including North African captives, were ill fed, ill dressed, and often inadequately housed. And one Muslim captive, working on the Guadarrama road in the vicinity of Madrid in the late eighteenth century, complained in a letter addressed to the ruler of Morocco that he and his fellow Muslim slaves were forced to work both day and night, "without rest or relief," that they were poorly fed and dressed, and that they were beaten to make them work harder.[86]

It would appear from the evidence that is available that the treatment of Christian slaves in North Africa was no worse than that of Muslim slaves in western Europe. The Muslims realized that it made good economic sense to keep their captives healthy, whole, and, as we shall see, Christian. Those captives thought likely to command the very highest ransoms were usually not sent out to work at all; as for the rest, some would be rescued while many others would not be, but all were of significant value as slaves.

The fact is that captive labor was of great importance to North Africa. It helped to compensate for the underpopulation that plagued the area throughout the Ottoman period, alleviating the shortage of both unskilled and skilled workers. Special emphasis was placed on certain abilities or talents and great pressure to serve the state was exerted on captives who possessed those skills. In 1754, Miguel González Dávila, an engineer, wrote that the Algerians were trying to force him to serve them in that capacity.[87] In the late seventeenth century the governor of Algiers, knowing his reputation as a great soldier, tried to persuade Don Baltasar Hernández de Rivadeneyra to convert to Islam, offering him such inducements as the rank of general in the army and marriage into the governor's family.[88] This incident demonstrates the severe shortage of talented manpower in Algiers, since it is clear that the governor placed more value on the military capabilities of Hernández than on the substantial ransom price that a high-ranking Spanish officer could command.

For some skilled captives there was no possibility of rescue at all, since their abilities were prized more than their potential ransom prices. In 1717, for example, the French consul in Tunis was unable to ransom a carpenter and a caulker because the Tunisian government needed their services for ship construction.[89] In the 1768–1769 redemption in Algiers, the dey refused to let certain captives go for any price because they served as masters of various works.[90]

Ransoms were also important to the North African economies. As we shall see, the Spanish redemptionists often spent large sums of money to rescue captives in North Africa. Much of this ransom money went to the state and represented a significant portion of the annual income. Laugier de Tassy noted that the Christian slave trade, and especially the ransoming of captives, was the principal form of commerce in Algiers.[91]

In conclusion, the available evidence suggests that the use and treatment of Christian slaves in North Africa were not uncommonly cruel, but adhered to the standards of the age. The Muslims recognized that their captives were a valuable commodity, both as slave labor and for their ransom value, and in the vast majority of cases acted to protect their investments.

Chapter 4
Religious Privileges

Although the treatment of Spanish and other Christian captives in North Africa was, in general, typical of the treatment of prisoners and slaves in western Europe, it was exceptional for the period in the matter of religion. Most of Europe at this time was torn by religious strife, which manifested itself in some states in the persecution not only of nonconforming nationals, but also of foreign merchants or visiting seamen who were adherents of an opposing faith. In North Africa, however, toleration in matters of conscience was public policy and applied not only to free non-Muslims who resided in or visited the region, but to Christian captives as well. The motivation for extending religious privileges to the captives was, in part, the Muslim tradition of respect for "people of the Book." Even stronger was the desire to retain the captives' economic value, which was usually lost, or at least considerably reduced, when a slave apostatized.

It is uncertain when and under what circumstances the Muslims first permitted clerics to enter their territories to meet the religious needs of Christian captives, but the practice seems to have been well established by the thirteenth century. In 1222, the Mercedarians were permitted to have a friar in Granada, with the title of "chaplain of the Christian merchants," who administered the sacraments and tended to the spiritual needs of the captives there. The Spanish Franciscans and Dominicans sent missions to North Africa for the same purpose. From the thirteenth century on, Trinitarian and Mercedarian friars were permitted to enter the Kingdom of Granada and the North African principalities in order to rescue Christians. Presumably, even during that early period, the friars took advantage of their presence among the captives to say mass and administer the sacraments. In addition, there were almost always captive clerics who could conduct religious services, although it is uncertain whether this was done with the permission of the authorities or clandestinely.[1]

The Churches

The first Christian church in the Algerian baños appears to have been the Iglesia de Santa Cruz, founded in the baño grande in 1551 by a Trinitarian friar, Sebastián del Puerto. The establishment of this church was made possible by the presence in Algiers at that time of a friendly governor, Hasan Paşa, son of Barbarossa.[2]

Churches were created in other baños as well, including those of some private individuals. In the seventeenth century Ali "Pichilin" had about eight hundred slaves, and his baño contained a church large enough to hold about three hundred worshipers. Attendance at services there was not limited to Pichilin's slaves, but was open to all captives. For example, even after Pichilin sold him to Cataborne Mustafa, Emanuel d'Aranda attended mass every day at his former owner's baño.[3] The five Trinitarian hospitals that were founded in the last third of the seventeenth century each had a small chapel in which services were conducted regularly.

A much-frequented church of the late sixteenth century was in the house of Maestro Pedro, the Catalán slave who was a master of the galleys of Algiers. Pedro had always gone out of his way to assist the other captives and over the years had seen to it that services were held regularly in his house. The female slaves, in particular, liked to worship there, and rarely went elsewhere, because they did not wish to encounter the Muslims stationed as guards of the baños. This arrangement came to an end when Pedro escaped in 1582.[4] Captives were also permitted to attend religious services at the house of the French consul, which had its own chapel. The only captives to whom regular observances were not available were those who lived and worked in the suburbs, and were not able to make regular visits into Algiers. During Christmas and Holy Week, however, they were usually permitted to go into the city to attend services at one of the baños.[5]

In Tunis, too, according to the account of Friar Jerónimo Gracián, the baño of the dey contained a church.[6] Gracián, who was informed that he had been bought by the dey especially for the purpose of conducting religious services for the captives, was placed in that area.[7]

In Morocco, unlike Algiers and Tunis, Christian captives did not always have easy access to facilities for religious devotion because the attitudes of the Moroccan rulers toward such observance were not consistently favorable. This was probably due to the fact that during the long periods of civil war that plagued Morocco through much of the sixteenth and seventeenth centuries, it was not uncommon for one of the protagonists to revive the psychology of the holy war in an effort to garner additional support.

The Franciscans were expelled from Morocco in 1544. The monasteries there remained closed for nearly a century, until 1636, when the sultan at Marrakesh granted a safe conduct for three Spanish Franciscans to travel to Morocco to minister to the needs of the captives. The friars arrived during Lent and began at once to organize the Holy Week observances. They held Palm Sunday services and processions in the *barrios* inhabited by the captives. When the sultan saw the extent of the religious activity, he decided that he had made a mistake in permitting the friars to come, and placed them under arrest. Fortunately for the friars, about six weeks later the sultan died. The new ruler, Mulay Muḥammad, whose mother was a Christian, released the clerics and issued a license to bring other missionaries to Marrakesh to reestablish the mission there. He granted them the use of one of their old churches, and, with financial assistance from the Spanish crown, the Franciscans erected a new monastery.[8]

The position of the Franciscan missionaries in Morocco was always precarious, since a change in political leadership was often accompanied by a change of fortune for them. In 1659 a new sultan, saying he needed the land and material for other purposes, ordered the demolition of the Franciscan church and monastery. He did not expel the mission, though, and they were able to obtain another house to use as a monastery.[9] In 1672, in the midst of civil wars in Morocco, the sultan ordered all of his captives transferred to Fez. The Franciscans were permitted to go along, and to reestablish their community there. Friars were sent out from it to Meknès and Tetuán; in both cities they lived in the prisons with the captives. In February 1677, however, the missionaries were once again expelled from Morocco, and were not permitted to return until 1684. By that time, all the sultan's captives had been moved to Meknès, where the new capital, which the captives were to help build, was being established. There the Franciscans were permitted to establish a monastery in the sagena.[10]

The periodic banishment of the Franciscans from Morocco, however, did not mean that the captives were deprived of spiritual direction. During all of this time the redemptionist orders were permitted to come to Morocco to ransom captives, and while there they performed religious services for the slaves, just as they did elsewhere in North Africa. In addition, there were almost always clerics among the captives who could provide these services.

Religious Observances

In Algiers at the time of Haedo, mass was said on a regular basis throughout the year, and with even greater frequency on the most solemn holy days, in the church of the baño grande. Services were also held regularly, if less frequently, at the other large baños. There was never a shortage of priests, since there were usually many of them in captivity. Haedo wrote that there were often forty or more clerics in the baño grande, "of every nation and quality . . . friars and secular clerics."[11] He added that in 1579 there were sixty-two ecclesiastics among the captives in Algiers.[12]

Following the establishment of the Trinitarian hospitals, the number of free friars in Algiers increased significantly. The Trinitarians performed daily services in the small chapels in the hospitals and in the churches of the baños as well. Francisco Silvestre, administrator of the hospitals in the late seventeenth century, remarked that there were so many clerics in Algiers, both captives and free Trinitarians, that it was not possible for all of them to say mass every day.[13] In addition, the Mercedarians and Trinitarians who came to Algiers to ransom captives also ministered to their religious needs. Haedo tells us that Friars Juan Gil and Antonio de la Bella, Trinitarian redemptors who arrived in Algiers in May 1580, came not only to rescue captives, but "to preach the faith . . . to give solace to and cheer the captives, for which more time was necessary than they spent in the redemption."[14] The instructions issued to the redemptionists by the masters-general of their orders always stipulated that their first concern on arriving in North Africa was to visit the baños and administer the sacraments to the captives. One reason for this early visit to the baños was to identify those captives who might be in greatest danger of apostatizing and so would be prime candidates for ransom.[15]

Many Spaniards who wrote about Algiers in the sixteenth and seventeenth centuries remarked that the regular religious observances available to the captives compared favorably with those in Spain. The numerous Catholic holy days throughout the year were celebrated, they pointed out, with the same pomp and solemnity as in Christian nations. The only difference, remarked Friar Jiménez, was that "the processions do not go out but remain inside the baños."[16] Friar Bernardo de Monroy, one of three Trinitarian friar-redemptors detained for many years by the Algerian government after a ransoming expedition in 1609, spent more than a decade ministering to the spiritual needs of Christian prisoners. He described his activities and those of his fellow friars in the baño grande: "Every Saturday at sunrise we sing the mass of the Holy Virgin . . . and at night, when the prison is closed, the . . . Litany of our Lady, devotions which we began on the first Saturday that we entered the prison. . . . Every day my fellow padres and I, together in the church, say the canonical hours with the punctuality with which they are said in the Trinitarian monasteries in Spain. We strive to have the Christians . . . well-drilled in the service of our Lord."[17] They also saw to it that the sacraments were given regularly, and Monroy noted that few days passed on which the friars did not administer those of penance and the Eucharist.

During Lent the entire Roman Catholic liturgy was available to the captives in the Algerian baños. On Ash Wednesday the friars placed ashes on almost all the Christians. Monroy preached, and he continued to do so daily throughout Lent. Those whose masters would permit them were invited to attend the *disciplina de sangre*, which was a flagellation ceremony for penitents, held every Friday during Lent after the baño was closed for the night. It was apparently a great effort for the captives to participate in this ceremony, since their chains and shackles made it difficult for them to kneel and move about, and Monroy remarked on the admiration of the Turkish and Moorish guards, who could hear the lashes and sighs of the penitents from their posts.[18]

During Holy Week religious fervor and activity reached its peak. The sacred period was preceded by a great flurry of preparation. "Those Christians who had some skill employed whatever time they could in making vestments for the altar, floral decorations, and other necessities, for which the administrator gave them the materials."[19] The Muslims loaned them ornaments with which to decorate the churches. A seventeenth-century Franciscan remarked that the adornment of the churches with silk and wax and oil lamps was so extensive "that it is no greater in any city in Spain."[20] Holy Week celebrations were vividly described by Father Monroy:

> When Palm Sunday arrived, we distributed the palms to the Christians, we held the procession and the entire office, with all possible solemnity. On Holy Wednesday we sang Tenebrae; many Christians attended, some merchants, but mostly captives. They remained for the disciplina, and most of them to sleep, because the baño was closed every day at sunset. Holy Thursday we said the office, I preached the Maundy, we enclosed the holy sacrament in the monument. . . . At night we said Tenebrae and we did not finish the disciplina, because it was . . . so copious . . . and there

were . . . many devout. . . . Friday arrived, we said the office, at night Tenebrae and disciplina de sangre for the devout of the brotherhood, and others who did not have a place the night before. Saturday the benediction . . . and the entire office, as all the other days. Sunday we arose very early to say Matins, Mass, and the Sermon of the Gifts of the Holy Virgin. . . . We held the procession with the holy sacrament, as we had every day of the Jubilee.[21]

During the processions the penitents paraded through the baño carrying candles and elaborate monuments.

The procession was held . . . with a cross of silver-plated wood, a banner with the arms of the King and the cross and pallium of our order. Some captives carried the monuments, while the others walked with candles in their hands, chanting . . . and a cleric carried the censer. . . . The alms that the captives gave were used to make the monuments very sumptuous. One consisted of twenty columns, with arches which were embellished with linen. . . . It had more than 100 lights, and was very long, for perspective.[22]

Other holy days were also celebrated with great festivity. For Corpus Christi the patios of the baños were decorated with palms and flowers, and the altars adorned with rich ornaments. Mass was sung in the morning, and a procession was usually held inside the baño in the afternoon. Many of the captives could play musical instruments, so most of the observances had musical accompaniment. On Christmas, a mass was sung at midnight and services were held throughout the day.[23]

Friar Jiménez noted that when he was in Algiers it was customary for the governor to give the captives cattle to slaughter for their Easter and Christmas Day meals. These were the only days of the year on which most captives ate meat. In addition, slaves of the governor or the state were not sent to work on Christmas, Easter, or important feast days.

This privilege, however, was often dependent on the governor's whim. On the eve of Corpus Christi in June 1719, the governor refused to exempt his captives from work because several of them had escaped earlier that day.[24]

In Tunis, as in Algiers, the slaves of the ruler enjoyed a rich spiritual life, with regular and frequent masses and festive celebrations of the holy days. From the day of his arrival until he was rescued, Friar Gracián celebrated mass every morning for those captives who were going out to work. At midday his companion, a Sicilian canon named Don Luis, said mass for the other captives. At night, after the baño was closed, Gracián would preach to the inmates. Gracián wrote that he was kept particularly busy during Lent, because it was necessary to preach every day and hear confessions very often, and many of the confessions were very long. He remarked that in 1595 Lent was made easier for him by the arrival the previous winter of a new group of captive clerics, which made it possible to say ten masses each day in the baño of the dey.[25]

Gracián's activities were not confined to the baño. If house slaves became ill, he was permitted to visit them, and to bring the holy sacrament if necessary. Gracián said that he always took the precaution of carrying the sacrament concealed underneath his cape, to avoid any demonstration of disrespect for it by Muslim children. But once he arrived at the house "they closed the doors from inside and did as in the land of Christians."[26]

Christian holy days were celebrated in Tunis with dances and processions, which were held not only inside the baño, but also through the streets of the city. Gracián remarked that the Muslims derived great enjoyment from these fiestas because of the eating and drinking that accompanied them and because they loved to watch the processions and public displays. They even helped decorate the church and patio of the baño for the feast days.[27]

In Morocco, from the late seventeenth century, holy days were very special events. There were several *cofradías* (brotherhoods) of captives in Meknès that organized processions for all the important feast days and the first Sunday of every month.

"On the principal feast days, the church is decorated, the walls are covered with draperies made of paper, but which appear to be of rich brocades, and the floor is carpeted with fragrant herbs and flowers."[28] The captives had all the accoutrements necessary for the processions.

> They have crosses, banners and flags . . . ; the holy sacrament is brought out in a pallium of very fine white damask. . . . The principal procession that they have is that of Corpus Christi day. . . . On this day the walls of the patio of the sagena, where the procession begins, are decorated with green stalks. In the center of the sagena they erect triumphal arches, decorated with herbs and flowers. . . . All of the captives participate in the procession, carrying candles. . . . A cleric leads . . . , holding an incense box. All walk chanting the hymns appropriate to that day.[29]

In order to hold their holy rites without interruption, the captives would ask the Moroccan in charge to close the iron gates of the sagena. On the principal feast days, they paid their overseers to take them out to work later than usual. Married captives, who did not live in the sagena, would come with their families on the evening of a holy day and remain in the compound overnight so they could attend the early morning service.[30]

The churches in the baños were maintained primarily out of funds collected in North Africa. In Algiers, a principal source of income was a tax on the tavern keepers, who were obliged to pay one *dobla* for each sack of wine or brandy that they sold. Alms collected from the captives were another important source of support. The majordomo of each church was permitted to take a daily collection among the captives in the baño and to go out into the city once a week to ask alms.[31]

Funds for the churches were also raised by the cofradías in Algiers. In 1594, two Trinitarian redemptors organized the Cofradía y Hermandad de la Santísima Trinidad in the baño grande. The record of the foundation of this cofradía, prepared in 1595, lists over seven hundred captives as brothers, all of them Spaniards. The following year the two friars helped establish cofradías in the baño de la bastarda and some of the other large baños. By 1639 there were seven such brotherhoods in Algiers. In addition to raising much of the money to support the churches, they sponsored daily masses, helped organize the processions for Holy Week and other feast days, and buried the dead.[32]

The North Africans also provided financial help and other assistance to the churches. Many Muslims donated money for masses or for wax or oil for the lamps. Gracián said that whenever the Turks entered his church they always gave a few coins.[33] We have already seen that during fiestas they gave the captives silks and brocades with which to decorate the churches.

In general, the North Africans showed great respect for the Catholic clerics and their faith. Gracián commented that he always found it rather astonishing to see the consideration that the Muslims had for the clerics.[34] In *Los baños de Argel*, the captive Ossorio was amazed that there were so many clerics in the baño celebrating the Easter mass. His companion, Vivanco, agreed that it was very admirable "that these faithless dogs let us keep our religion and say our mass."[35]

Silvestre related an incident when some Muslims came to the hospital one morning, seeking hidden arms. He said that although they searched the church in the hospital very thoroughly, they were extremely respectful of the sacred objects. "These Moors are worse than wolves toward the Christians," he wrote, "but they did not injure the celestial lamb, which is venerated by the Christians in our church."[36] Another seventeenth-century friar remarked that in times of epidemic, when the clerics had to make frequent visits with the holy sacrament to captives outside the baños, they were never abused or maltreated by either adults or children, nor was the sacrament ever subjected to insult. When they had to visit ailing captives who resided in the suburbs, they were never impeded by the guards at the city gates. Along the country roads, he added, they were "as safe as if they were guarded by the Turkish army."[37]

Even clerics who were captives were generally treated with respect and consideration. Those who were slaves of the sultan of Morocco were exempt from work.[38] As we have already seen, Friar Gracián received gentle treatment in Tunis. He was never sent out to work. The mother and mother-in-law of the dey often sent him and his fellow clerics fine linen shirts and saw to it that they were well fed. When Gracián finally was rescued, many Muslims gave him gifts before he departed.[39]

There were occasional exceptions to this attitude of respect for the Christian religion and the generally kind treatment of ecclesiastics. In 1579, for example, in the midst of a serious famine in Algiers, the governor turned to the marabouts for advice. They advised him not to permit the Christian slaves to hold services. The governor took their advice and prohibited the saying of mass. The prohibition lasted for only a few days, however, and religious services were soon restored.[40] In 1666, in response to the news that the Genoese had captured and burned a renegade who was an Algerian corsair, the divan ordered that all of the images and other sacred objects in the churches of the baños be burned. The overseers of the baños, however, warned the captives, and they were able to remove most of the images and objects from the churches and conceal them from the Algerians.[41] In the spring of 1594, all of the slaves in the baño of the dey of Tunis, except for Gracián, were sent with the fleet on an expedition through the Mediterranean. When they returned in November, Gracián's companion, the canon Don Luis, was "so weak and ill from working at the oar that he was useless to assist in any way, not even to say mass."[42]

Sometimes captive Spanish clerics were the victims of retaliation by the North Africans for offenses, real or imagined, committed against Muslim captives in Spain. Haedo told the story of Miguel de Aranda, a Benedictine friar from Valencia, who had been captured in 1576 while traveling from Tortosa to Tarragona by land. Aranda was put up for sale in the zoco of Algiers and was purchased by a Morisco family whose brother, a corsair, had been captured in Valencia and condemned by the Inquisition. The Moriscos were certain that they would be able to exchange Aranda for their brother. However, when word arrived in April 1577 that their brother had been publicly burned in Valencia, they decided to retaliate by burning the friar alive. They resisted all attempts to rescue him by the Mercedarian redemptors who were in Algiers at the time and requested permission from the governor of Algiers to burn him in revenge for the mistreatment of Muslims in Spain. In spite of opposition from some of his advisers to the burning of a seemingly innocent Christian, the governor apparently felt that it would be dangerous not to placate the Moriscos. The permission was granted and Aranda was burned alive on May 18, 1577.[43]

Another instance of retaliation against Spanish clerics for events in Spain occurred in February 1720 when the governor of Algiers, angered over a letter he had received in which some Muslim captives in Spain complained of being treated badly, ordered that the Spanish clerics be placed in heavy chains and taken out to pull carts filled with stones for the repair of the port. To increase the affront, they were required to wear their habits while they worked.[44] These incidents, however, were not typical of the treatment of captive clerics.

The attitude of the North Africans toward the Christian religion and the clerics was based partly on tradition. Beyond this, there were practical reasons for their permissiveness in matters of religion. The Muslims believed that the most devout captives made the best slaves. They thought that a slave who was spiritually content would be more submissive. The governor of Tunis once remarked that he would not give up Father Gracián for any amount of money because "he makes my Christians obedient."[45]

Furthermore, the North Africans wanted their slaves to remain in the Christian faith. The governor of Tunis would not permit his slaves to convert at all.[46] In Algiers, although captives were permitted to apostatize, in general the practice was discouraged. Even Gómez de Losada, who in his work repeatedly raises the specter of apostasy by captives in order to gain greater support for the redemption, admits that captives

who were expected to command a good rescue price were not
permitted to convert either by their owners or the divan, because the owners would lose the rescue price and the divan
would lose the departure fees for the captives.[47] Jiménez re-
counted an incident in October 1718 when the governor, himself a renegade, was informed that ten Christian captives wished
to become Muslims. He put them in chains with very heavy
balls attached "and kept them that way for several days until
they clamoured to be Christians."[48] The governor ordered that
any others who attempted to convert were to be given 500
lashes. The reason for this, Jiménez said, was that "he wanted
only the money for their rescues." Furthermore, he believed
that those who apostatized in captivity did so only to avoid the
onerous tasks and that they would not be true Muslims.[49]

At times, however, the Muslims did encourage conversions.
In 1559 thousands of Spanish soldiers were captives in Algiers
as a result of the Spanish defeat at Mostaganem the previous
year. The governor of Algiers, who was planning a military
expedition against other North African rulers, sought to profit
militarily from the presence of this potentially fine army and
offered to free all captives who would convert and accompany
him on the projected campaign. Large numbers of Spaniards
accepted his offer.[50] Sometimes attempts were made to convert captives who had skills that were highly valued in North
Africa. In 1719 the governor of Algiers offered "great advan-
tages" to a Spanish locksmith whose work he admired, if the
man would convert.[51] Owners also tried to convert individuals
of whom they were fond, and who would not be offered for
redemption. Women whose masters wanted to marry them
were sometimes under great pressure to become Muslims.
Bernarda de la Torre, an eighteen-year-old native of Almería
who had been captured in her village in 1666, was described,
when she was rescued in 1669, as having suffered great abuse
because she repelled attempts to persuade her to apostatize
and marry her master.[52] Young boys who were regarded as
good candidates for the elite janissary corps were also targets
of conversion efforts.

As a rule, though, the North Africans did not encourage

conversion. The reason for this was that the economic value of slaves who converted was significantly reduced, since the redemptionist friars would not rescue renegades, and limitations were placed on the type of labor that these captives could be forced to do. For example, they could not be sent to row in the galleys.[53] The owners of Christian slaves, therefore, did not want them to become Muslims.[54]

Thus, although Muslim tradition was a factor in North African religious policy, of greater significance were various economic considerations. The Muslims believed that their slaves would be better, more obedient workers if provided with the solace of religion. Even more important, they wanted to have either the unrestricted services of their Christian slaves or their ransom prices. Conversion by their captives would have deprived them of both.

Chapter 5
The Trinitarian Hospitals

The Hospitals in Algiers

In the second half of the seventeenth century the Trinitarians, a hospital as well as a redemptionist order, founded a network of hospitals in the baños of Algiers. The foundation of these institutions, under the auspices of the Spanish crown and with the encouragement of the Algerian government, may perhaps be viewed as a forerunner of collective international treatment of prisoners of war. Certainly the extent of support provided by both sides for the hospitals reflects the importance of the captives to the Algerians as well as to Spanish society.

Information concerning the administration of the hospitals and the type of care they dispensed is very limited. The most valuable sources are the narrative accounts of Friars Silvestre and Jiménez, who were associated with the hospitals in the late seventeenth and early eighteenth centuries, and an account book containing income and expenditure records, inventories of the hospitals and their pharmacies, and statistics on the numbers of patients treated for scattered time periods in the seventeenth and eighteenth centuries. A set of accounts covering the last four decades of the eighteenth century, which was maintained at the Trinitarian monastery in Madrid by the general administrator of hospitals in North Africa, was also utilized. These accounts are less valuable than those for the earlier period, since they provide information only on income received in and disbursements made from Spain and shed little light on the day-to-day operations of the hospitals in Algiers.[1]

The descriptive narratives as well as the inventories of pharmaceutical supplies and medical instruments suggest that the efforts of the hospitals were directed at curing patients; in that sense, they may be regarded as "modern," as opposed to hos-

91

pitals that offered only shelter and sustenance but did not specifically attempt to treat diseases or injuries.[2] The degree to which their curative efforts were successful is unknown.

The hospitals established in the late seventeenth century were not the first for captives in Algiers, but the history of the earlier ones is somewhat obscure. According to Haedo, the only hospital in the city in the late sixteenth century was a small one, created in 1549 by Hasan Paşa for the care of Muslims.[3] However, a reconfirmation of the privileges granted to the Trinitarian hospitals by the dey of Algiers in the eighteenth century states that the maintenance of such establishments in that city by the Trinitarians dates back to 1551.[4] This is supported by Francisco Jiménez, who claimed that the first Trinitarian hospital in Algiers was founded in 1551, in the baño grande.[5] I have found no pre-eighteenth-century references to this hospital, though, and Friar Silvestre claimed that there were no such institutions in Algiers prior to 1612, when one was established by the Trinitarian friars arrested by the Algerians in 1609. In May 1612, Bernardo de Monroy wrote that he and his companions had founded the Hospital of the Holy Trinity, with eight beds, in the baño grande. Their undertaking had the approval of the governor of Algiers and the guardián baji, the overseer of the baño.[6]

It appears that the hospital created by Monroy was neglected and fell into disuse sometime in the first half of the seventeenth century. It was not until later in the century that it was reconstituted and four other hospitals founded. The new hospital establishments were primarily the work of Pedro de la Concepción, a Trinitarian who arrived in Algiers in 1662. Prior to his departure for the Maghrib, he had spent three years, both in Spain and the New World, collecting funds for the hospitals' endowment. These funds were invested in *juros* (government annuities) and *censos* (mortgages) that were to provide the hospitals with a continuing income.[7]

Two hospitals were instituted in the baño grande and three in other large baños. The administrative center was in the baño grande and it was here that the administrator and the Trinitarian friars who assisted him were housed. A pharmacy was also set up in the baño grande to provide herbs and medicines for all the hospitals.[8]

Each hospital had a nurse and a cook, as well as a chaplain to administer the sacraments to those who were very ill. All who served in these positions were captives, for whom the administrator paid their owners 2 pesos a month. A doctor or a surgeon, and sometimes both, were attached to the main hospital in the baño grande, and made daily visits to the others. In the seventeenth century these were usually freed captives who had stayed on in Algiers to serve at the hospitals. In the eighteenth century, however, it was common for surgeons to be sent from Spain. The Mercedarians who came to Algiers to ransom captives in 1723 brought with them from Spain not only a surgeon for the hospital, but a pharmacist as well. In 1724 they again brought a surgeon with them, the first having died. Surgeons sent from Madrid were carefully chosen. In 1769, for example, the chief surgeon of the general hospital of Madrid, at the behest of the Trinitarians, examined various candidates for the position in Algiers and recommended Manuel Antonio Suárez, who had practiced in his hospital, as the best qualified. In spite of the care taken in making the selection, the individual chosen was not always successful in the post. In 1778 the administrator in Algiers reported that Felix Antonio Morales, a surgeon who had been sent from Spain in 1776, should be replaced, since he was not content, nor was the administrator satisfied with his work or his conduct. He was succeeded by Cipriano Cañada, who had served on the staff of the Madrid general hospital for ten years. In contrast, Alejandro San Millán volunteered to remain in Algiers for an additional two years when his six-year term expired in 1763.[9]

The documents do not indicate the capacity of the hospitals at the time of their founding. We do know that the main hospital in the baño grande was by far the largest. Alonso Cano, writing in 1770 when only this hospital remained, noted that it usually had sixty beds, but in times of epidemic its facilities could be expanded to accommodate more than one hundred patients.[10]

Only scattered data are available on the number of captives

cared for in the hospitals. A complete set of accounts from May 1686 to mid-June 1688 includes this type of information.[11] Unfortunately, it is not possible to determine how many individual cases were treated throughout the period; only a daily count of the patients is available. Thus, all that can be ascertained is the global figure, or number of patient days, of 16,445 for the entire time. As for the number of captives in the hospitals at any given moment, on a daily basis this usually ranged from ten to twenty during the fifteen months from May 1686 through July 1687.

These figures suggest either that the captives were a remarkably healthy group, or that many of those who became ill were not treated in the hospitals and perhaps were not treated at all. For at a time when the captive population in Algiers numbered in the thousands, only a small portion of these were in the hospitals at any one time. It is possible, indeed likely, that many others were cared for in their masters' homes.

The hospitals were prepared to handle many more patients, as they did from early August 1687, when an Algerian assault on Orán yielded large numbers of captives, many of whom were wounded. In the wake of the military engagement, the population of the hospitals swelled from fourteen on August 4 to sixty-two on August 5; the additional forty-eight were all wounded soldiers.[12] The figure remained high through the autumn and winter, when thirty to thirty-five patients were treated each day. Even as late as June 1688, the daily average was twenty-six. It is interesting to note that during the twenty-six months covered by these accounts there were no discernible seasonal fluctuations in the number of patients treated, a surprising discovery since plague was endemic to Algiers in the warmer months.

After the capture of Orán by the Algerians in 1709, which resulted in the influx of many additional captives into Algiers, the hospitals again were forced to handle far more patients than they were accustomed to. Although there is no indication of how many were treated after the war, it is clear from the expense records that the resources of the hospitals must have been strained. From mid-May to December 1710, a period of seven and one-half months, the hospitals' expenditures shot up to 21,881 reales, more than double the 10,042 reales spent during all of 1707, the last previous year for which a complete set of expenditures is available. In 1711 expenses totaled 34,712 reales, more than three times those of 1707.[13] Income kept pace with the increased expenses, as more financial assistance arrived from Spain in the wake of the Orán disaster.

Both the physical and financial resources were inadequate to deal, however, with a crisis that developed in 1756 when the captive population had declined and only the hospital in the baño grande remained. The year began with the onset in early February of a virulent epidemic that continued at least until August 24. During this period the hospital treated 444 victims of the disease, of whom 236 died. The situation became so severe in the months of June and July that the administrator was forced to rent a neighboring house that was converted into an infirmary for convalescents. The cost of caring for so many very sick patients as well as the expense of replacing mattresses and bedclothes that had been burned in order to eliminate all traces of the contagion placed a severe strain on the hospital's budget, and in October of that year the administrator, Friar Bernardo Pasqual, wrote to Spain pleading for more money.[14] To make matters worse, that autumn Algiers had attacked Tunis and in November the victorious Algerians returned to their city, bringing with them virtually all the Christian captives from Tunis, a total of about 950. Many of these arrived hungry, exhausted, and ill from the long trip and in need of the hospital's medical and social services. In a second letter, Pasqual remarked that his institution was now "truly a hospital," that there was not even sufficient room for his own bed because there were sick and dying captives all about.[15]

The annual costs of operating the hospitals and pharmacy varied. As we have already seen, a military campaign by the Algerians against Orán usually brought in its wake large numbers of wounded captives. Another factor that could seriously affect the hospitals' budget was the incidence of epidemic disease in Algiers. In 1664 the operating expenses of the hospitals totaled 12,960 reales. But in addition, thousands of captives died in an epidemic that year, and the hospital had to bear the cost of burying most of them at a peso each.[16] In epidemic years the hospitals' expenses often outpaced their income. A prolonged epidemic that began in 1675 and lasted for two years took the lives of more than five thousand captives. Because of the tremendous expenses incurred by the hospitals during this period, in March 1678 the Spanish crown granted the Trinitarians permission to ask alms in the Indies, over a period of four years, for the hospitals in Algiers.[17]

Detailed statements of hospital expenditures are also available for isolated time periods in the seventeenth and eighteenth centuries. For the twenty-five months from May 1, 1686, through May 31, 1688, the expenses of the five hospitals totaled 28,723 reales, an average of 13,787 reales a year.[18] Similar sets of accounts are extant for an extended period in the eighteenth century, from 1704 through 1707. During these four years the hospitals spent a total of 38,161 reales, for an average of 9,540 reales a year.[19] The expenses of the pharmacy were separate from those of the hospitals. These too varied greatly from year to year, but according to Silvestre were never less than 3,200 reales in the seventeenth century.[20]

To reduce operating costs, the administrator of the hospitals entertained and gave gifts to various Muslims who were regarded as "friends" of the hospital. When the corsairs' boats returned from their expeditions, these individuals would learn what merchandise and drugs were included in the booty and report this information to the administrator. He would then charge each of them with the purchase of certain needed items, which they were able to buy at a price considerably lower than what the administrator himself would have had to pay. For example, in February 1714 the hospitals purchased 110 pounds of salmon and in January 1715 2 *botas* (approximately 615 gallons each) of wine from the corsairs' booty.[21] Another way of lowering costs was to buy meat from the Jews that they had rejected for not meeting the requirements of their dietary laws. The account books contain frequent entries of purchases of this sort.

The hospitals were supported primarily by the income from

juros and censos, those purchased by Pedro de la Concepción as well as others acquired in subsequent years. Gifts were sometimes made to the hospitals in this form. In addition, the hospitals frequently received substantial donations and testamentary bequests in cash, which administrators, over the years, had used to purchase additional securities of this nature. During the latter part of the eighteenth century, investments of this type accounted for approximately 75 percent of the money raised in Spain for the hospitals.[22]

Although the Spanish crown did not grant a fixed income to the hospitals, it did take steps to facilitate the collection of funds for their maintenance. In 1672, for example, the crown established a memorial to the late queen mother that allowed alms to be asked in her name for the support of the hospitals.[23] From time to time, the crown also made outright gifts to the hospitals. In 1729, for example, it directed the Council of the Cruzada to grant them 7,500 reales. In 1761 the crown gave 30,000 silver reales. From the early eighteenth century it made an annual gift of one *arroba* (about 25 pounds) of mercury; the income from its sale was to be used to purchase supplies for the pharmacy.[24] The hospitals also received a portion of the income from vacant bishoprics in Spain. In 1763, for example, they received a total of 6,000 reales from the income of the bishoprics of Oviedo and León, and in 1767, 4,000 reales from the vacant bishopric of Plasencia.[25]

The pharmacy in Algiers was a favorite beneficiary of bequests and donations from pharmacists in Spain. Silvestre cites the case of one Madrid pharmacist who bequeathed more than 4,000 reales for the purpose of sending materials to the pharmacy in Algiers. In 1761 Don Bartolomé Ortiz, the personal pharmacist to the queen mother, gave the pharmacy a crate of medicines.[26]

The earliest continuous record of funds sent from Spain for the hospitals dates from 1759. During the decade 1759–1769, the last in which there were significant numbers of Spanish captives in Algiers, the remittances to the hospital from the general administrator in Madrid averaged about 66,000 reales a year. No comparable data were found for the earlier epoch—

the first three-quarters of a century after the hospitals' foundation—when the population served by them was at its peak. Nevertheless, the accounts that are available for the first two decades of the eighteenth century make it appear that the hospitals usually received adequate financial support, since they frequently show a surplus at the end of an administrator's tenure.[27]

The Muslims, knowing that the hospitals treated and often cured their slaves at no cost to them, also helped with their support. A captive friar from each baño, accompanied by the majordomo of each hospital, was permitted to go through the streets of Algiers once a week asking alms for the hospitals. Further, at the time they were founded by Pedro de la Concepción, the Algerian government conceded to the Trinitarians certain taxes and fees, known as *garramas*, for their support. These included a charge of 2 pesos on every Christian ship that arrived in the port of Algiers to take on or discharge merchandise and an additional levy of 2 reales on each mariner who went ashore. The hospitals also received 2 reales of the 40-peso tax charged for each rescued captive who departed from Algiers. Finally, the Algerian government granted to the hospitals an annual garrama of 6.5 pesos on each of 6 botas of wine produced in the baño grande.[28] The garramas did not defray a significant portion of the hospitals' expenses. Silvestre said that in the seventeenth century the highest annual income from these fees was 1,040 reales.[29] In 1704 these concessions yielded a total of 1,020 reales, but during the following three years they dropped by 40 to 50 percent.[30] Furthermore, the income from the garramas was not reliable. In years in which few or no ships arrived in Algiers or no redemption was made, the garramas fell significantly. Even the garrama on wine was not dependable. In 1706 the governor appropriated it for his own account, claiming that he was short of funds, and in 1707 the grape harvest was so poor that there was no garrama on wine.[31] But the Algerian government provided other forms of support for the hospitals as well. It required each baño in the city to provide, free of charge, one Christian captive to serve in the hospitals. In addition, it permitted the hospitals to import both money and merchandise from Spain free of the usual duties.[32]

The primary purpose of the hospitals was to serve the Christian captives. They had to attend to their needs before making themselves available to the Algerians. The medical treatment of Muslims by those affiliated with the hospitals was generally discouraged, because of complications that might ensue should the treatment fail, although they were permitted to treat Jews. The services of the pharmacy were also limited to the captives. It was not permitted to supply medicines to anyone else, even if he paid for them. The only exception to this rule might be a person who needed some small item, such as a salve, and who in return would permit the pharmacist to take from his garden the herbs and flowers he required.[33]

A captive could not be treated at or enter the hospital without the consent of his master or of the divan. If treatment was given without this permission and the captive died, the hospital was liable to his owner for the redemption price he would have asked for the slave. Every captive who did enter the hospital had to bring with him a blanket and a peso. The blanket was to be used on the bed while he was ill. If the patient lived, the blanket would be returned to his master; if he died, he would be buried in it. As for the peso, it too would be returned to the owner if the patient survived, but if he died it would be used to pay the four captives who would bury his remains.[34]

The Trinitarians did not have hospitals for women in Algiers, nor could women be treated in those already mentioned. Silvestre said that this was because the Muslims would not permit it. Many masters did, however, permit the doctors to treat their female slaves in their homes, and the hospital administrator was often allowed to visit them and to administer the sacraments when necessary.[35]

The function of the hospitals was not limited to the care of the sick. Equally important was their role as religious centers and residences or friaries for a group of free Trinitarians who were assigned to Algiers. With the establishment of these hospitals, the already extensive religious activities of the Christian captives expanded and became more highly organized. Trinitarian friars coordinated the observance by the captives of religious days, and an examination of the account books of the hospitals shows substantial outlays for meats and other protein-rich foods on important feast days. The accounts for the feast of the Holy Trinity in 1686, for example, include expenditures for numerous beef cattle, chickens, lambs, and goats for the celebration.[36]

In addition, the clerics associated with the hospitals performed a variety of social services for the captives. It was not unusual for the administrator to give alms to captives who were hungry or in need of clothing; there are numerous entries of this nature in the account books. The friars frequently visited those who were kept imprisoned. Father Jiménez, who kept a detailed diary of his experiences, related many incidents of visits to incarcerated captives.[37] The hospitals also bore the expenses of burying all Catholic captives who died outside the hospitals.[38] The Trinitarians at the hospital assumed, too, the responsibility for the education of the children of captives. In the summer of 1761 the general administrator sent to Algiers a box of primers to be used to teach children to read. Later that year 100 catechisms were sent, also to be used for the children's education.[39]

The administrator, for his part, became a spokesman for all the captives, but especially for the Spaniards who, up to that time, had no official to represent them. Jiménez tells of frequent visits by the administrator to the governor or other Algerian officials on behalf of the captives. Sometimes he would go to request that the Christians be excused from work on certain feast days. At other times he would intercede on behalf of particular captives to prevent them from being punished or to mitigate their punishment. On August 31, 1719, for example, he visited the guardián baji to plead with him not to castigate some Spanish slaves who had been found outside the city washing their clothes.[40]

The administrator's role went even beyond this. Laugier de Tassy, writing in the eighteenth century, compared the Casa del Hospital de España, as the Trinitarian residence was known, to the consulates that other states, but not Spain, maintained in Algiers. "When the king of Spain wishes to conduct business with the government of Algiers, he avails himself of the services of the administrator of the royal hospitals."[41] The administrator also acted as a mediator in any conflict between the friar-redemptors and the governor of Algiers over the course of a redemption.[42]

Hospitals in Morocco and Tunis

Hospitals for captives were established in other North African states much later than in Algiers. In 1691 the Spanish crown founded a royal hospital and friary in Meknès, which the Moroccan emperor placed under his protection in return for an annual gift. At that time there were about one thousand Spanish captives in Meknès, most of whom had been captured while in military service. The hospital establishment, which was supported by a royal grant of 2,228 pesos a year made at the time of its founding, was to house a total of twelve Franciscan missionaries. But John Windus, an Englishman who visited Morocco in the 1720s, wrote that the hospital, which had a 100-bed capacity, had only four missionaries and a doctor.[43]

In 1720 Father Jiménez left the hospital in Algiers in order to found a similar one in Tunis. To encourage the establishment of the new hospital, the *bey* (ruler) of Tunis provided the site and conceded to it privileges similar to those enjoyed by the hospitals of Algiers. These included the right to import into Tunis, duty free, money, equipment, and supplies for the hospital. The bey also granted the hospital a gift of 200 pesos a year, as well as the income from a 2-peso tax to be levied on every Christian ship arriving at the port of Tunis and a charge of 2 reales on each rescued captive. Furthermore, he committed himself to provide four Christian captives to serve at the hospital full time, and four captives to bury Christian slaves who died.[44] The hospital in Tunis was also aided by contributions from Spain, including an annual grant of 200 pesos from the Council of the Cruzada, which was given from 1729 through 1746.[45]

There are many lacunae in our information concerning the hospitals that the Spaniards maintained for captives in North Africa. Inventories of the Trinitarian hospitals from the eighteenth century show that they were well provided with medical and pharmaceutical instruments and equipment, as well as numerous medical treatises.[46] But the documents tell us virtually nothing about the quality of medical care that was dispensed, nor do they indicate how far-reaching this care was. It is clear, though, that the Trinitarian hospitals became integral to the way of life of the Christian captives, not only as sources of health care that had not heretofore been available, but also as providers of important social services. That they were encouraged and supported by the Muslims for over a century may indicate that they achieved some degree of success.

Of greater importance, however, in explaining the Muslims' enthusiasm for the hospitals is the fact that these institutions subsidized the North African slave system. By providing basic medical and social services, the Christians assumed the marginal expenses of slavery that would otherwise have been borne by the slaveowners, and thus helped make slaveowning a lucrative enterprise.

More significant yet in ensuring that corsairing and the taking of captives would be profitable were the ransom payments. It is to the system that provided this assurance—redemptionism—that we now turn our attention.

PART III
THE REDEMPTION

Chapter 6
Procedures and Financing

The campaign to ransom captives from North Africa had a prominent place in early modern Spain. This, of course, was not a new development; the problem of rescuing Spaniards from Muslims had existed since the first Moorish invasion in the eighth century. But in the past the ransoming process had been conducted somewhat informally with relatively little interference from the crown, whereas in from the late sixteenth century, as the number of captives in North Africa increased all aspects of the redemption came under the state's control.

At the same time, the scale of the redemptions grew; the sums raised to ransom captives through the early years of the seventeenth century seem trifling when compared to the funds that were available later. Just as the seventeenth century was the great age of the corsairs, so too were the seventeenth and eighteenth centuries the great age of the redemptionists. By then, if not earlier, the redemption of captives was a "big business" in Spain as well as in North Africa. This traffic was not reciprocal. Although some of the many Muslim captives in Spain were ransomed individually, there was no large-scale Muslim ransoming effort. The reasons for this are not altogether clear, but since most North African slaves in Spain had been engaged in corsairing, it appears unlikely that the Spanish government would have allowed them to regain their freedom. Economic conditions within North Africa may also have been a factor.

Medieval Redemptionism

During the early years of the Middle Ages, there was no organized system for the redemption of captives held by the Muslims. Instead, individual prisoners or their families were

105

expected to arrange for their ransoms. Occasionally, the relatives or friends of captives traveled into Islamic Spain to rescue them, but most redemptions of this period were negotiated by merchants engaged in trade with the Muslims, who were paid a fee for their services.[1]

Later, the method of rescue by merchants became more highly organized. In the twelfth and thirteenth centuries some Spanish towns developed a system of licensing professional ransomers. Various town fueros of this period refer to the rights and obligations of *exeas* in the fulfillment of commissions of redemption. These individuals, who were named by the crown or councils, were privileged persons, traveling under safe-conduct across the military frontier between Christian and Islamic Spain. They were usually merchants who maintained regular traffic with the Moors and who were charged with ransoming captives as well. For their services, the exeas were paid 10 percent of the ransom price.[2]

Although the obligation for providing the rescue money continued to fall on the captives or their families, there were other sources of funds as well. Members of the Military Order of Santiago, founded in Castile in 1175, and the Order of Montegaudio, founded in Aragón shortly thereafter, collected alms for the redemption of captives.[3] In addition, some towns helped pay for the rescue of their citizens; in Valencia, for example, a tax was levied in the thirteenth century for the purpose of providing ransoms for captured soldiers.[4] Various societies and brotherhoods also guaranteed their members that they would be ransomed if they were captured by the Muslims. In the twelfth century the fishermen of Tarragona organized such a brotherhood, which continued to function until the middle of the next century.[5]

At the beginning of the thirteenth century, two religious orders dedicated to the redemption of captives were instituted in Spain. The Order of the Holy Trinity was established in Aragón in 1201, and in 1218 James I of Aragón granted a charter to the Order of the Merced. Shortly thereafter, both orders established houses in Castile.[6] Later, other smaller redemptionist orders were created. In 1569, Pedro García Orense, a municipal official of Burgos, left his entire estate, more than ten million maravedís, for the redemption of captives. The redemptors from Burgos, known as the Congregación del Santo Cristo de Burgos, made nine expeditions, the first in 1593 and the last in 1676, in which they rescued 1,035 captives, 543 from Algiers and 492 from Morocco, for a total cost of 64,495,950 maravedís.[7] In the eighteenth century the Third Order of San Francisco, established in Madrid in 1722, made several general redemptions with income from a foundation created by a noblewoman, Lorenza de Cardeñas Manrique de Lara.[8] But both this order and the Congregación operated on a rather small scale, and from the thirteenth century the redemption of captives from the Muslims was dominated by the Mercedarians and Trinitarians. The two orders were not, however, equal in size and wealth. Insofar as redemptionism was concerned, the Mercedarians were always wealthier and more powerful than the Trinitarians, who had been founded, and continued to serve, as a hospital order.

The Role of the State

Until the reign of Philip II, the state supported but did not interfere with the activities of the redemptionist orders.[9] The situation changed under Philip, when the government regulated every step of the ransoming of captives. The Council of Castile issued minutely detailed instructions to every party of friar-redemptors that traveled to North Africa. These instructions required that the friars be accompanied by a notary appointed by the council, which directed the redemption to pay him a salary of 20 silver reales a day, from the time they left Madrid until the final report was submitted to the royal authorities. The notary had to be present at all times; it was his responsibility to keep a written account, in triplicate, of all transactions, and to verify their accuracy. The records kept by the notaries were extremely thorough, and provide complete details of the daily activities of the redemption.

Ransoming expeditions were initiated by the Council of Castile, upon petition by the general of either of the redemptionist orders, when the order had accumulated sufficient funds. After approving the petition, the council would grant a license to undertake the redemption and to publicize it throughout the kingdom. This document stated the purpose of the expedition, named the friar-redemptors, and outlined the route they were to take. It authorized the collection of *limosnas*, alms that went into the general funds of the expedition, as well as *adjutorios*, which were contributions earmarked for the rescue of specific individuals. (The Council of Aragón granted a separate license to publicize the redemption and collect funds in that kingdom.)

Although the instructions of the council required that those rescued with limosnas "be natives of these kingdoms," the friars were usually permitted to accept adjutorios for any captive, without restriction. In the seventeenth century, however, after the Portuguese revolt, a provision was added to the instructions prohibiting the acceptance of funds for captives "from the rebel kingdom of Portugal."[10] No restriction was ever placed on the rescue of captives from the rebellious Catalán kingdom.

The notary recorded all funds collected by the friars, as well as the names of the donors, and the purpose for which the money had been given. One copy of this record was turned over to "the person named by the Council to know the amount of money that they have for the redemption." The notary and the auditor made it possible for the council to keep close watch over the entire procedure.

In addition to the license, the crown also issued a special passport addressed to all local royal officials. It named the redemptors and stated their task: "to travel to the Barbary kingdoms in order to rescue the poor captives who are in the power of the infidels." In this document the officials were directed to provide the friars with any assistance necessary to travel to North Africa without paying duties or fees in the port of embarkation. That these orders did not always ensure the cooperation of local officials suggests how weak royal authority was at this level. In 1632, one of the Trinitarian redemptors had to address a special plea to the duke of Medina Sidonia that he direct his customs officials to comply with the royal decree and proceed with the registration and preparation of the merchandise and money for the redemption.[11] In the Mercedarian expedition of 1739, contrary to royal instructions, the governor of Cartagena and various other officials demanded from the redemption the payment of departure fees totaling 825 silver pesos for 50 Muslim slaves whom the king had donated, to be exchanged for Christian captives. In granting the Muslims for the exchange, the crown had stipulated that they were to be free of all duties.[12] Although the crown directed the officials involved to return the money "under pain of royal indignation," a similar incident occurred in 1751, when the officials of the port of Cartagena again imposed exit duties on 110 Muslims whom the crown had given to the Mercedarians for an exchange.[13]

Royal officials along the route to the port of departure were sometimes ordered to provide protection for the expeditions. A directive of 1660 addressed to such officials stated that the friars were traveling to Tetuán with a large sum of money and that "in view of the lack of security on the roads at this time due to the large numbers of soldiers and vagrants that congregate on them, and of the many robberies that they perpetrate every day, the treasury of the redemption is not able to proceed without great danger of being lost." These officials were enjoined, therefore, to provide guards and convoys to accompany the friars within Spain.[14]

Because of severe restrictions on the export of specie from the country the amount of money that the redemptionists took out of Spain was carefully monitored and regulated.[15] The passport stipulated the quantities that the friars were permitted to export, and a new passport was required if they wished to exceed this sum. The Mercedarians who traveled to Algiers in 1669, for example, were granted a passport in May of that year permitting them to take 800,000 reales. A month later a second passport authorized an additional 400,000 reales.[16] In the redemption of 1675, the first passport, issued in October 1674, granted the redemption the right to export 100,000 pesos. A supplementary passport, issued the following January, permitted them to take 20,000 pesos more which they had collected since October.[17]

Prior to their departure from Spain, the friars had to register their treasury with the officials of the port from which they were sailing, in the presence of two notaries appointed by port officials. The contents of each box were weighed and counted, after which the boxes were numbered, sealed, and loaded on board their vessel. This information was recorded, and many of these inventories still can be found in the record books of the redemptions. Within six months after the ship had been laded, the redemption was required to submit a report of its finances to the Council of Castile, and within thirty days after the return with the rescued captives it was to account for its expenditures. A substantial fine, usually 2,000 ducats, was provided for failure to submit these reports on time, but there is no evidence that this penalty was ever imposed.

The extensive government regulation of redemptionist activity reflects in part the bureaucratizing tendencies of Philip II. But it also suggests the possibility that in the past the unscrutinized activity of the redemptionists may have led to abuses which these stringent controls sought to eliminate.

Income of the Redemption

The Mercedarian and Trinitarian orders, which both in Spain and in the New World were frequently engaged in jurisdictional struggles, almost never collaborated in a redemption.[18] In the early seventeenth century a reform movement within the Trinitarian order led to the development of a separate branch, the Descalzos, which carried on redemptionist activity separate from that of the older order. Because of this proliferation of groups dedicated to redemptionism, it was not uncommon for an expedition by one to follow closely on the heels of another. Consequently, the effort to raise funds to ransom captives was an ongoing activity in early modern Spain.

The proclamation of a redemption was accompanied by a great deal of publicity. Placards announcing the event were posted throughout Spain; in addition, brief accounts by former captives or the redemptionists themselves, which served to remind potential donors of the sufferings of those in captivity and the risks taken by the friars, were printed and widely circulated.

The printed propaganda was augmented by public ceremonies. For example, the publication of the Mercedarian redemption of 1723 was heralded by a procession held in Madrid on October 9, 1722, in which members of the high nobility, including the dukes of Lesera and Osuna, participated. The streets along the route were crowded with onlookers and the royal family watched from the balconies of the Buen Retiro palace.[19] The participation of such high-level public figures suggests the degree to which the crown supported, and encouraged the public to support, redemptionist activity.

Funds for the rescue of captives were raised from various sources, both public and private. Much of the money for ransoms came in the form of adjutorios, which were given by the families or friends of designated captives and earmarked only for them. But the redemption of captives was also one of the favorite charities in early modern Spain for donors at all levels of society.

The Spanish crown provided strong financial support to the redemption. The most important single source of funds within the government was the Council of the Cruzada, which had at its disposal income from *abintestatos*, estates that passed to the crown from individuals who died intestate and without qualified heirs, and *mostrencos*, property that was considered abandoned and ordered sold.[20] The council also administered various endowments and ordinary bequests for the rescue of captives. In 1621, for example, it had at its disposal 10,000 reales that Don Martín de Córdoba, a former official of the council, had left to it with instructions that the entire principal be used for the rescue of Spanish women and children held captive by the infidel.[21]

The council made grants of various types. It contributed to every redemption a lump sum, usually about 500 ducats, that was not earmarked for specific captives, but could be used at the discretion of the redemptionist friars. In ten expeditions between 1662 and 1698, the council gave a total of 5,900 ducats for this purpose.[22] Most of the money that the council gave for ransoms was intended to aid specific individuals. These grants were usually made in response to petitions by relatives, friends, or officials of the captive's town or village. Occasionally the requests came from the captives themselves, who were permitted—indeed, encouraged—to write to Spain for the rescue money.[23] Requests for aid had to be supported by evidence that the person was in fact, or had been, a captive, in the form of letters written by the captive from North Africa, testimony from trusted witnesses (such as the administrator of the hospitals), and an explanation of the circumstances under which the person had been captured.

Contributions by the council for the rescue of individuals were not usually for the entire ransom price. Although those taken prisoner while in royal service or from the Indies fleet were preferred, aid was also given to ordinary civilian captives, and to those of low as well as high social status. In 1639, for example, the council gave 400 ducats for the rescue from Tetuán of four fishermen from Vigo in Galicia. In 1642 it gave 500 ducats toward the ransom of a family of ten from the village of La Guardia, also in Galicia, who had been captured in their village some years earlier and had written from Algiers asking for assistance in paying for their rescue.[24] At the opposite end of the social spectrum was Francisco de Alarcón, son of the governor of Ceuta and a captive in Tetuán. In 1650 the council allocated 22,000 reales for his ransom, and in 1655 the crown directed it to aid him with an additional 11,000 reales. Don Francisco was finally rescued for 112,000 reales and fourteen Muslim captives in Spanish hands.[25]

Some of the petitions to the council reflect the financial state of the Spanish gentry. In 1627, a request on behalf of Don Alonso de Herrera of Jerez de la Frontera, a captive in Salé, stated that although he was among the principal caballeros of his city, he was "very poor" and could not afford to pay his own ransom, which his North African master, aware of his noble rank, had set at 5,600 reales. In 1644 an agent of the duke of Ciudad Real wrote to the council on behalf of Don Juan Francisco Ortiz Colonia of Madrid, a twenty-four-year-old army officer who had been captured while serving with the royal armada. The letter said that although Ortiz was of an important noble family, he too was poor.[26] Although poverty is a relative condition, it is possible that in terms of the high ransoms asked for them both men were poor and truly in need of assistance.

The council also allocated funds for specific classes of captives, such as the residents of a particular village or region. The files contain frequent expressions of concern, by both the crown and the council, for the rescue of the captives seized in Gualchos in 1640. In 1641 the Council gave the Trinitarians 40,809 reales toward their ransom.[27] In the same year, a total of 9,600 reales was given to assist in the rescue of various individual captives.

Many captives who had already been rescued but had incurred debts in order to pay all or part of their ransom were aided by the council. In 1648, for example, the council gave 50 ducats to Lorenzo de Mesa, who had been rescued from Tunis eight months earlier, but had gone into debt for more than 4,000 reales for his ransom. In June 1637 the Cruzada aided the family of Mathias Puchal of Ibiza, who had been a captive in Algiers with his two young daughters, his thirty-six-year-old sister, and her daughter. He had negotiated his family's ransom with his master for a total of 11,000 reales and had been permitted to return alone to Ibiza to raise the money. He had succeeded in paying 10,000 reales of it to a Genoese in Valencia, who was his master's correspondent, and the council granted him the remaining 1,000 reales. In 1713 the council gave Antonio Orgaz 500 reales to help repay a debt of more than 1,700 reales that he had incurred when he was rescued by the Mercedarians eight months earlier.[28]

The council aided not only captives who were ransomed through the traditional channels, but sometimes those who gained their freedom in less orthodox ways. In 1702 Roque de Robles of Jerez de la Frontera requested help in paying a debt to some Muslims who had helped him escape from Meknès in December 1701. In his petition he noted that if the money were not paid to his accomplices as promised, in the future the Moors would be less willing to help captives escape. The council apparently saw his point, for it granted 100 reales to him, as well as to Sebastián Antonio of Montilla, who had escaped at the same time, and 400 reales to Simón González de Donís, who fled in March 1701 and owed 800 reales to those who had aided him.[29]

Other government councils also provided important sums. In 1583 the Council of Castile gave 1,125,000 maravedís to the Mercedarians.[30] In 1661, 121,792 reales from the fees collected by various councils were given to the Trinitarians.[31] Until the mid-seventeenth century, the Council of Orders regularly allocated a portion of the income of the Order of Santiago for the redemption of captives who were natives of villages and towns under its jurisdiction, with the proviso that no more than 52,500 maravedís were to be applied from these funds to any individual captive. In the event that there were not sufficient captives from the territories of Santiago, then the friars were to rescue subjects of the other two military orders, Alcántara and Calatrava. The sums given by the Council of Orders ranged from 628,000 maravedís in the Mercedarian redemption of 1575 to 49,844 maravedís in 1654,[32] the year of the last record found of a contribution of this nature, but the amount was generally about 200,000 maravedís. This was not an enormous sum of money for the redemption—at a maximum price of 52,500 maravedís each, it permitted the rescue of only four, or perhaps five, captives—but it was given regularly until the mid-seventeenth century. The other military orders occasionally made generous contributions to the redemption as well. The Order of Alcántara maintained a foundation in honor of one of its deceased commanders, Luis de Villacajas, which gave the Trinitarians 397,184 maravedís in 1617 and 204,000 maravedís in 1621 for the rescue of its subjects or those of the other orders. If these could not be located, the money was to be used to rescue children or men captured in military service.[33]

Alms collected in the New World made a valuable contribution to the redemption. Indeed, it was these funds, channeled through the Council of the Indies, that made possible the large ransoming expeditions of the second half of the seventeenth century. Priority in the use of this money was given to captives whose rescue had been requested by the Spanish

crown, those from the Indies, and those captured in the carrera.[34] Otherwise it could be utilized at the discretion of the
friars. The fact that they fell into the category of limosnas,
rather than adjutorios, whose use was restricted, lent special
importance to the large sums raised in the Indies. Table 5
illustrates the relationship of contributions from the Indies to
the total amount of limosnas in some of the redemptions of the
second half of the seventeenth century. In 1648 alms from the
Indies represented only 28.8 percent of all limosnas, but by
1667 receipts from the New World accounted for 72.2 percent.
The records of the Mercedarian redemption of 1702 did not
provide a breakdown of funds into limosnas and adjutorios,
but in that year the contributions from the Indies represented
70.4 percent of the entire treasury of the redemption.

Because funds from the New World constituted such a large
portion of the redemption's treasury, the Council of the Indies
had the right to audit its financial records.[35] Furthermore, the
council occasionally initiated redemptions. In 1664 the *Margarita*, one of the vessels of the Indies fleet on which a number
of important people were traveling, was captured by Algerian
corsairs. On October 20, 1665, Juan de Solar, on behalf of the
council, wrote to José Sánchez, master-general of the Mercedarians, advising him that the most recent fleet from the In-

Table 5. Sources of Income for the Redemption, 1648–1702[a]

Year	Limosnas Collected in Spain	Limosnas from New World	Percentage of All Limosnas	Adjutorios	Total
1648	396,241	160,892	28.8	152,737	709,870
1651	224,908	210,186	48.3	87,175	522,269
1660	222,320	257,922	53.7	261,166	741,408
1664	174,427	400,768	69.6	180,089	755,284
1667	123,163	320,000	72.2	383,882	827,045
1669	136,816	283,160	67.4	498,054	918,030
1702	n.a.[b]	99,218	n.a.	n.a.	140,843

SOURCES: BNM, MSS. 3631, 3597, 4359, 4394, 3586, 3593, 3587.
[a]All amounts are in silver reales, except those for 1702 which are in pesos.
[b]n.a. = not available.

dies had brought 34,000 pesos in alms for the ransom of captives. He expressed the desire that the order move quickly to rescue the captives of the *Margarita*. About a month later, Sánchez replied that the redemption would be published that winter for the following spring. Solar objected to this schedule, emphasizing that the *Margarita* had carried "priests, captains, and other high officials, as well as children," and that it was necessary "that the redemption be made with all brevity." He threatened that "if you will not speed it up as necessary the Council will decide that it [the redemption] should be made in some other way."[36] The implication here was that they might turn to the rival order, the Trinitarians. But Sánchez simply responded that his order was proceeding as quickly as possible, and he pointed out that "not all seasons are appropriate for redemption, because navigation is so dangerous." He added that while the 34,000 pesos from the Indies seemed like a great deal of money, the captives from the *Margarita* would be ransomed at so high a price that "it will not be enough to rescue ten of them," particularly since many were negotiating their own ransom prices, which the friars would be compelled to pay. It was necessary, he argued, not only to publish the redemption, but to give the order time to gather additional limosnas for it. He closed his letter by admonishing Solar that in the council's concern for the important captives from the *Margarita*, they were ignoring many others from earlier Indies fleets, "captains and soldiers who have served well and remain without recourse when it seems that they ought to be preferred."[37] The council continued to press for a speedy departure, but the friars did not go to Algiers until May 1667.[38]

The royal family was a frequent contributor to the redemption. Spanish kings regularly gave sums to be used for the rescue of military captives, while their queens usually designated their contributions for the ransom of children. For example, the Trinitarian redemption book of 1582 shows a donation from Philip II of 3,000 ducats to be used to ransom the "most able-bodied" captives, while the will of his late queen, Elisabeth of Valois, gave 1,666 ducats for the rescue of those persons who were "in the greatest danger of losing the faith, such as children or, lacking these, women."[39] In 1621 Philip IV gave 66,000 reales to the Trinitarians for their redemption in Tetuán, toward the rescue of soldiers, and in 1662 the king gave 12,216 reales for the same purpose.[40]

Occasionally the crown would grant to the redemption money that had been confiscated by the state. This occurred in 1575, when the Mercedarians were awarded 159,240 maravedís that had belonged to some Moriscos who had fled from Valencia to North Africa. Priority in the use of this money was to be given to the rescue of nine residents of a village in Valencia, who were believed to be held captive in Algiers.[41]

Some of the wealthy and powerful established trusts or endowments that were permanent sources of income for the redemption. The Mercedarian monastery of Santa Barbara in Madrid, for example, administered an endowment established by its founder, Doña Elvira Manrique de Lara. This fund yielded 24,392 reales for the redemption of 1660; 12,256 reales in 1664; 18,400 reales in 1669; 12,800 reales in 1675; and 9,360 reales in 1678.[42] A foundation in memory of Lope de Mendieta of Córdoba provided both Mercedarians and Trinitarians with large sums during most of the seventeenth century. The records of seventeen expeditions between 1609 and 1677 show contributions from this fund totaling 219,479 reales.[43] Another important source of money was a foundation at the chapel commemorating the constable of Castile in the cathedral of Burgos. The records of twelve redemptions in the sixteenth and seventeenth centuries, beginning with that of the Mercedarians in 1583, show receipts of 292,899 reales from this fund.[44] Other trusts also provided income for the redemption. One was a fund in memory of Don Fadrique de Toledo, duke of Alba, at the monastery of San Leonardo de Alba, which regularly donated large sums for the rescue of servants of the current duke of Alba or residents of towns and villages under his jurisdiction. If these could not be found, the money could be used for other captives. The importance of such trusts to the redemption can be seen by the fact that in the Trinitarian expedition of 1662 the income from fourteen of them provided 180,320 reales out of a total treasury of 460,000 reales.[45]

Many private trusts were administered by agencies of the crown. The trust in the name of Lope de Mendieta, for example, was overseen by the Council of Castile. Trusts were also supervised by the Council of the Cruzada. Traditionally such funds had been under the jurisdiction of the redemptionist orders themselves, but in the late sixteenth century the councils took control of a number of them.[46] In this way, the state could use the redemption to reward certain individuals, since the government-appointed administrators took fees for their services. It is not possible to say whether this new procedure resulted in a loss to the redemption, since those who administered the trusts on behalf of the orders may also have taken fees. Only a thorough analysis of the accounts pertaining to these trusts would provide this information.

Some trusts continued to be supervised by various branches of the redemptionist orders. In 1648 foundations under the control of Andalusian houses of the Merced yielded 35,205 reales.[47] In 1675, thirty-six trusts administered by the Mercedarian monasteries at Seville and Granada contributed a total of 11,015 pesos to the redemption.[48] In 1678, sixteen trusts managed by the Mercedarian monastery at Seville provided 42,787 reales.[49] Although the administrators of the trusts occasionally stipulated that all or part of their contributions were to be used for the rescue of specified captives, in general the use of these funds was unrestricted; that is, they were limosnas.

Limosnas were also derived from smaller contributions that members of the orders obtained by personal solicitation in towns and villages throughout Spain. These probably came to a substantial amount, but it is not possible to determine how much of the redemption's income they represented, as such sums were usually recorded together with the contributions of the various monasteries of the orders.

From the time of their establishment in the late Middle Ages, the Mercedarians and Trinitarians had been the recipients of numerous royal *mercedes*, grants that provided them with substantial incomes.[50] Thus, both orders were quite wealthy and their monasteries contributed a portion of their revenues for the ransom of captives. In the Mercedarian redemption of 1651 alms collected by the friars and the contributions of the Mercedarian monasteries came to 141,821 reales, out of a total treasury of 478,858 reales.[51] In 1660 the same sources yielded 222,320 reales, and in 1669, 78,904 reales.[52]

Although most of the limosnas received for the redemption had no restrictions placed on their use, some of the contributors did direct that an attempt be made to utilize them on behalf of certain categories of captives. The most common priority was the rescue of children and/or women. Donors sometimes stipulated that precedence be given to captives from a particular locality, usually the hometown of the donor. In 1575 the will of Doña Leona Fernández of Córdoba gave 430,000 maravedís for the rescue of captives from that city, with preference to be given to women and children.[53] In 1582 the Trinitarians received 30,000 maravedís from the dean of the cathedral of Toledo and 10,875 maravedís from Hernando de Salazar of the same city for the rescue of natives of the archbishopric of Toledo.[54] In 1632 Antonio de la Justa gave 1,100 reales for the ransom of natives of the city of Granada, and in 1651 Francisco de Valencia donated 3,265 reales for captives from the archbishopric of Valladolid.[55] These are only a few examples of such contributions. Although donors of these funds stipulated the type of captive whose rescue was preferred, this money was nevertheless part of the limosnas, since if such captives could not be found the redemptors could generally use it as they wished. The same was true of the assistance provided by the Council of the Cruzada. In the event that the captive for whom the money was destined had died, could not be located, or for some reason could not be ransomed, the redemptors were free to apply the funds to the rescue of other captives, at their discretion.

The friars did not have this flexibility with most adjutorios, which usually had to be returned to the donor or given to the captive for whom they were earmarked if he or she could not be ransomed. These were generally donated by the captives' relatives or friends. For example, Leonor de Cortinas and Andrea de Cervantes, the mother and sister of Miguel de Cervantes, gave the Trinitarians 300 ducats toward his rescue in 1579.[56] Occasionally localities maintained funds for the rescue of their own citizens, and adjutorios might be provided for these. In 1648 the city of Cádiz gave the Mercedarians 800 *vellón* (copper coinage) reales toward the ransom of Francisco de la Cruz of that city, who had been captured the year before while fishing.[57] In 1651 the Basque community in Seville gave 2,680 reales for the rescue of one of its members, Melchior de Riola.[58]

The redemptors frequently received adjutorios in North Africa from the captives themselves.[59] In the Mercedarian redemption of 1678, for example, various captives contributed to their own ransoms a total of 14,840 reales; in the Trinitarian redemption of 1579, twenty captives gave 668,600 maravedís; and in 1618 captives paid a total of 11,023 reales for their own rescue.[60] In 1669 the Mercedarians received 81,769 reales from captives in Algiers, and in 1674 the Trinitarians were given 16,080 reales by various captives for the same purpose.[61]

Once in a while the North Africans helped with the rescue of certain individuals. In 1582 "a Turkish renegade" in Algiers was identified as the source of a 17,000-maravedí contribution toward the ransom of Estevan de Palermo, and in 1713 the rescue of a captive named Joseph Muel was aided by contributions of 50 pesos from the guardián baji, chief overseer of the baño de la bastarda, and 25 pesos given by "the Jew Samuel."[62] The redemption books provide no explanation of why these contributions were made.

The percentage of the redemptions' treasuries that was represented by adjutorios varied from time to time. It could be quite substantial and, indeed, in the Mercedarian expedition of 1669 represented more than half the total (see Table 5). Because the application of these funds was generally restricted to designated captives, rescues in which adjutorios accounted for a large portion of the treasuries were often difficult, since the money did not actually belong to the redemption. When the friars arrived in North Africa, they were required to register their funds with the local government authorities. The Muslims recognized no difference between limosnas and adjutorios, and the Algerians in particular were insistent that virtually the entire amount be spent. In cases where the designated captives could not be rescued, the friars were forced to go into debt by using their adjutorios to rescue others, and once back in Spain they had to raise the funds to repay the donors.

In addition to the limosnas and adjutorios they received for the rescues, the redemptionist friars were able to augment their funds by taking a portion of their cargo in goods, which they sold in North Africa or exchanged for captives. In the sixteenth century this was mandatory. In order to limit the amount of specie taken out of the country, the crown directed the redemptors to take two-thirds of their treasury to North Africa in merchandise, such as hats, cloth, pearls, cochineal, or anything else on which they thought a profit might be made. This practice not only decreased the impact of paying ransom to the enemy, but also significantly increased the value of the cargo, since the merchandise was sold at a good profit, even with the expenses involved in purchasing, handling, packing, and transporting it. In the sixteenth century some of this merchandise was purchased by the redemptors out of funds given for the redemption; the rest was given instead of cash by donors.

An examination of the purchase prices of goods in Spain and their sale prices in North Africa reveals that a handsome profit was made on such merchandise. In their redemption of 1575 in Algiers, the Mercedarians bought and sold pearls and various kinds of cloth (see table 6). Various expenses relative to the acquisition of the items in table 6 totaled 83,523 maravedís, leaving a net profit of 581,579 maravedís, 39.5 percent of their original investment.

In 1583, the Mercedarians used 2,111,086 maravedís of their total treasury of 3,882,094 for merchandise. They purchased 217.5 ounces of pearls for 918,102 maravedís and sold them for 1,080,639, and 1,214 varas (one vara equals 2.8 feet) of cloth from Baeza and Córdoba for 826,106 maravedís that they sold for 1,245,020. In addition, they bought 318 dozen hats from Toledo for 366,878 maravedís. They were able to sell only 193 dozen of these, but the price was 380,834 maravedís, so

Table 6. Merchandise Sold by Mercedarians, 1575

Item	Purchase Price	Sale Price	Profit
600 varas damask cloth from Toledo	366,979	432,148	65,169
949.5 varas wool and broadcloth from Baeza	614,676	941,299	326,623
679.25 varas cloth from Valencia	250,473	380,827	130,354
66 ounces pearls	239,940	382,896	142,956

NOTE: All prices are given in maravedís.
SOURCE: BNM, MS. 2963.

there was still a small profit made on them. They took the remaining 125 dozen hats back to Spain with them, to be sold on a subsequent expedition. Expenses related to the purchase, preparation, and transport of the merchandise totaled 107,792 maravedís. Thus, this redemption earned 487,615 maravedís from the sale of its merchandise, a profit of 23 percent on its original investment.[63] Trinitarian redemptions in the sixteenth century show similar profits on merchandise.[64]

In 1609 a change was made in the instructions the Council of Castile issued to the redemptors, to the effect that they were no longer to convert their funds into merchandise, but instead use cash for the redemptions. Certain types of goods that were very much in demand in North Africa were excluded from this restriction, and it was left to the discretion of the redemptors whether to take such items. The reason given for the change was that the acquisition of goods was more trouble than it was worth because the friars were not good businessmen and the costs incurred in connection with the merchandise were too high.[65] As we have seen, this view was incorrect, since their profits were, in fact, substantial. In any case, the effect of this new regulation was merely to free the friars of the requirement that two-thirds of their cargo be in merchandise. They continued to take goods in the seventeenth century, although they represented a smaller portion of their treasuries than in the past. In the redemption of 1615, the

Mercedarians took with them to Tetuán 208 dozen hats that they had purchased in Toledo for 637,296 maravedís, with related costs of 39,978 maravedís. They sold them all to a Jewish merchant named Moses Mexías for 938,400 maravedís, a net profit of 261,126 maravedís.[66] In 1621 the Mercedarians purchased 192 dozen bonnets in Toledo for 14,976 reales. They incurred expenses of 1,322 reales in purchasing, packing, and transporting the hats to Algiers, where they sold them for 22,402 reales, a profit of 6,104 reales.[67] In 1632 they took to Morocco 96 dozen hats from Toledo, 442 varas of cloth from Baeza, and 6⅓ arrobas of cochineal, for which they paid a total of 32,278 reales plus related expenses of 1,010 reales. The merchandise was exchanged for captives in Salé, where it was valued at 41,297 reales, for a net profit of 8,009 reales.[68] Table 7 shows additional profits made on the sale of merchandise in North Africa during the seventeenth century.

Other redemptions in which large profits were made on merchandise were those of 1648, when the Mercedarians earned 141,425 reales on hats from Toledo, cloth from Segovia, and cochineal and 1656 when the Trinitarians realized a profit of 53,566 reales on cloth, hats, and other assorted items.[69]

This trade was not always lucrative. In 1627 the Mercedarians had difficulty selling their colored hats since, it was reported, they were being made better and for less money in Algiers. As a result, they had to sell them at a small loss.[70] Nonetheless, from the sixteenth century until the last quarter of the seventeenth, the treasuries of the redemptions profited considerably from the commercial activities of the redemptionist friars. At the end of the seventeenth century and in the eighteenth, the practice had ceased and the only merchandise taken was that intended as gifts for various North African officials.

Expenses

The amount of money available for the rescue of captives varied with each redemption and ranged from fewer than 200,000 reales in some of the expeditions of the late sixteenth and early

Table 7. Profits on Sale of Merchandise by Redemption in Seventeenth Century

Year: Merchandise	Purchase Price	Sale Price	Related Expenses	Profits
1633: 192 dozen hats of Toledo, 396 pounds cochineal, 400 pounds tobacco, 82.75 varas cloth	46,546	68,977	1,900	20,531
1636: 531 dozen hats of Toledo, 7 arrobas cochineal	45,765	68,090	1,430	20,895
1640: 1,049 dozen hats of Toledo, 1,041 varas Córdoban cloth, 11 arrobas and 9 pounds cochineal, 63.5 ounces pearls	118,582	249,312	4,935	125,975
1645: 1,030 dozen hats of Toledo, 509 varas cloth from Baeza, 2 arrobas cochineal	63,167	166,293	5,744	97,382

SOURCES: BNM, MSS. 3819, 6573, 6160; AHN, Códices, Libro 129B.
NOTE: All prices are given in reales.

seventeenth centuries, to approximately a million reales in the 1660s, to a high of 694,463 pesos in the last redemption of 1768–1769. Most of this money was used to pay the ransoms and various duties and taxes levied in North Africa for the import of the cargo of the redemption and the departure of the captives. Algiers imposed an import duty on the value of the cargo that ranged from 11.5 percent in the sixteenth and early seventeenth centuries to 3 percent in the eighteenth. In addition, there was a tax on each departing captive that was fixed at 328 reales in the seventeenth and eighteenth centuries. Fees of this nature were not levied in Tetuán or other parts of Morocco, but the individual rescue prices there tended to be somewhat higher. For example, in the redemption in

Tetuán in 1645 the Mercedarians rescued 210 captives for 446,772 reales, for an average price of 2,127 reales per captive, while in their expedition to Algiers in 1649 the Trinitarians rescued ninety-two captives for a total of 120,488 reales, an average of 1,310 reales per captive. In addition, though, this redemption had to pay 15,580 reales for a 9.5 percent duty on their cargo and 30,176 reales for the 328 real departure fee for each captive, which raised the average cost per captive to 1,807 reales.[71]

Other costs incurred by redemptionists in North Africa included the rental of housing for the friars and the rescued captives, plus other maintenance expenses. In their redemption in Algiers in 1618, the Trinitarians paid 344 reales for the rental of a house and 1,600 reales for food for the friars and the rescued captives prior to their departure.[72] In addition, the friars incurred various expenses before leaving Spain and upon their return. Among these were the costs of such things as bedding, candelabra, and other items needed for the journey, which they frequently sold in North Africa at the conclusion of the redemption, as well as wine, vinegar, and biscuit. Examination of the expenses of various redemptions shows that in general incidental costs were kept to a minimum, and the bulk of the treasury was used for the actual ransoms (see table 8).

The apparent financial probity of the friars who carried out the expeditions does not necessarily lead to the conclusion that the orders or their hierarchies did not profit from redemptionism. Only a thorough examination of the financial records of the orders themselves would reveal how much of what was collected actually went toward the ransom of captives and how much was diverted to other uses.

The ransoming of captives in North Africa had widespread support in early modern Spain at both the official and popular levels. The generosity of Spaniards to the redemption reflects the concern of contemporary society for those in captivity, as well as its response to the propaganda and publicity concerning the plight of the captives. The response was conditioned, too, by fear of the fierce popular image of the "Barbary cor-

Table 8. Expenses of the Redemption

Year-Location	Number Rescued	Total Expenses	Cost of Rescue of Captives, Taxes and Duties in North Africa	Percent of Total Expenses
1575-Algiers	140	8,103,088 M	6,453,648 M	79.6
1609-Tetuán	64	4,294,906 M	4,005,000 M	93.2
1612-Tetuán	127	9,805,932 M	9,255,480 M	94.3
1618-Algiers	144	365,555 R	324,276 R	88.7
1632-Tetuán	69	148,784 R	136,977 R	92.0
1640-Tetuán	219	548,471 R	519,382 R	94.6
1651-Algiers	232	489,452 R	449,424 R	91.8
1660-Algiers	366	799,376 R	708,379 R	88.6
1667-Algiers	196	1,025,692 R	997,076 R[a]	97.2
1669-Tetuán	127	306,571 R	272,582 R	88.9
1674-Tetuán	128	264,206 R	249,420 R	94.4
1678-Algiers	450	869,232 R	798,190 R	91.8
1686-Algiers	320	771,192 R	724,704 R	93.9
1692-Algiers	156	35,416 P	31,764 P	89.6
1702-Algiers	482	139,372 P	126,107 P	90.4
1711-Algiers	280	120,481 P	115,770 P	96.0
1723-Algiers	414	136,074 P	130,126 P	95.6
1730-Algiers	345	125,492 P	121,133 P	96.5
1739-Algiers	394	113,070 P	111,262 P	98.4
1759-Tangier	88	59,205 P	54,436 P	91.9

SOURCES: BNM, MSS. 2963, 4390, 3862, 6573, 4359, 3586, 7752, 3597, 4363, 3587, 3591, 3549, 3592, 3590, 1635; AHN, Códices, Libros 125B, 128B, 142B, 143B, 147B.

NOTE: M = maravedís; R = reales; P = pesos.

[a]The high cost of this redemption was due to the fact that several captives were rescued for extraordinarily high prices, among them Lorenzo Santos de San Pedro, for whom the Mercedarians paid 240,000 reales (see chapter 8).

sairs." Furthermore, contributions to this cause were not without a return to the donor. From the early fifteenth century, a succession of popes had declared the giving of alms for the rescue of Christians in Muslim lands to be deserving of "spiritual benefits" and had set aside certain holy days on which donations might be asked for this purpose.[73]

In spite of this broad-based support, the redemption was

not without its critics. As we have seen, from the mid-seventeenth century the continuous outpouring of money to North Africa caused thoughtful Spanish observers to question the wisdom of continuing to ransom captives. They claimed that to do so only encouraged the corsairs. These criticisms were usually answered by members of the redemptionist orders themselves; they published long treatises in which they attempted to demonstrate the importance of the redemption.[74]

The orders obviously had a vested interest in continuing redemptionist activity. And while they were probably correct in their assertion that its termination would not have brought an end to North African aggression against Spain, the loss of the strong incentive provided by rescue money would almost certainly have reduced the frequency with which attacks occurred.

Why, then, did the crown continue to give such strong support to an activity that regularly exported specie to enemy states? Why was it so important to continue this large-scale campaign to rescue captives from the Muslims? Did the crown have a stake in redemptionist activity? The answers are by no means obvious. The documents examined in the course of this study provide no indication that the interest of the crown was financial, that it encouraged public contributions to the redemption in order to be able then to tap these resources for its own benefit. Simple humanitarian considerations certainly played a part in the crown's continuing support for the redemption, as did tradition—the fact that Spanish monarchs had always supported this institution, which had deep roots in Spain. The crown may also have been motivated by a desire to identify itself with a popular cause.

Were cultural factors also an element? Perhaps so. It is a fact that the ransoming of Christian captives from the North Africans was carried out not only by Spain, but by most European states, either through religious redemptionists or government representatives. And although there were Spanish prisoners of war in European states—they rowed in the French galleys, for example—there is no evidence of any public fund-raising campaign on their behalf. For all Europeans there was something special about captives in Muslim lands, and the important difference may have been cultural.

In this context, one motivating element behind the state's strong support for the redemption may have been a desire on its part to maintain the public impression of a continuing religious war with Islam in order to direct popular attention to a foreign enemy and divert it from the very real problems facing Spain at this time. It is true that throughout the seventeenth century Spain had many European enemies, but given shifting alliances it was difficult to sustain intense hatred toward any one of them. The Muslims, however, were the traditional foe and it was easier to play on old prejudices and fears. Furthermore, since they usually attacked nonmilitary objectives and captured so many civilians, the conflict with the North Africans struck many Spaniards on a more personal level than did more traditional types of warfare. Finally, the other enemies—the French, for example—shared with the Spaniards a common cultural and sometimes even religious heritage. But the Muslims of North Africa looked different, had different beliefs and standards of behavior, lived differently—they were totally alien and therefore to be feared and hated. Here was an enemy that could be brought into focus, and the continuation of redemptionist activity served to sharpen that focus.

Chapter 7
Negotiations in North Africa

Before an expedition for the rescue of captives could be undertaken, the redemptionists had to obtain a passport and safe conduct from the authorities of the North African state to which they wished to travel. Negotiations for the passport were conducted either by a member of the redemptionist order who traveled to North Africa for that purpose, by an official of one of the Spanish territories in North Africa, or, from the late seventeenth century, by the administrator of the Trinitarian hospitals in Algiers. In the eighteenth century, after the accession of the Bourbons in Spain, the French consuls in North Africa sometimes obtained these passports. The orders did not usually experience difficulty in acquiring these documents, since the redemption was welcome in North Africa. But once they arrived there, the friars frequently encountered serious problems in dealing with local officials, especially in Algiers.

The North African passports stated in the first place that the redemption and its cargo were not to be molested on the high seas by Muslim corsairs. They also laid down the terms under which the rescue was to be made. On both counts these documents were inadequate. The passport from Algiers promised the redemptors security from attack by corsairs from the Turkish regencies, Algiers, Tunis, and Tripoli, but there was no guarantee that they would not be seized by Moroccan pirates. Nor could the Moroccans assure the safety of their redemptions against corsairs from the regencies. In the Trinitarian expedition to Tetuán in 1669, for example, Algerian corsairs seized two vessels traveling from the Spanish presidio at Ceuta to Tetuán, one of which carried the Trinitarian friar Juan de Jesús María, along with three boxes of silver containing 8,500 pesos. This money was to be turned over to slaveowners in

Tetuán, with whom the ransoms had already been negotiated, in exchange for captives. Because of the loss of these 8,500 pesos, Friar Diego de la Purificación and seventeen of the rescued captives had to remain in Tetuán as hostages.[1] They were not permitted to leave until 1674, when another team of Trinitarians traveled to Tetuán with the money owed.[2] At times the Algerians could not enforce their safe conduct against violations by the other regencies. In 1711, one of two ships returning to Cartagena from Algiers with captives rescued by the Mercedarians was seized by pirates of Tunis. Twenty months later, with the aid of the dey of Algiers, the Ottoman sultan, and the French consul in Tunis, the group was freed in return for a payment of 14,000 pesos.[3]

Insofar as the terms of the redemption were concerned, the passport required the friars to rescue a specified number of captives from the North African rulers and states and stipulated the prices to be paid for them. The number varied from redemption to redemption. Although these captives, known as *forzosos*, were to be selected by their owners, all had to be Spaniards. Beyond this, the friars were free to negotiate for the other prisoners they wished to ransom. They were not to be required to take either captives who were not Spanish, or bienvenidos, the deserters from Spain's African presidios who came voluntarily to Muslim lands in the hope that they would be ransomed and returned to Spain. Passports of the sixteenth and early seventeenth centuries provided for a refund of the purchase price of any captive who apostatized after being rescued. This provision was never enforced, and it did not appear in the passports of the later seventeenth and eighteenth centuries. These documents did state, though, that the redemption was not to be required to pay the departure fees for rescued captives who died or apostatized. The passports also stipulated that if it could be proven, after a captive had been ransomed, that he had debts in North Africa, the redemption would not be obliged to pay these, but could instead have the ransom price refunded in order to rescue another captive who was free of debt.

The terms of the passports were rarely observed. The behavior of the Algerian officials in particular, especially in the seventeenth and eighteenth centuries, was highly erratic and unpredictable. An anonymous Mercedarian of the late seventeenth century wrote that it was impossible to give fixed rules for the conduct of the redemption in Algiers, because the state "is not governed by law or reason, nor do they keep their word if it conflicts with their interest. The government changes so often and depends on the disposition of the governor in power."[4]

Among the most frequently violated guarantees were those that stated that the friars would not be required to rescue non-Spaniards and that, after rescuing the stipulated number of forzosos, they would be free to choose the other captives to be ransomed. Abuses of this nature appear even in the earliest recorded redemptions. In the expedition to Algiers in 1575, the notary commented that the governor had insisted that the Mercedarians rescue large numbers of foreigners and that, in order to satisfy him, most of their rescue price had been paid by Juan de Torres, a Jesuit who resided in Algiers.[5] In the Trinitarian redemption of 1582, many foreign captives were ransomed with limosnas generales. The notary explained that they had been rescued at the insistence of the Algerian governor.[6]

These violations were objectionable on two counts: first, having to pay for the rescue of additional forzosos sometimes meant going into debt either by using funds donated for particular captives who could not be rescued or else borrowing from North African merchants; second, the forzosos were not usually the captives whom the friars were most eager to ransom. They were often non-Spaniards or Spaniards who were old or infirm. As the seventeenth-century Franciscan, Melchor de Zuñiga, remarked, "the redemption in Algiers cleans the land of the useless and those who help use up the supplies."[7]

Upon arriving in Algiers, the redemptors were greeted by port officials and escorted to the governor's palace. There they were presented to the ruler, who inquired as to the sum of money they had brought with them. He then appropriated an amount to cover the import duty and the prices to be paid for the state-owned forzosos. From the palace, the friars and the remainder of their treasury were taken to the *casa de la limosna*, the house that was assigned for their use while they were in Algiers. Although the passport stipulated that they would be permitted to retain control of the rest of the money, in fact they usually were not free to dispose of it as they pleased because the guard of the casa locked it in a room to which he retained the key.[8] This control of the redemption's treasury by Algerian officials constituted a form of pressure on the friars to accede to the demands of the governor.

Typical of the difficulties experienced by the friars were those encountered by the Mercedarians in 1713, when they traveled to Algiers with the intention of ransoming Spanish officers who had been captured when the Algerians took Orán in 1709.[9] The redemption began with the rescue of the forzosos under the jurisdiction of the council, the cristianos del común, of whom the passport required eight to be taken at 1,000 pesos each. But the dey presented the friars with eleven youths, ranging in age from eighteen to twenty years old. Only four of them were Spaniards; the rest were Genoese, Florentine, and Portuguese. The redemptors protested that they were obliged to ransom only Spaniards, and objected to spending such a large portion of their funds for foreigners when there were so many Spanish soldiers from Orán in captivity. They threatened to return to Spain with their money rather than rescue these captives. The following day the ruler told them that instead of the original eleven he would bring fourteen Spaniards. When the friars arrived at the palace, they found not fourteen Spaniards, but eighty-nine of the "oldest and most useless" slaves, of various nationalities, all of whom the dey wanted them to rescue. The friars said that they would take only the fourteen forzosos, as agreed, and that if they wanted any more they would negotiate for them on an individual basis. The dey then designated fourteen Spaniards out of the eighty-nine. He continued, however, to try to persuade the friars to take the rest.[10]

Several days later, the redemptors presented to the dey a list of seventy-one slaves whom they wished to rescue from the council. Negotiations began with the friars offering 225 pesos each, the usual price for such slaves. The dey replied that he would not sell them for less than 1,000 pesos each, since many of those chosen were among the most valuable people in the baños. The friars refused to pay this sum, which would have constituted more than 75 percent of their entire treasury, and they returned to the casa de la limosna. Shortly thereafter word arrived from the dey that if they wished to proceed with the redemption they would have to ransom the eleven youths they had rejected on the first day. If they refused, they could take their money and return to Spain. The redemptors decided that since they had already paid the entry tax on the treasury, the price of chartering the ship, and other costs, it would be best to go along with the demands of the dey and rescue the eleven boys at a price of 818 pesos each. They did this in the hope that the redemption would be permitted to proceed smoothly.[11]

They were then allowed to ransom the officers and privately owned slaves on their list. This included twenty-four captains and lieutenants from Orán at 1,000 pesos each. They were not able to negotiate the rescue of Don Baltasar de Villalba, governor of Almarzaquivir in Orán. The dey insisted that he was not free to come to an agreement concerning this prisoner; the case would have to be referred to the divan, the governing council of Algiers.[12]

On February 18, after they had rescued half the officers they wanted, the dey ordered the redemption halted until the friars rescued eighty more captives from the council, whom he had designated. When they protested the injustice of this and threatened to return to Spain, he reduced the number to sixty. At the same time, those officers who remained in captivity pleaded with the friars not to abandon them, but to comply with the dey's demands.[13] Thus, they were under pressure not only from the ruler, but from the captives as well. On February 19, the friars told the dey that his order that they rescue these captives was unjust, as was his price of 9,000 pesos for the eleven youths. They asked him to abandon his unreasonable demands and permit them to resume the negotiations for the remaining officers and private slaves. The ruler, unaccustomed to having his authority challenged, became furious with them. The redemptors pointed out that "from the moment the redemption began he had not kept his word nor the good faith of the passport" and asked for permission to leave. He told them to go, but as they were preparing to depart, they received an order forbidding them to embark. Several days later the French consul came to the casa de la limosna to tell the friars that he had persuaded the dey to reduce the number of slaves in his order to forty, all of whom would be captives from Orán. He pointed out that since the dey controlled their treasury, they ought to go along. The redemptors were reluctant to give in, but finally agreed to submit provided they were allowed to choose twenty of the forty. These forty captives were rescued for 225 pesos each; all were Spaniards except one, a German who had been captured at Orán. They were then permitted to rescue the rest of the officers on their list at 1,000 pesos each.[14]

The redemption continued without difficulty for a few days, until the dey called in the friars to tell them that many important citizens had complained that they were not ransoming their slaves according to custom. The friars responded that no such custom existed and that even if it did they could not abide by it because they had no money left. In that case, the dey replied, they must borrow it, and he directed a Jewish merchant named Samuel to arrange a loan. After first protesting that if they were going to borrow money it would not be for slaves that they were forced to take, but rather for those whom they wanted to rescue, the friars submitted. As a result of the ruler's demands, this redemption, in which 204 captives were rescued, overspent its 92,300 peso treasury by 18,823 pesos, which it had to borrow.[15]

By acquiescing in these violations of the conditions of their passport, the friars established what the Algerians regarded as a precedent for future redemptions. In their expedition to Algiers in 1723, the Mercedarians were confronted with demands that they accept the same terms as they had in 1713, in spite of the fact that these again diverged from the stipulations of the passport.[16] Other difficulties arose out of efforts by the Algerians to obtain what they regarded as more realistic prices than those provided for in the passport, which had been drawn up according to tradition rather than the conditions of the moment. One controversy concerned a demand by the dey for higher prices than had been paid in the past for the cristianos del común. The dispute lasted for several days, and was finally resolved when the dey agreed to accept 400 pesos for each of fifty-one captives in this category. This price was considerably lower than the 1,000 pesos he had demanded for them at the start, but a good bit higher than the customary price of 225 pesos each for such captives.[17]

The actions of the ruler in this episode were not as unreasonable as the accounts would make them appear. In the past, the slaves of the council had usually been those who were least apt to be rescued, either because they had skills that were needed in Algiers and thus would not be offered for redemption, or, more typically, because they were not likely to be selected by the friars. In the latter case, the Muslims did not set the prices very high. But with the capture of Orán in 1709, the situation had changed. Now many of the cristianos del común were Spanish soldiers, to whom the redemptors gave high priority. The Algerians felt they were worth more than the 225 pesos that the friars were accustomed to paying for cristianos del común. The dey was merely trying to obtain a price that he felt reflected the true value of the slaves. The sum finally agreed upon, 400 pesos, was undoubtedly what he had in mind when he began the negotiations at 1,000 pesos.

The redemption of 1723 was especially difficult not so much because of the specific demands of the Algerian officials, as the extremely volatile and capricious nature of the dey, Muḥammed ben-Asein. On their first day in Algiers, when the redemptors were brought before him in order to begin the negotiations, they found him irate. The reason for his anger, they soon learned, was a letter from a Muslim woman whose daughter had been baptized in Cartagena. The bishop of Cartagena would not permit the girl to return to Algiers, and the dey threatened to detain one of the redemptors until the girl was brought to him. The friars protested that they had nothing to do with the case, and could not secure the return of the girl. The dey finally calmed down, but as Melchor García Navarro, one of the Mercedarians, remarked, "our concern lasted until we left Algiers," because the dey would frequently take the letter out of his pocket and repeat his threats.[18]

Despite the difficulties encountered in this redemption, the Mercedarians returned to Algiers the following year. The expedition of 1724 was originally destined for Tunis, where no rescue had been made for many years, but because of delays in obtaining a Tunisian passport they decided to go to Algiers instead. One of the factors that prompted this decision was a letter from Friar Navarro advising them of the assassination on March 18 of the unreasonable and tyrannical Muḥammed ben-Asein, and the promise by his successor that he would observe the passport.[19]

The redemptors found the new dey friendlier and more cordial than the previous ruler, but it became apparent soon after their arrival that he would no more abide by the provisions of the passport than had his predecessor. Although this dey lacked the choleric temper of Muḥammed ben-Asein, nevertheless, as in 1723, the passport was violated at every turn.[20] But broken promises were so typical of the redemptions in Algiers that it is surprising that the Spaniards expected them to be kept.

Although the Algerians frequently threatened the friars with imprisonment and bodily harm, these threats were rarely carried out. In his account of the difficult redemption of 1723, García Navarro told how, in a rage over the dey's tyrannical behavior, he spoke disrespectfully to him. Rumors raced through the palace that García Navarro would be executed for such an offense. In recounting this, the redemptor remarked that he was not worried, because he knew that the dey "did not want the friar to die, but to live and return to Algiers with more money."[21]

The safety of the redemption had not always been such a certainty. In 1609, three Trinitarians, Friars Bernardo de Monroy, Juan de Águila, and Juan de Palacios rescued 130 captives in Algiers. As they were making plans to return to Spain, word arrived that the eight-year-old daughter of a wealthy and powerful citizen of Algiers was being detained in Sardinia, where her ransom from captivity had been arranged, on the grounds that she had expressed the desire to convert to Christianity. The child's father was furious when he learned of this and demanded that the governor hold the redemptors in order to obtain her release. The ruler complied, placing the friars under arrest and informing them that neither they nor their rescued captives would be permitted to leave Algiers until she was returned. Various Spanish officials tried to obtain the girl's return to Algiers, but the church claimed that since she was a Christian she could not be sent back. Offers to exchange high-ranking Muslim captives in Spain for the friars and the ransomed captives also failed. Negotiations for the redemption's release continued without success until at least 1620, and it appears that the redemptors eventually died in Algiers.[22]

Because of the detention of this expedition, no Spanish redemptionists traveled to Algiers between 1609 and 1618; all passports issued in these years contained a prohibition against any redemption in that city.[23] But since there were so many Spanish prisoners in Algiers, attempts were made during this period to obtain selected ones through intermediaries. The Mercedarians who traveled to Tetuán in 1612, for example, arranged for the ransom of ten captives from Algiers to be negotiated by a Jew of Tetuán, Abran Mexías. Although they had hoped to rescue more, they were unable to because of unfriendly relations between Tetuán and Algiers.[24] In 1615 the Mercedarians again asked the cooperation of the governor of Tetuán in permitting merchants to travel to Algiers to redeem captives designated by the friars.[25] These arrangements were sanctioned by the Spanish crown, which issued safe conducts and licenses for vessels from Gibraltar or Ceuta to transport Muslim or Jewish merchants to and from Algiers for the purpose of ransoming captives, without being molested by officials of Spain's North African garrisons.[26] But only small numbers of captives were rescued by this means. The more common method of ransoming captives from Algiers during these years was for the Algerian slaveowners themselves to come to Morocco with their slaves.

The ban on travel to Algiers by Spanish redemptionists was lifted in the fall of 1617, in the wake of the seizure by Algerian corsairs of two Spanish ships with some five hundred soldiers on board, off the coast of Cartagena. Because of this, an expedition originally destined for Morocco was ordered by the crown to journey to Algiers instead.[27] In an effort to avoid the difficulties that Monroy and his companions had experienced, the friars tried to avoid personally going to Algiers. A French merchant in Valencia, Anthony Mansuer, who regularly conducted business in the North African city, was to effect the redemption for them. But the Algerians would not negotiate with Mansuer; they wanted the friars themselves to come to Algiers with their treasury, and in June 1618 a passport and safe-conduct arrived for them.[28] The passport contained the guarantees characteristic of these documents; just as typically, the redemption was riddled with violations of those guarantees. For example, of eighteen forzosos rescued, only twelve were Spaniards. More serious yet were the problems that arose when the time came to depart.

On July 12, having completed the redemption, the friars asked for a license to leave with the rescued captives. Unfortunately for them, only two days earlier the Spanish navy had seized ten vessels from the Algerian corsair fleet. Because of this, the Algerian authorities were not inclined to accommodate the friars, and told them to return the following Saturday. They returned on July 21, amid rumors that Spain was planning to launch an armada against Algiers, and once again the license was denied. The following day, nine Dutch warships fired on the city, damaging some houses and vessels in the port. The Dutch consul was arrested and all Christians were forbidden to go out into the streets. The door of the casa de la limosna was locked. Events continued to thwart the efforts of the redemptors to leave Algiers. On August 6 a renegade who had fled the city only a few days earlier and was brought back from Mallorca along with other captives reported that the king of Spain was rumored to be planning a great armada against Algiers, in cooperation with the ruler of Cuco (about 15 leagues from Algiers), the Moriscos from Andalusia, and some renegades. As a result of this report, restrictions were placed on the Moriscos' movements and the redemption was not permitted to leave.[29]

The departure of the party was delayed until September 1, nearly two months after the friars' business had been completed. During this period, they were forced to rescue nine additional captives, including an Augustinian monk who was brought to them while they were waiting to embark.[30] The cost of maintaining themselves and the rescued captives during the long delay, plus the additional ransoms made during this period, caused this redemption to accumulate approximately 20,000 reales in debts.[31]

Sometimes the difficulties encountered by the redemptors were caused by the captives themselves. It was not unusual for captives, especially wealthy ones, to negotiate their own ransom prices in the hope of obtaining an early release. This price was generally higher than what the friars would have offered, but invariably they had to accept it.

One such incident occurred in the Mercedarian redemption of 1686, in a case involving the son and daughter of the regent of Mallorca, Don Melchor Cisternes.[32] In 1684 the son, Don Plácido, had negotiated a ransom price of 7,500 pesos for himself and 12,000 pesos for his sister, Doña Inés. Don Plácido was permitted to return to Mallorca to raise the money, while his sister remained hostage in Algiers. Now, two years later, not only had he failed to remit the promised sum, but he had not been heard from since he left Algiers. The Mercedarians, the governor understood, were carrying more than 8,000 pesos Don Plácido had raised, and would have to pay the entire amount promised, plus interest, or at least the 7,500 pesos plus interest for the ransom of Don Plácido. The friars replied that they knew nothing of these arrangements, that they had been given only 200 escudos for each of the Cisternes by Felipe Pizal in Madrid.[33] They pointed out that the more than 20,000 pesos asked would suffice to rescue 150 poor captives, and suggested that since the governor still held Doña Inés, he collect the money from her family. The governor proposed that both he and the friars write to her father concerning the matter. He permitted the friars to proceed with the redemption, but required that they set aside 7,500 pesos plus interest to cover Don Plácido's ransom.[34]

On April 16, Andrés de Oyos y Morales, secretary to the Mallorcan regent, arrived in Algiers. He informed the friars that he had brought with him 8,500 pesos to rescue Doña Inés. As for Don Plácido, he had gone to Sicily in the royal service without having said or done anything about his ransom price. The friars told the secretary that the Algerian governor would certainly demand that the money he had brought be used to pay the debt of Don Plácido. Oyos replied that these funds were solely for the rescue of Doña Inés, and he intended to so advise the governor.[35] The governor supported Oyos' position; from his point of view, it was preferable to take the ransom for Don Plácido from the redemption and then obtain an additional amount for his sister from their father. He was, therefore, willing to support the secretary in his claim that the funds were only for the rescue of the girl. There was no way out of the dilemma, and the friars had to pay this extremely high rescue price for Don Plácido, whom under ordinary circumstances they would not have rescued without substantial adjutorios. In addition, they had to supplement the money that the Mallorcan regent had sent for Doña Inés.

Although the greatest difficulties experienced by the redemptionists occurred in Algiers, their transactions in Morocco were not free of problems. Many of the redemptions in Morocco were made in the coastal city of Tetuán. Only infrequently did the friars travel inland. Instead, slaves from other parts of Morocco were brought to Tetuán. Occasionally, it was possible to carry out a redemption without traveling to Muslim territory at all, by negotiating the terms in the nearby Spanish presidio of Ceuta.

In the Mercedarian expedition of 1609, the governor of Ceuta, the marqués de Villareal, refused to allow the friars to travel to Tetuán because of the civil wars in Morocco.[36] Instead, he sent a messenger to Tetuán with letters for the *almocadén* (governor) and Moses Mexías, a Jew who frequently acted as agent for the slaveowners, with names of those captives the friars wished to rescue. Moses Mexías brought eighty-seven captives and their owners to a field just outside of Ceuta, where the Mercedarian friars negotiated ransom prices and made arrangements for the redemption without leaving Spanish territory.

In 1621 the Trinitarians attempted to transact business in Tetuán in the same manner.[37] They arrived in Ceuta at the beginning of March, and once again travel to Tetuán was prohibited because of unrest there. Furthermore, the friars preferred to make the redemption under the walls of Ceuta because they feared that some of the problems they had recently encountered in Algiers would occur in Tetuán as well. But this time the almocadén of Tetuán refused to go along with their plans. He wanted the friars to come to his city in person, and by late April he was able to issue a safe-conduct in the name of the sultan. The document granted them the right "to come to Tetuán freely . . . and remain there for the time necessary . . . for their rescue and return . . . with captives or without them, freely, without being harmed or assaulted; nor may they be detained or seized for the debts of past redemptions nor for any disputes between the sultan and the governor of Ceuta." They were not to be "obliged nor forced to rescue any captives other than those covered by their instructions and royal orders."[38]

On May 5, one of the redemptors, Friar Diego de Ortigossa, and the notary traveled to Tetuán, accompanied by two soldiers from Ceuta. Arriving in the Muslim city, Ortigossa found that the almocadén and his sons had a total of 128 captives, all of whom they wanted him to buy. The friar protested that he could not afford to ransom so many, and after much discussion it was agreed that he would take thirty-seven captives from them at 2,000 reales each. A further problem arose when the almocadén insisted on including some foreigners and bienvenidos on the list. Ortigossa refused to accept this and asked for a license to return to Ceuta without making any redemption. At this point, the almocadén modified his terms, and the matter was resolved with Ortigossa agreeing to include five Frenchmen among the thirty-seven, provided they were Roman Catholics. All the others had to be legitimate captives and not deserters.[39] The problem of foreign captives arose again in 1625, when the almocadén insisted that of thirty captives to be rescued from him and his brothers, seven had to be French. The friars finally agreed to take four Roman Catholic French captives.[40]

Although examples of difficulties with the redemption in Morocco do exist, abuses were far less frequent there than in Algiers. The reason for this was undoubtedly the proximity of the Spanish garrison at Ceuta, which was in a position to act quickly on behalf of the redemption if it were really in danger. A related advantage was that, because of the short distance, it was possible for expeditions to Morocco to leave their money in Ceuta, where payment could be made to the Muslim slave-owners on Spanish soil, after the rescue had been completed. Thus, although the Moroccans might inconvenience the friars, they did not have the leverage of the Algerians, who had custody of the funds.

The redemption was not able to institute a similar procedure in Algiers. From a purely practical point of view, the Algerian slaveowners could not be expected to travel the approximately two hundred miles to Orán to receive their payment. Another obstacle was that the Algerian government was not willing to give up the duty imposed on all money and goods brought into the city. Finally, they undoubtedly recognized the advantage that their control of the treasury gave them in negotiations with the friars.

The growing abuses in Algiers in the eighteenth century prompted a Mercedarian redemptor, Pedro Ros Valle, to write a treatise in 1734 on "the unhappy state to which the redemption in Algiers has arrived, due to the tyrannies of that government."[41] In this essay Ros Valle expressed concern over not only the passport violations, but also the rising prices that the Algerians were demanding for captives. With the constant increases, it would be impossible to rescue the more than a thousand Spaniards who were still in Algiers at that time. Even a treasury of 100,000 pesos would be inadequate to pay for the approximately sixty women and children held captive. The

Algerians, he asserted, were operating under the assumption that people who came from the middle ranks were actually of the highest estates, and they could be expected to ask as much as 10,000 pesos each for them. He also noted that the Algerians were placing deserters among the forzosos from the council. The redemptors had tried to deal with the problem of rescuing deserters by obtaining lists of them from the governor of Orán. But this was of little use, since "if the money is inside Algiers, the will of the governor prevails."[42]

He proposed that in future negotiations for a passport, the Spaniards insist on the stipulation that the friars and their treasury travel to Algiers in Spanish warships, and that the money remain on board until the redemption was completed. Furthermore, the redemptors should not be required to pay an import duty on the money, the 40-peso per head departure tax, or any of the smaller fees for which they were traditionally obligated, but only the costs of the rescue itself. If these terms were rejected, the negotiators should refuse to agree to another redemption. Ros Valle was certain that once the Algerians realized that the rescue money would not come through sources other than the religious orders, they would accept these terms, since otherwise "the governor's position and life will be endangered."[43]

In his treatise, Ros Valle performed a service similar to that of the critics of the redemption, counseling a more rational approach to the emotion-laden problem of Spanish captives in North Africa. Although his solution was different from that of the redemption's critics, he recognized, as they did, that the principal motivation behind the North African offensive against Spain was not religious, but economic, and that the problem should be approached with this in mind. Further, he displayed a keen sensitivity, lacking in so many of his contemporaries, to the fragile political situation in eighteenth-century Algiers, where the heavy dependence on ransoms meant that while a ruler might abuse the Spanish friars in order to enhance his public image, he could not lose the redemption and retain his office.

Parts of Ros Valle's proposal were adopted by the Spaniards

in their last redemption in Algiers, made by the Trinitarians and Mercedarians together in 1768–1769. In negotiating for the passport for this redemption, the Spanish representatives insisted, and the Algerians agreed, that the expedition should come in four warships and that the treasury and Algerian captives to be exchanged would remain on board until the negotiations had been completed and the rescued Spaniards delivered. During this redemption the Algerians made several attempts to violate the conditions of the passport, but the friars were able to resist because the treasury was not in Algiers and the warships were on hand to come to the defense of the redemptors if necessary.[44]

By approaching the redemption in terms of the realities of Algerian political and economic conditions, the Spaniards were at last able to alter the relationship between Algerian rulers and redemptionist friars that had governed the course of this institution for at least two centuries. The failure on the part of the Spaniards to recognize these realities earlier meant that whereas the redemptors should have had the upper hand in negotiating with the Algerians, instead they were always at a disadvantage.

Chapter 8
The Rescue

It is not possible to estimate the number of Spaniards who were held captive in North Africa during the years covered by this study. Figures given by contemporary observers such as Haedo are speculative at best and include all captives, not only Spaniards.[1] Indeed, it is not even possible to say how many were rescued. During the course of this study the records of eighty-two redemptions made between 1575 and 1769, in which some 15,500 captives were rescued, were examined.[2] But how many more of these redemption records have not been found? Even in the absence of concrete data, it would probably be correct to say that most of those taken prisoner lived out their lives in captivity.

The possibility of rescue depended on a number of factors. Some captives who had valuable skills, such as gun founders or shipbuilders, were unlikely ever to be rescued. Many were sent to Constantinople, where the redemption never went.[3] The only hope for these captives was to escape or possibly to be returned to North Africa. Manuel Castellano, seventy years of age, of Valencia de Alcántara, and Francisco Rodríguez, sixty, of Portugal, had both been captured in 1578 after the Portuguese defeat in Morocco. They were sold to slaveowners who took them to Constantinople where they spent thirty-five years. In 1613 they were sold to new masters in Tetuán, and two years later they were redeemed by the Mercedarians.[4] But even for many captives who remained in North Africa, redemption was unlikely. We have already seen that captive labor was important to the North African states, especially Algiers, and it was essential to maintain an adequate supply. According to Cervantes, cristianos del común who worked on public construction projects in Algiers had almost no chance of being rescued.[5] And some captives belonged to slaveowners who, for various reasons, personal or otherwise, would not allow them to be ransomed.

Other factors that determined whether or not a person would be rescued were the preferences of the redemptors. Both the Council of Castile and the generals of the redemptionist orders directed the friars to give priority to individuals for whom they had adjutorios and to make up any differences between these funds and the ransom prices out of limosnas, provided the amounts were not too large. Thus a captive for whom some money had been given, or who was willing to pay something toward his ransom, even if it were less than the total price, was more apt to be rescued than one for whom the friars had received nothing.

The limosnas that the order had collected were to be used for other Spanish captives, with priority assigned, as we have seen, to those captured in the royal service or the Indies fleet. Preference was also to be shown to those who were believed to be in danger of apostasy. The friars were warned by their general to examine each case carefully, since many captives, in order to be rescued, would threaten to convert. In any event, they were to try to ransom women and children, who were regarded as weakest in the faith and most likely to apostatize under pressure.

An unstated reason for preferring these captives was undoubtedly their potential contribution to society. Although the instructions never dealt with this, the friars tended to avoid spending limosnas to rescue elderly captives who were unlikely to contribute to Spain's population, economy, or military might. In the case of those captured in the royal service or from the Indies fleet, although this was never stated, it was their potential for future service as much as their past records that made these captives desirable. Preference was also to be given to ecclesiastics.

Slightly more than 5 percent of the rescued captives surveyed were females. Since many women were sent to Constantinople, and others were not permitted to be rescued, it is not possible to state whether this bears any relationship to the proportion of women in the captive population. The redemptors did make every effort to ransom women when they were available.

As far as children were concerned, 8 percent of the rescued captives in the survey were younger than sixteen years of age. In general the emphasis in the redemption was on youth. The mean age of the captives rescued was thirty-four. Eighty-eight percent were fifty years or younger, and 80 percent were between sixteen and fifty, the prime years for military service.

Certain captives were not to be rescued at all. After the expulsion of the Moriscos from Spain in 1609, the instructions of the superiors of the orders contained a warning to "watch with great vigilance that the captives you redeem are not Moriscos expelled from this kingdom."[6] Before they began the redemption in Morocco in 1615, the Mercedarian friars reminded the Muslim slaveowners that those rescued had to be "legitimate captives . . . and not . . . the Moriscos expelled from Spain."[7] Apparently the Spanish authorities were concerned that the exiled Moriscos would use the redemption as a means to return to Spain. The friars were not to ransom foreigners, unless they had received adjutorios for them, or deserters from Spain's North African presidios. However, as we have seen, it was not always possible to adhere to these strictures.

In the sixteenth and seventeenth centuries, the price for a typical captive ranged from about 1,000 to 2,000 reales. In the eighteenth century these prices rose to between 275 and 350 pesos, with up to 500 pesos asked for soldiers and 1,000 pesos for officers. In many redemptions the friars carried large sums that were earmarked for specific captives, often people of high rank whom the Spanish crown or one of the governing councils had directed them to rescue. They made a special effort to ransom these individuals and when they were successful paid very high prices for them. One such captive was Lorenzo Santos de San Pedro, a member of the Council of Castile, who had been taken prisoner by Algerian corsairs in 1668 while returning to Spain from a *visita* (inspection tour) of the Canaries. The original asking price for Santos was 100,000 pesos, but in 1669 the Mercedarians were able to obtain his release for 30,000 pesos, all of which were adjutorios from the crown and his family and friends.[8] Another high-priced captive was Friar Pedro de la Concepción, who was captured by Moroccan pirates in 1641 just outside of Cádiz in a vessel that was taking him and three other Franciscans to Larache, where he was to serve as superior of the Franciscan monastery and administrator of the hospital of the presidio. The Mercedarians were not able to rescue him until 1648, when they negotiated a ransom price of 224,000 reales. All but 6,400 reales were adjutorios given by the crown and various other high-ranking persons, as well as by the Franciscans. At the same time, one of the friars who had been captured with him, Antonio Vanegas, was rescued for 10,400 reales, of which 3,200 were adjutorios.[9] Another friar, Alonso Morena, was not rescued until 1654, when the Trinitarians paid 13,600 reales for him.[10]

In the summer of 1663 Algerian corsairs captured one of the vessels of the Indies fleet, under Captain Juan de Villalobos. A number of prominent people were aboard Villalobos' ship and in 1664 some of them were rescued for very high prices. Villalobos himself was ransomed for 24,000 reales. By order of the crown, this was paid out of the limosnas of the Indies, which were rather substantial at this time. Among the passengers were José de Luna y Peralta of Navarre, a member of the Council of Castile and the *audiencia* (court of appeal) of Seville, and *visitador* (inspector) of Hispaniola, which was his destination in the New World when he was captured, and Pedro de Carabajal y Vargas of Trujillo in Extremadura, also of the Council of Castile and a judge of the audiencia of Santo Domingo, who was traveling with his wife. Luna y Peralta was rescued for 40,000 reales and Carabajal and his wife for 28,000 reales each. All three were ransomed by order of the crown which, as in the case of Villalobos, directed that their redemption prices be taken from the limosnas sent from the Indies.[11] In 1667 Algerian corsairs again captured Villalobos' ship on its return voyage from the Indies. Once more his rescue price was 24,000 reales, but Villalobos paid two-thirds of this himself and the remainder was taken from the limosnas of the Indies.[12]

The friars were not always successful in rescuing those for whom they had large sums of money. The North Africans usually knew both the identities of their captives and how much money the friars had in adjutorios for them, and they would often hold out for even higher prices for the most valuable prisoners. This occurred in the case, already referred to, of Don Miguel de Sesa, the Aragonese nobleman who was a captive in Tetuán from 1596 to 1609. In spite of the fact that eight redemptions came to Tetuán with 340,000 maravedís given by the king of Spain for Sesa's ransom, he could not be rescued because his owner was asking twice that amount for him. When he finally was ransomed for 561,000 maravedís in 1609, the Mercedarians had to add more than 200,000 maravedís of their own money.[13] In 1579 the Trinitarians attempted to ransom Don Jerónimo de Palafox of Ariza in Old Castile, who had been captured in 1575 while traveling from Sicily to Naples in the royal service. Although the redemption had brought 500 gold escudos for him, Friar Juan Gil's many attempts to obtain Palafox' release failed because the Algerians, who said he was "a man for whom a great ransom price was due, a nobleman," were asking 1,000 escudos, which had to be paid in gold. In the next Trinitarian redemption, in 1582, he was rescued for 1,000 gold escudos with the help of a 500-escudo adjutorio from the Spanish crown.[14]

The Trinitarians encountered similar difficulties with the rescue in 1579 of the young Miguel de Cervantes, then an obscure soldier who had been captured in 1575 while returning to Spain from service in Naples. Because Cervantes was an officer, the governor of Algiers believed he was wealthy and not only demanded a 500-escudo ransom for him, twice that paid for any other captive in this redemption and more than five times the average, but insisted on receiving it in gold as well. He threatened to send him to Constantinople if he were not rescued. So that "he should not be lost in the land of the Turk," the friars borrowed from various merchants in Algiers 220 escudos to add to the 280 that they had already received in adjutorios for him.[15] During the sixteenth century the payment of such large ransoms in precious metals was difficult because the redemptors brought two-thirds of their treasuries in merchandise, which was sold for Algerian currency or else exchanged directly for captives.

In 1667, the Mercedarians were unable to obtain several captives from the *Margarita*, whose rescue had been directed by the crown and the Council of the Indies. The *Margarita*, as previously noted, had been carrying a number of prominent individuals when it was seized in 1664, and the council had provided one-third of the total treasury of 995,961 reales for the primary purpose of ransoming them. The redemptionists were directed by their general to make a special effort to secure the release of Francisco Castejón y Belvis, brother of Bernardo Castejón, a member of the audiencia of Seville. They had received contributions of 42,000 reales for him, including 17,600 from the Council of the Cruzada, given at the direction of the crown. If necessary, the redemption was to add another 40,000 reales out of limosnas. Castejón's freedom was said to be the "major concern of the entire court, from the queen . . . to the ministers, so that if you were to bring all of Algiers without this nobleman, it would be as though you had done nothing." They were next to be concerned with the rescue of Tomás de Concha, captain of a dispatch boat of the Indies fleet captured along with the *Margarita*, whose redemption was especially important to the count of Peñaranda, president of the Council of the Indies. Peñaranda had directed them to pay approximately 4,000 reales from the limosnas of the Indies for him.

They were unable to obtain either of these captives. According to a letter from Pedro de la Concepción, administrator of the Trinitarian hospitals in Algiers, if they had rescued them "undoubtedly the entire redemption would have been endangered." The governor, who apparently knew of the priority assigned to the rescue of these men, had demanded a total of 40,000 pesos for them and the captain of the *Margarita*, Fernando Montellanos. But other slaveowners objected to one-third of the entire treasury being spent on three captives. They wanted the Mercedarians to ransom their slaves instead, and threatened to riot and set fire to the churches in the baños if these redemptions were carried out.[16] The friars did rescue other important captives from the *Margarita*, among them Clara de Acevedo, the thirteen-year-old daughter of Juan Antonio Acevedo, a member of the Council of Castile, for whom they paid 5,000 pesos, most of which were adjutorios.[17] In 1668 the Mercedarians were able to rescue Castejón for 16,442 pesos, of which about half were adjutorios.[18]

In order to keep their ransom prices down, high-ranking captives sometimes attempted to conceal their true identities. One who succeeded was Don Pedro de Solís y Trujillo, who in 1648 was rescued under the pseudonym of Pedro Alejandro for the reasonable price of 2,860 reales.[19] But it was usually not possible for captives to do this. Father Jiménez once remarked that the Algerians were very crafty at learning if their captives were nobles or ecclesiastics or held other titles.[20] In 1732 the marqués de Valdecañas was captured with his battalion by the Algerians. In January 1733 he wrote to Don Lorenzo Figueroa Fajardo in Madrid, informing him that he was alive and a slave of the dey of Algiers, and that in an attempt to conceal his high noble status, he had identified himself as Juan Márquez, a captain of the regiment of Aragón. The danger that the Algerians would learn who he was increased daily from the time he reported that he was alive since, as one correspondent noted, his mother the marquesa had broadcast "all over Madrid that her son is a slave of the dey of Algiers, is well-treated, not even being kept in chains, and is suffering only from poor diet and difficulty in sleeping." On July 17 the *Gazette of Holland* carried the news that he was probably alive and a captive in Algiers. Attempts were made, through the Swedish consul in Algiers, to rescue him quickly, along with others of his regiment in order not to arouse suspicion, but these failed. In 1735 Friar Pedro Ros Valle warned that the redemption must proceed cautiously, since if Valdecañas' identity did become known to the Algerians, they would not give him up for 1,000 Muslims, even if they were all corsair captains. It proved impossible to keep the secret; the marqués was finally given away by two soldiers of his regiment who had apostatized, and in 1736 the Algerians asked a ransom of 100,000 pesos for him, which the Mercedarians were not able to pay. In spite of Ros Valle's pessimism, he finally was ransomed in 1738, in exchange for two Algerian corsair captains and a substantial sum of money.[21]

The Spanish crown or ruling councils sometimes directed the redemptors to pay special attention to the ransoming of particular groups of captives. In 1639 the crown ordered the Council of the Indies to give 1,000 ducats to the Trinitarian redemptors for the rescue of captives seized when Calpe in Valencia was attacked by Algerian corsairs in 1637. In addition to this money and substantial sums given by the Council of the Cruzada, the crown also released ten Muslim slaves from the galleys to be exchanged for some of the captives from Calpe. Because of the incomplete nature of the documentation, it is impossible to say how many people from the raid on Calpe were rescued, but the redemption lists examined contain the names of seventy-seven of them.[22] In 1642 the Trinitarians were directed by the crown to make a special effort to obtain the release of the victims of the attack on Gualchos in 1640, for which, as noted earlier, the Cruzada had given substantial assistance.[23] In that redemption twenty-one of the captives from Gualchos were rescued, including six women and nine children, for a total of 54,055 reales.

A royal decree of September 22, 1638, ordered that in recognition of "the valor, fidelity, and constancy of the people of Fuenterrabía" in defending their town against the French earlier that year, the Trinitarians were to give preference to captives from Fuenterrabía.[24] This was followed by a royal order of January 28, 1639, providing the names of ten Fuenterrabían captives in Algiers whom the friars were to try to rescue. In 1642 the crown directed that 9,900 reales given by the patriarch of the Indies be applied to the redemption of captives from Fuenterrabía. During the next seven years they were able to locate seven of the captives on the list, including Sebastián de Mendizábal, thirty-six years old, who had been captured just outside San Sebastián on a French boat that he had helped seize during the attack on Fuenterrabía. He was rescued by the Trinitarians in 1646 for 2,985 reales.[25]

In 1667, in reply to a complaint by officials of the Basque province of Guipúzcoa that they were having difficulty meeting their quota for the royal levy of mariners because so many seamen from the province had been captured by the North Africans, a royal order was issued directing the redemptors to attempt to ransom mariners from that province.[26] Of a total of 401 captives rescued by the Mercedarians in 1667 and 1669, 27 were from Guipúzcoa. Only eight were identified by occupation, and all of these were mariners. But the rest had been captured at sea, and may well have been seamen.[27] Guipúzcoans represented nearly 7 percent of the total rescued in these two redemptions. Yet Guipúzcoans accounted for only 2.5 percent of all rescued captives surveyed. Thus the few years after the royal order saw a substantial increase in the percentage of captives from this region who were rescued.

An interesting aspect of the redemption was the occasional ransom of the black slaves of Spaniards. These were usually paid for by their Spanish owners. Juan de Villalobos paid 300 pesos for the rescue of a black slave from Puerto Rico named Juan Moreno, who had been captured with him in 1667.[28] José de Mesa, who was rescued in 1670, paid 492.5 pesos for the release of his mulatto slave, Francisco Guerra, who was captured with him.[29] In 1662 Juan Alonso Alvarado of the Canaries paid 1,200 reales for his black slave, Francisco, and in 1667 Pedro Blanco, prebend of the cathedral of Seville, paid 2,000 reales for the rescue of his black slave, Juana.[30] In 1669 the president of the Council of Castile gave 800 reales for the ransom of a young black slave named Pedro, who belonged to his nephew.[31]

There is at least one instance in the redemption books of the rescue of captives who had been *forzados* (penal laborers) on Christian galleys. In 1667 the Mercedarians rescued Pedro Domingo de Caruche of Luque in Andalusia, a forzado in the galleys of the duke of Oria, for 200 pesos, and Joseph Servilio of Naples, who had served in the same capacity in the galleys of the duke of Tursis, for 150 pesos. Both were rescued with limosnas.[32]

We have already noted the concern for the rescue of children in captivity. It was particularly difficult to ransom children, since the North Africans were frequently not willing to let them go at all. In 1612 the Mercedarians attempted to obtain the release of two children whose parents had already been freed. One was a girl named Isabel, a native of Barcelona, whose father had been rescued earlier by the Trinitarians. In 1611 the redemptors from Burgos had offered 3,000 reales, but her owner was not willing to give her up at that time. The Mercedarians tried again to ransom her in 1612, but were unsuccessful. They were, however, able to rescue an eight-year-old boy from Gibraltar named Cristóbal. The previous year his father had been freed, but the child's owner, Alay Joseph, had refused to permit his rescue. This time the Mercedarians had 4,000 reales in adjutorios for him and were able to secure his release. They also rescued the six-year-old daughter of Francesca Trujilla of Menorca, who had been born in Algiers and never been baptized.[33] In 1670 the Trinitarians paid 342 pesos for the month-old daughter of two rescued Spaniards who had been born while her parents were still captives and had not been baptized.[34] In 1645 the Mercedarians rescued a seven-year-old girl from Málaga who had been captured when she was eighteen months old and did not know who her parents were. They paid 8,400 reales for her.[35]

So, although the North Africans were reluctant to let young children go, in fact the friars were able to rescue many of them.[36] And while the prices just cited were high, in general the prices for children were not substantially higher than those for other captives. In the Trinitarian redemption of 1614, in which the average rescue price was 69,157 maravedís, the friars paid only 64,600 maravedís for each of eleven children under twelve years of age.[37] In 1625, four children under twelve years of age were rescued for 3,000 reales each. The average rescue price in this redemption was 2,342 reales.[38]

Children were not the only captives whose masters would not permit them to be rescued. In many cases, owners asked more than the friars could pay, even for captives who had adjutorios. Some owners simply did not want to let their slaves go because they needed them for the work they performed or for various other reasons. Numerous attempts were made to ransom Don Baltasar de Villalba, governor of Almarzaquivir in Orán, who was a prisoner in Algiers from 1709. The Mercedarians who came to Algiers in 1713 offered 6,000 pesos for him, but were unable to obtain his release. In 1717, the Mercedarians were prepared to pay 9,000 pesos for him, even though he was "old and useless," but they were still unsuccessful. The dey told the Trinitarians who came the following year that even if they could pay the 100,000 pesos he had demanded for Don Baltasar, he would not let him go. Another attempt to negotiate his release was made by the Mercedarians in 1723, when Villalba was eighty-four years old. The dey agreed to discuss his rescue, but then asked 30,000 pesos for him, an exorbitant price for someone who might not survive the return voyage to Spain. The following year the new governor proposed to refer the matter of the old man's rescue to the divan, if the redemption would first pay him 20,000 pesos plus thirty Muslim slaves from the Spanish galleys. The offer was refused and the matter dropped. According to García Navarro, the Algerians did not want him to be rescued because of a superstitious fear that if he were freed Almarzaquivir would be lost again. Villalba died in captivity in Algiers on June 20, 1728, at the age of eighty-eight.[39]

Difficulties were encountered in obtaining less prestigious captives also. Diego Galán's master would not permit him to be rescued because he regarded the boy as a member of the family. When Galán suggested to him that he would like to be ransomed, he threatened to dismember the redemptionist friars if they even proposed it.[40] Galán finally obtained his freedom by escaping. In 1625 Juan Nieto of Osuna, for whom adjutorios of 1,500 reales had been given, could not be bought because his master "did not want to give him."[41] For the same reason, in 1651 the Mercedarians had to return an adjutorio of 320 reales given for Nicolás de Anís of Sanlúcar.[42]

Sometimes captives whose owners would not part with them during their lifetimes were rescued after their death. When Ali Pichilin, the great slaveowner of seventeenth-century Algiers, died in the 1640s, his widow offered for redemption large numbers of slaves whom her husband had refused to sell. In 1649 the Trinitarians purchased nineteen slaves from Pichilin's widow for 1,200 reales each. Ten of these had been in captivity for from eight to twenty years.[43] In 1651 the Mercedarians paid a total price of 8,640 reales for eight more of Pichilin's captives, whose average time in captivity was nineteen years. Four of them had been captives for more than twenty years. They were Simón Rodríguez of Seville, age forty, captive for twenty-two years; Andrés de Carmona of Carmona, age fifty, captive for thirty years; Lorenzo Pérez of the Canaries, age fifty, captive for twenty-three years; and Gaspar Bas of Alicante, age fifty, captive for twenty-three years.[44] These men, after spending their prime years as slaves in Algiers, were now brought back to Spain to begin new lives.

Although Ali Pichilin's slaves were sold after his death, many others were simply freed when their masters died. In 1582, the Trinitarians paid only the departure tax for seven captives who had been freed when their master, known as Friosino Corso, died. All of them had been slaves for more than ten years and one, a fifty-year-old native of Barcelona called Mateo Catalán, had been in captivity for twenty-eight years.[45] In 1662 the Trinitarians again paid only the departure tax for four slaves freed in this way.[46] The redemption books contain numerous other instances of captives freed by their masters either before or after their deaths.

Some slaveowners would not permit their captives to be rescued for money, but would exchange them for Muslims who were slaves in Christian lands. In 1674 the Trinitarians obtained Francisco de Castro, fifty-six, of Tarifa, a captive in Tetuán, in exchange for his master's wife and daughter, whom they had purchased in Spain for 2,264 reales. In previous redemptions Castro's owner had refused to negotiate his redemption for cash, insisting that he would give him only in return for the two women.[47] The master of Pedro Varona, an army officer who was captured in Orán in 1736, would not allow the redemption to ransom him for cash, but demanded that Varona be traded for his relative, who was a slave in the Spanish galleys.[48] Although Spanish policy generally permitted the exchange of Muslims for Christians on an individual basis, the release of Muslim corsair captains was prohibited. Exceptions were made occasionally, as in the case of the marqués de Valdecañas.

Sometimes the crown or high-ranking individuals would give slaves to the redemption for the purpose of making a trade. This occurred in 1656 when the Trinitarians rescued Jerónimo Belasco y Castañeda, a commander of the Order of St. John, for 2,500 pesos plus a Muslim from the Spanish galleys whom the king had given in order to assist in the rescue of this captive.[49] An exchange attempt that failed occurred in 1587, when Philip II granted the duke of Maqueda permission to give the Trinitarians one of his slaves, Jusuf Benalhamar, who was to be exchanged for two boys whom Benalhamar owned in Algiers. A group of Moriscos from Valencia, described as "trustworthy persons," posted 600 ducats as surety for this transaction. But when the redemptors arrived in Algiers with him, Benalhamar refused to give them the captives. They took him before an Algerian court, where he claimed that he did not have to give the friars anything because he had paid the duke of Maqueda for his freedom. When the friars asked why, in that case, he had signed an agreement to free the boys, he replied that he had done it because the duke had not wanted people to know that "so great a nobleman would take money from his captive." He was upheld by the Algerian court and the two boys were not released.[50]

Exchanges of Muslim captives for Christians on a large scale did not become commonplace until the mid-eighteenth century, when the crown began to turn over large numbers of North African galley slaves to the redemptors for this purpose. This first occurred in 1739, when the Mercedarians paid ransoms for 350 captives and then exchanged 50 Algerians chosen by the dey for 50 Spanish soldiers named by the crown. The arrangements had been proposed two years earlier by members of the Algerian government. According to the Mercedarian who negotiated the passport for this redemption, transactions of this sort had been suggested in the past by the redemptors and rejected by the Algerians. García Navarro, however, wrote that the king of Spain was reluctant to trade Muslim captives for Christians because he did not want to surrender the chance to convert them to Christianity.[51] While both reasons may have played a part in the failure to initiate such exchanges earlier, by the middle of the eighteenth century the Spanish crown was committed to the principle of exchanging Muslim captives for Spaniards, and issued orders to that effect.[52]

At about the same time as this policy was adopted in Spain, the Moroccan rulers insisted that no redemption could be made there unless it included an exchange of captives. In 1740 the governor of Tangier refused to permit the Mercedarians to come to his city without such an arrangement. Philip V agreed to this, and in 1741 the friars traveled to Tangier with sixty Muslim slaves from the Spanish galleys, whom they traded for the same number of Spaniards. In addition, they gave 650 pesos for each Spaniard.[53] Another exchange took place in Tangier in 1759, when of eighty-eight Spaniards rescued, thirty-six were obtained for one Muslim slave and 550 pesos each.[54]

The attitude of the Algerian government toward exchanges remained ambivalent, since it was torn between its heavy dependence on cash ransoms and the demands of its subjects for the return of Muslim captives in Spain. Just as captive labor was important to the Algerian economy, so were ransoms. Proof of their importance is the fact that at all times not only was the redemption welcome in Algiers, it was eagerly courted, and it was a simple matter for redemptionists to obtain passports and certificates of safe-conduct. Although the terms of these documents were frequently violated and the behavior of Algerian officials often erratic, in only one known instance, in 1609, did harm come to the friars at the hands of the Algerian rulers. Otherwise, as the experience of García Navarro in 1723 demonstrates, the safety and security of the redemption was almost never in doubt. As Pedro Ros Valle noted, the dey "would do nothing—neither burn, mistreat, nor kill the redemptors, nor even rob them of their money outright—although there were some who thought he would—because they like the redemption so much and do not wish such a good thing to end."[55]

The importance of ransom payments to the Algerian economy was so manifest that even the friar-redemptors, whose writings generally emphasized the risks involved in their work in order to engender greater support and sympathy, admitted that in fact there was little real danger because the Muslim rulers did not want to chance losing the income from future redemptions. For, as we have seen, the friars often spent enormous sums of money in North Africa, and most of it went to the state. In 1730, for example, of 121,133 pesos that the Mercedarians spent in Algiers, 77,984 were paid to the state and its high officials.[56] Of course, even the sums paid to private individuals stimulated the Algerian economy, as did the amounts spent by the redemptionists to support themselves and their entourage, as well as the rescued captives, while they were in Algiers.

Budgets for Algiers during the period in question are virtually nonexistent, but one was provided by Alonso Cano, a Trinitarian who took part in the 1768–1769 redemption and recorded his observations of the Algerian government, politics, and economy.[57] According to the figures presented by Cano, only 38 percent of the income of the Algerian state was collected within Algiers, with the rest coming from the provinces of the regency.[58] Of the total of 202,300 pesos raised in Algiers, more than half came from corsair-related activities. Cano estimated that the ransom of captives alone accounted for an average of about 30,000 pesos a year, or about 14 percent of the total income obtained in Algiers.[59] In view of the large ransoms paid during the eighteenth century, Cano's estimate would appear to be low. Furthermore, the income brought in by the corsairs' activity was not easily replaceable. With the decline in privateering at the end of the eighteenth century, the Algerian government attempted to impose taxes to compensate for the lost income. The result was popular discontent and several unsuccessful uprisings.[60]

The last and largest redemption in Algiers by the Spaniards took place in 1768–1769. Negotiations for this transaction began in 1766, through the good offices of the Moroccan ambassador to Spain and Pietro Capriata, the Venetian consul in

Algiers. Capriata's letters to the king of Spain in the early part of the year indicate that the dey, who had taken office in February, was eager to negotiate the release of all remaining Spanish captives for cash only, with no exchange. But he changed his mind after two attempts on his life, and on June 3 Capriata wrote that although the dey would prefer the money to Muslims, he feared there would be a general uprising against him if the redemption were executed without an exchange. Although the initial reaction in Madrid to the Algerian insistence that corsair captains be included in the trade was negative, the crown finally relented and the redemption was arranged.[61] Its purpose was to rescue all legitimate Spanish captives remaining in Algiers, as well as Roman Catholics of other nations who had been taken prisoner under the Spanish flag. Deserters were not to be rescued. Although many of the captives would be ransomed for cash, an integral part of this transaction was the exchange of Algerians for Spaniards.

The redemptors arrived in Algiers with a total of 1,246 Algerian slaves whom they wished to exchange. Although the Algerian officials at first demurred at a trade of this magnitude, telling the friars that they "did not want Moors, but money," they agreed to complete the exchange before any rescues for cash were negotiated. Among the Algerian captives were twenty-six corsair captains, who were to be exchanged for the same number of Spanish naval officers or boat owners. The rest were to be traded at the rate of two Algerian seamen for one Spanish seaman.[62]

During the course of the redemption, the Algerians repeatedly attempted to revise their agreement with the Spaniards in order to secure as many cash ransoms as possible. When the rescue was completed, a total of 631 captives had been exchanged for 1,236 Algerians, and 819 captives had been ransomed for cash. The total amount of the cash ransoms was 694,463 pesos.

The reluctance of the Algerian rulers, in spite of popular pressure, to live up to the original understanding attests to the importance to their economy of ransom payments. The remark to the Mercedarian friars that they wanted money and not

Muslims for their Christian slaves demonstrates not a lack of feeling for their compatriots, but rather the realities of the economic structure of the Algerian state.

The Return Home

The return of the captives to Spain was not always a joyous experience for them. The reason for this was that they often had to endure a period of quarantine before they were permitted to mingle with the population of the port of arrival. In the sixteenth and early seventeenth centuries, this requirement was not imposed on returning redemptions. The captives were simply registered upon arriving at the port and then permitted to enter the city.[63] Nor was quarantine usually required for captives returning from Morocco, who always went first to Ceuta and then usually to a port in Andalusia. But in the aftermath of the frequent and devastating epidemics that struck Spain in the seventeenth century, more stringent health measures were imposed on those coming from the eastern Maghrib. This is not surprising, for plague was virtually endemic to that region.[64]

At times, local health officials simply required assurance that the North African city from which the redemption had come was free of contagion. This assurance could take the form of a certificate from Spanish or other European officials in North Africa, or might be nothing more than an oath by the redemptors and their notary that there was no epidemic in the city and that all those who had embarked for Spain were in good health. This occurred in December 1662, when the Trinitarian redemption arrived in Cartagena from Algiers. After the oath was taken, the entire group submitted to a medical examination and then was permitted to enter the city.[65]

For most of the last third of the seventeenth century, the health certificate was not enough, and the returnees were usually required to undergo quarantines of varying duration. In 1679, when plague was present in parts of Spain, the Trinitarian redemption arrived in the port of Cartagena on November 26, was not permitted to disembark until December 18, and then was confined, under guard, for fifteen days. During the quarantine period the entire group was visited and examined every few days by doctors and surgeons employed by the city's health board.[66] Another redemption that came to Cartagena from Algiers in 1692 was allowed to leave the ship the day after their arrival and quarantined for only five days.[67]

Some returning redemptions were subject to long and harsh quarantines. In 1664 an epidemic struck Algiers prior to the departure of the expedition and no health certificate was issued. When the ship carrying the returnees arrived at the port of Alicante, several physicians came on board to examine them. They found no symptoms of disease and permitted the captives to disembark and go into quarantine in a *lazaretto* (pesthouse) less than a league from the city, where they were visited daily by the physicians. Although no signs of illness were observed, when the viceroy of Valencia learned of this arrangement he ordered the entire group to return to their ship for the remainder of the quarantine period, which lasted fifty days. During this long period at sea, the captives frequently expressed regret at having been rescued.[68] A similar incident occurred in 1678 when, within three days of their arrival at the lazaretto of Alicante, the redemption's notary died of unknown causes. Fearing that he had succumbed to plague, the authorities directed the returnees to leave the lazaretto and go into quarantine on a small, uninhabited island 3 leagues out to sea. Although the island had no trees for protection, it did have several caves. One of the rescued captives described these as so damp and full of vermin that they were unable to enter them, so they spent their days in the open, unprotected from the elements. Food and drink were brought to them from the mainland, but neither in sufficient quantities. If the sea was stormy, no provisions arrived at all. In addition to the thirst, hunger, and exposure, the captives were also in danger of being recaptured by corsairs on that unprotected island. The general of the Mercedarians brought the matter to the attention of the crown, and shortly thereafter the group was moved to another place.[69]

Upon their return to Spain, or after being released from

quarantine, the rescued captives were expected to participate in a series of religious processions in various cities. While traveling from Algiers in 1627, for example, the Mercedarian friars and the rescued captives stopped in Mallorca, where a procession was held on November 14. They arrived in Valencia four days later, had a second procession there, and then went on to Zaragoza, where a third such ceremony took place. Captives whose homes were in the kingdom of Aragón then left the group, but those who lived in Castile continued to Madrid, where the fourth and last procession was held on Christmas Day.[70]

The emotional impact of a returning redemption was very powerful, and an important factor in generating contributions for future ransoming expeditions. The instructions that the generals of the orders issued to the friars make it clear that this was the purpose of the ceremonies. In 1730 the general of the Mercedarians directed the redemptors to return after the procession to the cathedral of Valencia for a service in which the captives were to participate. One of the redemptionist friars would deliver the sermon, in which the desperation of those who remained in the power of the infidel was to be emphasized and an appeal made to the faithful for alms to enable the Mercedarians to return for them. Then, in full view of the congregation, all the captives were to receive communion together. Subsequently, the redemptors from Castile were to travel to the royal court in Madrid with some of the captives "so that the king and his ministers could witness the zeal of the friars in this holy ministry, and the others might recognize how successfully their alms are being used in a work of such pious charity."[71] The redemptors from Andalusia were instructed to travel to Seville with another group of captives for the same purpose. Then the captives could go home.

We do not know what became of most of the captives after they returned to Spain. People like Don Lorenzo Santos de San Pedro returned to their old positions in the government. After his rescue in 1664, Juan de Villalobos resumed his career as a ship's captain in the carrera de las Indias and presumably did the same after being rescued from his second captivity in

1667. Many others went back to their homes and resumed their former lives.

But for some, especially those who had been in captivity for many years, there may not have been a home or a past to return to. The redemption issued a document to each captive certifying that the individual had indeed been a captive in North Africa. This was virtually a license to solicit alms, and the former captive turned beggar was a common figure in early modern Spain.

Conclusion

It is not possible to calculate the cost to Spain of the "little war" with the Muslims of North Africa. The sums spent to ransom captives were not large in terms of overall national expenditures, but they did have to be paid in precious metals during a period that was dominated by vellón coinage. Nor, perhaps, was the cost of defense against the corsairs great, although it was large enough so that it could not be afforded. Of course, these burdens were proportionately heavier for the coastal localities. In addition, the economic activity of these regions bore the greatest brunt of the corsair offensive.

As for the demographic consequences, contemporaries regarded the captivity of Spaniards by North Africans as a factor in the population decline of the seventeenth century. The *arbitrista* (author of proposals for economic and political reform) Pedro Fernández Navarrete included among the causes of depopulation "those who, because of our neglect, are in slavery or captivity."[1] The Junta de Reformación of the early seventeenth century also placed part of the blame for the demographic decline on the capture of large numbers of Spaniards.[2] In fact, it is unlikely that the number of people in captivity in North Africa at any given moment constituted a significant drain on Spain's population, although it is arguable that given the demographic crisis of the seventeenth century any further attrition was significant.

More important than the actual numbers seized was the psychological effect that the phenomenon had on Spanish society. In this sense, it can be compared with modern urban crime, in that the actual number of victims is relatively small, but society as a whole is terrorized. While it is true that large numbers of captives were seized in Spain's coastal regions, the demography of those areas suffered more from the departure of those who were frightened away than of those who were captured. As for the residents of those areas of the coasts that remained populated, the corsair conflict became an integral part of their lives and was woven into the fabric of their societies—it forced them to adopt a peculiar life-style, affected their economies, and threatened their livelihoods and their lives. The letter from Gibraltar cited at the opening of this book gives some insight into the effects that this struggle had on coastal localities. (The people of Gibraltar never felt secure—"neither at night nor during the day, neither in bed nor at mealtimes, neither in the fields nor in our homes.")

The psychological impact of the conflict was not confined to coastal regions. The problem of captives in North Africa was a phenomenon that deeply pervaded all of Spanish society and influenced the Spanish outlook on life. For the massive campaigns to raise funds for the ransom of captives, the printed and widely circulated accounts of their sufferings and of the difficulties encountered by the redemptionist fathers in North Africa, the processions held when the ransomed captives returned, the visibility of former captives begging alms, the chains and shackles hung in churches and public buildings throughout Spain, all served to confirm for many Spaniards that the long struggle with the Muslim world was not over.

**NOTES
BIBLIOGRAPHY
INDEX**

Notes

Introduction and Historical Background

1 AGS, Estado, leg. 495, July 25, 1614.
2 On the growth of piracy in the Mediterranean in the wake of the cessation of great-power hostilities, see Fernand Braudel, *The Mediterranean and the Mediterranean World in the Age of Philip II*, 2 vols., trans. S. Reynolds (New York, 1973), 2:865–891.
3 Ibid., p. 866. On Christian pirates, see pp. 873–882. See also the brilliant study by Albert Tenenti, *Piracy and the Decline of Venice, 1580–1615* (Berkeley, 1967). Another work that juxtaposes Christian and Muslim piracy is Peter Earle, *Corsairs of Malta and Barbary* (London, 1970).
4 For the development of the crusading ideal among Muslims in North Africa, see J. M. Abun-Nasr, *A History of the Maghrib* (Cambridge, 1971), pp. 119–158.
5 For discussions of Ferdinand's foreign policy, see J. H. Elliott, *Imperial Spain 1469–1716* (New York, 1966), pp. 130–135; John Lynch, *Spain under the Habsburgs*, 2 vols. (Oxford, 1964), 1:28–34; Fernand Braudel, "Les Espagnols et l'Afrique du Nord de 1492 à 1577," *Revue Africaine* 69 (1928); Braudel, *The Mediterranean*, 2:669–672. Andrew Hess suggests that Spain's new interest in the Atlantic, as a result of Columbus' first voyages, also distracted it from further expeditions to North Africa. Andrew C. Hess, *The Forgotten Frontier: A History of the Sixteenth-Century Ibero-African Frontier* (Chicago, 1978), pp. 36–44.
6 Braudel, "Les Espagnols," p. 220.
7 Ibid., pp. 212–213; Hess, *Forgotten Frontier*, pp. 45–50. Hess argues that the peculiar organization of Maghribian society at this time, based heavily on kinship relationships, made it especially vulnerable to the military force of the early modern Spanish state. Ibid., pp. 11–25.
8 On the Spanish-Ottoman confrontations of this period, see Brau-

169

del, *The Mediterranean*, 2:904–1105; Hess, *Forgotten Frontier*, pp. 71–90. On naval engagements, see John F. Guilmartin, *Gunpowder and Galleys: Changing Technology and Mediterranean Warfare at Sea in the Sixteenth Century* (London, 1974).

9 For the political development of the Ottoman regency in North Africa, see Abun-Nasr, *History of the Maghrib*; C.-A. Julien, *History of North Africa*, trans. J. Petrie, ed. C. C. Stewart (London, 1970); Hess, *Forgotten Frontier*, pp. 156–178.

10 Elliott, *Imperial Spain*, pp. 238–239; Braudel, *The Mediterranean*, 2:843–844. For a discussion of the years between Lepanto and the 1580 truce, see Andrew C. Hess, "The Battle of Lepanto and Its Place in Mediterranean History," *Past & Present* 57 (November 1972): 53–73, and *Forgotten Frontier*, pp. 90–99. He argues for the Moroccan victory at Alcazar as the decisive turning point for the withdrawal of both sides from the western Mediterranean.

11 Abun-Nasr, *History of the Maghrib*, pp. 211–213; Julien, *History of North Africa*, pp. 230–233.

12 For a discussion of the growth of corsair influence in Moroccan politics, see Jerome B. Weiner, "Fitna, Corsairs and Diplomacy: Morocco and the Maritime States of Western Europe, 1603–1672" (Ph.D. diss., Columbia University, 1975).

13 On the Morisco problem in the context of the international situation, see Joan Reglá, "La cuestión morisca y la coyuntura internacional en tiempos de Felipe II," *Estudios de Historia Moderna* 3 (1953): 217–234; Andrew C. Hess, "The Moriscos: An Ottoman Fifth Column in Sixteenth-Century Spain," *American Historical Review* 74, no. 1 (October 1968): 1–25; Braudel, *The Mediterranean*, 2:792–797; Lynch, *Spain under the Habsburgs*, 1:205–235; Antonio Domínguez Ortiz and Bernard Vincent, *Historia de los moriscos. Vida y tragedia de una minoría* (Madrid, 1978), pp. 57–72.

14 Hess, *Forgotten Frontier*, p. 187. The full text of Dr. Guilmartin's remarks on the subject may be found in the *Newsletter* of the Society for Spanish and Portuguese Historical Studies 3 (1977): 267–270. Braudel's *The Mediterranean* contains a suggestive discussion of the efforts by the Islamic world to gain access, often by means of warfare, to western technology and manpower, 2:798–802, 864–865.

15 Albert Mas, *Les Turcs dans la littérature espagnole du siècle d'or*, 2 vols. (Paris, 1967), 1:357–358.

Chapter 1: The Captives and Their Captors

1 For a discussion of the role of Christian captives in the North African states, see part 2.

2 The following record books were utilized for the quantitative survey: BNM, MSS. 1635, 2963, 3549, 3551, 3586, 3587, 3591, 3593, 3628, 3631, 3634, 3819, 3837, 3870, 3872, 4359, 4405, 4394, 4363, 6160, 6547, 6573, 7752; AHN, Códices, libs. 118B, 119B, 120B, 121B, 122B, 124B, 125B, 126B, 127B, 128B, 129B, 130B, 131B, 132B, 133B, 134B, 135B, 136B, 137B, 138B, 139B, 140B, 142B, 143B, 144B, 145B, 147B, 148B, 149B. A list of the other redemption records examined may be found in chapter 8.

3 This assumption is borne out by the statistics for 1750–1769. During this period, military and Indies fleet captives represented only a small percentage of the total. Although there is no evidence of an upswing in coastal piracy at this time—indeed, piracy was in decline throughout the eighteenth century—captives from the Spanish coasts accounted for a higher percentage of the Spanish captive population than at any previous period in the survey. Nearly all of these captives were rescued in the redemption of 1768–1769, which was made to ransom all captives remaining in Algiers. The only Spaniards who were not rescued at this time were those whose talents the Algerians regarded as too valuable to give up at any price and deserters from the Spanish garrisons. Thus, the survey for this period presents a particularly accurate picture of the captive population at that time.

4 This is a very conservative estimate. In order to avoid overstating the percentage captured on land, it was never presumed, in calculating this, that a captive had been seized on land unless that was specifically stated in the redemption book. In cases where captives were recorded as having been captured "on the coast of" a particular place, the assumption was that the capture had occurred in coastal waters.

5 For a discussion of this piracy, see Braudel, *The Mediterranean*, 2:880–882.

6 Hess, "The Battle of Lepanto," p. 62.

7 Tenenti, *Piracy and the Decline of Venice*, p. 17.

8 Sebastián García Martínez, *Bandolerismo, piratería y control de moriscos en Valencia durante el reinado de Felipe II* (Valencia, 1977), pp. 69–71; AGS, Estado, leg. 1531, f. 29, letter of Pedro

de Mendoza to Cristóbal de Salazar, August 19, 1584; AHB, Registre de deliberaciones, Cota II-93, f. 11v., July 19, 1584.

9 Braudel discusses the problem of underpopulation that affected the Muslim world in *The Mediterranean*, 1:398–402.

10 Abun-Nasr, *A History of the Maghrib*, p. 173.

11 On the northern European contribution to the corsair war in the Mediterranean, see Tenenti, *Piracy and the Decline of Venice*, pp. 56–86.

12 For a full account of the threat, both real and perceived, of Morisco collaboration with Muslim corsairs and attempts to deal with the problem, see García Martínez, *Bandolerismo*.

13 AGS, Estado, leg. 2636, consultas of December 4, and 31, 1601; ACA, Consejo de Aragón, leg. 607, dtos. 41/5, 41/8, 41/22.

14 Diego de Haedo, *Topografía e historia general de Argel* (Valladolid, 1612), f. 89. Haedo, a Spanish Benedictine, was a captive in Algiers from 1579 to 1582. His work, while often polemical, is generally regarded as one of the most reliable eyewitness accounts of Algerian society in the late sixteenth century. See Hess, *Forgotten Frontier*, p. 196.

15 García Martínez, *Bandolerismo*, p. 69.

16 On the Morisco-Ottoman contacts, see Hess, "The Moriscos."

17 García Martínez, *Bandolerismo*, p. 27.

18 AHN, Estado, lib. 1012d, ff. 303, 85v.

19 Julien, *History of North Africa*, p. 305.

20 AGS, Estado, leg. 494. See also leg. 493.

21 BNM, MS. 4393, f. 36; ibid., MS. 3586, f. 73.

22 Lynch, *Spain under the Habsburgs*, 2:164.

23 AGS, Estado, lib. 365, dto. 9, "Relación del reino de Galicia."

24 AHN, Estado, leg. 3498-lib. 163, ff. 157, 179, 181.

25 MN, Colección Navarrete, vol. VI, f. 120, dto. 21, "Victoria de los Monges del Monasterio de Ntra Señora de Oya. . . ." Dr. J. F. Guilmartin first drew my attention to this document.

26 AHN, Estado, leg. 3498-lib. 163, f. 91.

27 Ibid., f. 51.

28 RAHM, MS. 9–6436, f. 2.

29 Antonio Domínguez Ortiz, *La sociedad española en el siglo XVII*, 2 vols. (Madrid, 1963, 1970), 1:96–97.

30 BNM, MS. 1802, f. 33.

31 Ibid., MS. 3872, f. 134, 144; MS. 1802, f. 50.

32 Ibid., MS. 3819, f. 26.

33 AHN, Códices, lib. 133B, f. 53.

34 *Ibid.*, lib. 132B, f. 22.

35 MN, Colección Vargas Ponce, vol. XXII, dto. 56, f. 111.
36 A royal order of December 3, 1671 authorized Trinitarian friars to go to the Canaries to ask *limosnas* (alms) for the redemption, since, although there were large numbers of captives from the Canaries, there were no religious redemptionists there to solicit alms. AHN, Códices, lib. 153B, n.f.
37 AGS, Cruzada, leg. 286, petition of January 4, 1656.
38 AHN, Códices, lib. 139B, f. 26.
39 Ibid., lib. 135B.
40 AGS, Cruzada, leg. 287.
41 BNM, MS. 3870, f. 27.
42 Ibid., MS. 4359, f. 32.
43 Ibid., MS. 4405, f. 21.
44 ACA, Consejo de Aragón, leg. 556, dtos. 10/1–10/5. For an account of the raid on Calpe by a Christian captive who rowed in the Algerian galleys, see Francis Knight, *A Relation of Seaven Yeares Slaverie Under the Turks of Argeire* (London, 1640), p. 9. Information on individuals captured during the raid may be found in AGS, Cruzada, leg. 288; AHN, Códices, lib. 131B, 134B; BNM, MS. 3631; ACA, Monacales de Hacienda, lib. 2705, Redemption of July 1639 by Mercedarians of Catalonia, Aragón, and Valencia.
45 BNM, MS. 4405, f. 19.
46 Ibid., MS. 3870, f. 34.
47 AGS, Casa de Medina Sidonia, cartulario 79–1, f. 26.
48 AHN, Códices, lib. 132B, 133B.
49 See Miguel de Epalza, "Moriscos y Andalusíes en Túnez durante el siglo XVII," *Al-Andalus* 34 (1969): 247–327, and John D. Latham, "Towards a Study of Andalusian Immigration and Its Place in Tunisian History," *Les Cahiers de Tunisie* 5 (1957): 203–249.
50 AGS, Estado, leg. 494, consultas of January 9, and March 24, 1610.
51 Latham, "Towards a Study of Andalusian Immigration," p. 245.
52 See García Martínez, *Bandolerismo*, and Bernard Vincent, "Les Bandits Morisques en Andalousie au XVIe siècle," *Revue d'histoire moderne et contemporaine* 21 (July–September 1974): 389–400.
53 MN, Colección Navarrete, vol. 5, f. 185, dto. 31.
54 Ibid., f. 165, dto. 28.
55 Ibid., vol. VI, f. 88, dto. 14.
56 AGS, Estado, leg. 494, consulta of May 29, 1610.
57 John Digby to Buckingham, April 5, 1619, SIHMA, vol. 2, pp. 511–512.

58 The Moriscos were not trusted by the Algerians because they felt that their loyalties were divided between their old and new lands. Thus, in 1618 when the rumor spread in Algiers that Spain was planning to send an armada against the city, all Moriscos were forced to surrender their arms, they were forbidden to wear Turkish-style dress, and restrictions were placed on their movements. (AHN, Códices, lib. 125B, ff. 69–72).

59 Kenneth Brown, "An Urban View of Moroccan History—Salé, 1000–1800," *Hesperis-Tamuda* 12 (1971): 47.

60 Brown, "An Urban View," pp. 51–52; Weiner, "Fitna," pp. 158–159; Charles Penz, *Les Captifs français du Maroc au XVIIe siècle 1577–1699* (Rabat, 1944), p. 11. For further information on the "corsair republics," see Roger Coindreau, *Les Corsaires de Salé* (Paris, 1948); Henri de Castries, "Les Moriscos de Salé et Sidi el Ayachi," SIHMF, vol. 3, pp. 189–198, and "Les Trois Republiques du Bou Regreg; Salé, la Kasba, Rabat," ibid., vol. 5, pp. I–XXVIII.

61 Brown, "An Urban View," pp. 51–52.

62 Weiner, "Fitna," pp. 155, 196.

63 Ibid., pp. 153–155, 197.

64 Ibid., pp. 178, 185.

65 Pierre-Priam du Chalard to Louis XIII, October 13, 1635, SIHMF, vol. 3, p. 504.

66 AHN, Códices, lib. 128B.

67 Julien, *History of North Africa*, p. 254.

68 "Relación verdadera de las prevenciones máquinas y aparatos con que la Armada del Cristianísimo Rey de Francia . . . va sobre la ciudad de Argel," in Ignacio Bauer y Landauer, *Papeles de mi archivo: Relaciones de Africa*, 4 vols. (Madrid, 1922), 4: 142–160; Friar D. Agustín Sanz de la Llosa, "Verdadera y nueva relación . . . del feliz suceso que ha tenido una escuadra de cinco navíos Olandeses de guerra . . . ," ibid., pp. 77–81; Abun-Nasr, *History of the Maghrib*, p. 175.

69 MN, Colección Vargas Ponce, vol. XXXII, dto. 64, f. 87; J. Carrera Pujal, *Historia política y económica de Cataluña, siglos XVI al XVIII*, 4 vols. (Barcelona, 1947), 3:297.

70 Carrera Pujal, *Historia política*, 2:414.

71 BNM, MS. 3572, f. 326–334; Friar Serafín de Freytas, "Por la redempción de cautivos sobre que no se deve impedir por la redempción que llaman preservativa, agosto, 1631," BNM, MS. 3536, ff. 10–12; Friar Gabriel de la Asunción, "Memorial del general de la Orden de Descalços de la Santísima Trinidad, redención de

cautivos, contra el arbitrario dada por el Capitán Guillermo Gar-
ret, sobre la erección de una escuadra de seis navíos, que guardan
las costas que miran a Berberia, y preserven estos reinos y sus
habitadores," in Bauer y Landauer, *Papeles de mi archivo*, 2:53–
86.
72 AHN, Estado, leg. 3380, "Dictamenes originales de los capitanes
generales de Cataluña, Valencia y Andalucía sobre remediar las
piraterías de moros en nuestras costas."

Chapter 2: The Response to the Challenge

1 Francisco-Felipe Olesa Muñido, *La organización naval de los estados mediterráneos y en especial de España durante los siglos
XVI y XVII*, 2 vols. (Madrid, 1968), 2:943. See also. I. A. A.
Thompson, *War and Government in Habsburg Spain, 1560–1620*
(London, 1976), pp. 18–19.
2 Haedo, *Topografía*, f. 61; MN, Colección Navarrete, vol. IV, f.
74, dto. 4.
3 Salvador Raurich, "La piratería berberisca en las costas de Cataluña," *Revista General de Marina* 124 (March 1943): 318.
4 Olesa Muñido, *Organización naval*, 2:941.
5 H. Sancho de Sopranis, "Cádiz y la piratería Turco-Berberisca en
el siglo XVI," *Archivo del Instituto de Estudios Africanos*, no. 26
(September 1953), pp. 7–77.
6 Raurich, "La piratería berberisca," p. 318.
7 Olesa Muñido, *Organización naval*, 2:941.
8 AHN, Estado, lib. 1012d, ff. 89v., 90, 115, 116–117v. See also
Braudel, *The Mediterranean*, 2:874.
9 AHN, Estado, lib. 1012d, f. 104v.–105, carta 183.
10 ACA, Consejo de Aragón, leg. 555, dto. 9/3, consulta of February
10, 1625.
11 Ibid.
12 ACA, Consejo de Aragón, leg. 996–999 contain numerous documents concerning licenses granted to Mallorcans, dating from the
mid-seventeenth century.
13 AGS, Guerra Moderna, leg. 1530, letter of Friar Francisco Navarro, April 11, 1724.
14 García Martínez, *Bandolerismo*, p. 29.
15 *Cortes de los antiguos reinos de León y de Castilla* (Madrid, 1861–
1903) 5:543.
16 Ibid., 5:857–858.

17 Ibid., 5:858–859.
18 *Actas de las Cortes de Castilla, 1563–1627* (Madrid, 1887–1925), 1:26.
19 Ibid., 3:428–429.
20 For a discussion of the limited value of galleys against the North African corsairs, see Guilmartin, *Gunpowder and Galleys,* pp. 98–100.
21 AGS, Guerra Antigua, leg. 63, f. 6, July 30, 1556; f. 39, August 20, 1556.
22 Ibid., leg. 68, f. 27.
23 Ibid., leg. 69, f. 28, March 20, 1558; f. 38, July 18, 1558.
24 Ibid., leg. 68, f. 124.
25 Thompson, *War and Government,* p. 21.
26 AGS, Guerra Antigua, leg. 73, ff. 91, 93.
27 AHN, Códices, lib. 133B, f. 21.
28 AGS, Guerra Antigua, leg. 75, f. 93.
29 Ibid., f. 159.
30 Ibid., leg. 70, f. 165.
31 Ibid., leg. 72, f. 182.
32 Ibid., leg. 73, f. 110.
33 AGS, Estado, leg. 2636, consultas of December 4, and 31, 1601; ACA, Consejo de Aragón, leg. 607, dtos. 41/5, 41/8, 41/22.
34 The documents relating to Bravo de Laguna's survey are contained in AGS, Guerra Antigua, leg. 83. A good summary of this documentation can be found in H. Sancho de Sopranis, "El viaje de Luis Bravo de Laguna y su proyecto de fortificación de las costas occidentales de Andalucía de Gibraltar a Ayamonte," *Archivo del Instituto de Estudios Africanos* 9, no. 40 (March 1957): 23–78.
35 AGS, Guerra Antigua, leg. 83, f. 53.
36 Sancho de Sopranis, "El viaje," pp. 55ff. Documents concerning the lawsuit may be found in AHN, Consejos, leg. 7143. See also Thompson, *War and Government,* pp. 24–25.
37 García Martínez, *Bandolerismo,* pp. 32, 42, 69, 72–73.
38 ACA, Consejo de Aragón, leg. 556, dto. 11/2, consulta of April 30, 1637.
39 Ibid., leg. 558, dto. 21/5, letter of marqués de los Vélez to the king, January 26, 1635.
40 Ibid., leg. 561, dto. 43/2, consulta of September 22, 1665.
41 Ibid., dto. 56/1, consulta of November 14, 1695.
42 AGS, Medina Sidonia, cartulario 78–1, ff. 152, 158, 183.
43 Sancho de Sopranis, "El viaje" and "Cádiz y la piratería."

44 AHN, Estado, leg. 3498–lib. 163, f. 157, May 8, 1617.
45 Ibid., f. 177.
46 Ibid., f. 179.
47 Ibid., ff. 127–131.
48 Braudel, *The Mediterranean*, 2:855.
49 Ibid., p. 858.
50 AGS, Estado, leg. 493, consulta of November 23, 1606; leg. 494, consulta of March 15, 1612; leg. 495, consultas of March 10, and April 9, 1620, letter of duke of Maqueda, September 30, 1619.
51 Ibid., leg. 2636, consulta of May 25, 1600.
52 Ibid., leg. 494, consulta of March 7, 1610.
53 Ibid., leg. 495, consulta of February 17, 1613.
54 Ibid., leg. 493, November 23, 1606; leg. 494, March 15, 1612.
55 Braudel, *The Mediterranean*, 2:862; RAHM, MS. 9/6436.
56 AGS, Estado, leg. 494, consulta of February 1611.
57 RAHM, MS. 9/6436.
58 AGS, Estado, leg. 495, letter of duke of Maqueda, September 30, 1619.
59 AGS, Guerra Moderna, leg. 1531, expediente de 1744, "Desertores de las plazas de Orán y Ceuta en los años de 1742, 43 y 44"; "Desertores de las plazas de Ceuta y Orán en los años de 1745, 46 y 47;" ibid., leg. 1532, expediente de 1750, "Desertores de las plazas de Orán y Ceuta en los años de 48, 49 y 6 primero meses de 50."
60 BNM, MS. 3572, ff. 210–211.
61 AGS, Guerra Moderna, leg. 1533, expediente de 1752.
62 Ibid., expediente de 1755, "Relación de las personas que desde el 2 de abril de 1753 han desertado de los presidios de Africa al campo de los moros . . . 2 de feb. de 1755."
63 Ibid., Cruzada, leg. 287, petition of Don Antonio Correa de Afranca.
64 Ibid., leg. 286–288.
65 AHN, Osuna, leg. 3406, letters to Francisco Ortiz, March 10, 1514, May 12, July 7, July 29, 1515, and to Juan Hurtado de Mendoza, April 10, 1514. I am indebted to Professor Helen Nader for this reference.
66 BNM, MS. 1802, ff. 27–32, 54–55; Domínguez Ortiz, *La sociedad española*, pp. 96–97.
67 AHB, Registre de deliberaciones, Consell de Cent, Cota II–94, f. 150v; MN, Colección Sanz de Barutell, art. 6, no. 75.
68 AHN, Consejos, leg. 7143.
69 MN, Colección Navarrete, vol. VI, dto. 4, f. 74.

70 AHN, Estado, leg. 3498–lib. 163, f. 130.
71 AGS, Medina Sidonia, cartulario 79–2, ff. 72–73.

Chapter 3: Life in Captivity

1 AGS, Guerra Antigua, leg. 73, f. 110.
2 On the treatment of captivity in Golden Age literature, see Mas, *Les Turcs*, pp. 357–383. The typical pattern for redemptionist literature was to discuss all slave societies, back to early antiquity, and show by example that slavery in North Africa was worse than in any of them. Good examples of this type of writing are Gabriel Gómez de Losada, *Escuela de trabajos* (Madrid, 1670) and Pierre Dan, *Histoire de Barbarie et de ses corsaires* (Paris, 1637). Although not written by a redemptionist, the work of Haedo, who had been a captive, also fits this format, as does that of the Franciscan, Francisco de San Juan del Puerto, *Missión historial de Marruecos* (Seville, 1708).
3 Braudel makes an interesting argument for his theory that the West rejected efforts by Islam to make cultural contact. *The Mediterranean*, 2:798–802. Western governments may have encouraged the recounting of captive "horror stories" in order to convince their subjects of the dangers of any contact with Islam.
4 Haedo, *Topografía*, f. 14.
5 Ibid., f. 17.
6 Ibid., ff. 17, 46; Melchor de Zuñiga, "Descriptión i república de la ciudad de Arjel," BNM, MS. 3227, f. 46. On the participation of the bey of Tunis in corsair enterprises in the eighteenth century, see Lucette Valensi, "Esclaves chrétiens et esclaves noirs à Tunis au XVIIIᵉ siècle," *Annales: économies, sociétés, civilisations* 22, no. 6 (1967): 1270–1271.
7 Jerónimo Gracián, "Los trabajos y vida del padre maestro Gracián, desde que salió de Madrid expulso de los Descalzos," in *Escritos de Santa Teresa*, ed. Vicente de la Fuente, *Biblioteca de autores españoles*, vol. 55 (Madrid, 1952), p. 459. Gracián was seized while returning to Spain from Rome, where he had unsuccessfully appealed his expulsion from the Carmelite order on grounds of heretical writings.
8 Haedo, *Topografía*, f. 19; Diego Galán, *Cautiverio y trabajos de Diego Galán, natural de Consuegra y vecino de Toledo, 1589–1600*, ed. M. Serrano y Sanz (Madrid, 1913), p. 11; Emanuel d'Aranda, *Relation de la captivité et liberté de sieur Emanuel d'Aranda* (Paris, 1665), pp. 16–17.

9 Galán, *Cautiverio*, p. 11. Emanuel d'Aranda, more than half a century later, described a similar experience in *Relation*, p. 16.

10 Miguel de Cervantes Saavedra, *El trato de Argel*, in *Obras completas*, ed. A. Valbuena Prat (Madrid, 1970), p. 141.

11 BNM, MS. 2794, "De la vida y costumbres de los Turcos," n.f. See also Julien, *History of North Africa*, p. 308; Earle, *Corsairs*, pp. 76–78.

12 Zuñiga, "Descriptión," f. 46; S. Bono, *I corsairi barbareschi* (Turin, 1964), pp. 222–223; Earle, *Corsairs*, p. 78; Godfrey Fisher, *Barbary Legend: War, Trade and Piracy in North Africa, 1415–1830* (Oxford, 1957), p. 99.

13 Galán, *Cautiverio*, p. 12; Zuñiga, "Descriptión," f. 46; Haedo, *Topografía*, f. 19.

14 Galán, *Cautiverio*, p. 13.

15 Cervantes Saavedra, *Trato*, pp. 140–144; Gómez de Losada, *Trabajos*, p. 35.

16 Miguel de Cervantes Saavedra, *Los baños de Argel*, in *Obras completas*, ed. A. Valbuena Prat (Madrid, 1970), p. 351.

17 AHN, Códices, lib. 125B, f. 45.

18 Ibid., lib. 135B, ff. 38–39.

19 Ibid., ff. 46, 57.

20 BNM, MS. 3634.

21 Gómez de Losada, *Trabajos*, p. 211.

22 Ibid.

23 The origins of the use of the term *baños* to refer to the Muslim prisons is somewhat obscure. Most etymologists agree that it arose from a former bathhouse used to house captives in Constantinople.

24 Gómez de Losada, *Trabajos*, p. 33.

25 Alonso Cano, "Nuevo aspecto de la topographía de Argel," RAHM, MS. 2/71, pp. 41–42; Zuñiga, "Descriptión" f. 136; Haedo, *Topografía*, f. 42.

26 Miguel de Cervantes Saavedra, *Don Quijote de la Mancha*, in *Obras completas*, ed. A. Valbuena Prat (Madrid, 1970), p. 1416; Zuñiga, "Descriptión," f. 136; Galán, *Cautiverio*, p. 19.

27 Cano, "Nuevo aspecto," pp. 41–42; Zuñiga, "Descriptión," f. 136; Haedo, *Topografía*, f. 42.

28 So called because after Hasan Paşa defeated the Spaniards at Mostaganem in 1558, he armed a "bastard galley" and chose the most robust captives from the Mostaganem expedition to row it. He did not want these oarsmen to mix with his other captives, who were in the *baño grande*, so he put them in this new *baño*,

which became known as the *baño de la bastarda*. Haedo, *Topografía*, f. 42.

29 Cervantes Saavedra, *Don Quijote*, p. 1416; Haedo, *Topografía*, f. 42.

30 For taverns in Algiers: BNM, MS. 2727, f. 15; BNM, MS. 2387, f. 334; Haedo, *Topografía*, f. 42; Francisco Antonio Silvestre, *Fundación histórica de los hospitales que la religión de la Santísima Trinidad . . . tiene en la ciudad de Argel* (Madrid, 1690), pp. 14, 111; Zuñiga, "Descripción," ff. 131, 139. On the conviviality of the taverns: Aranda, *Relation*, pp. 25–26. For taverns in Morocco: San Juan del Puerto, *Missión historial*, p. 231; *Relation de ce qui s'est passe dans les trois voyages que les religieux de l'ordre de nostre dame de la mercy ont faits dans les états du roy de Maroc pour la rédemption des captifs en 1704, 1708 et 1712* (Paris, 1724), p. 46; Germaine Mouette, *The Travels of the Sieur Mouette in the kingdoms of Fez and Morocco, during his eleven years captivity in those parts*, in *A New Collection of Voyages and Travels in all Parts of the World* (London, 1710), pp. 17–18, 25.

31 Haedo, *Topografía*, f. 42.

32 Zuñiga, "Descripción," f. 139; Aranda, *Relation*; Silvestre, *Fundación histórica*, p. 127.

33 Zuñiga, "Descripción," f. 139; Haedo, *Topografía*, f. 42. This item appears in the expense ledgers of all the redemptions in Algiers.

34 Francisco Jiménez de Santa Catalina, "Viage de Argel," 7 vols., RAHM, MS. 9–27–7E 193–199, 2:238.

35 AGS, Guerra Moderna, leg. 1536, expediente de 1776, letter of Don Manuel Joseph Nieto Martínez, Algiers, October 12, 1776.

36 San Juan del Puerto, *Missión historial*, p. 231.

37 Ibid.; *Relation de trois voyages dans Maroc*, p. 46.

38 *Relation de trois voyages dans Maroc*, p. 47.

39 Ibid.; San Juan del Puerto, *Missión historial*, p. 72.

40 Julien, *History of North Africa*, pp. 308–310; Earle, *Corsairs*, pp. 72–80; Fisher, *Barbary Legend*, p. 99. Contemporary observers, such as Haedo, also made frequent references to the importance of captive labor in North Africa.

41 Mouette, *Travels*, p. 41; Aranda, *Relation*, p. 13; Haedo, *Topografía*, ff. 16, 18, 46; Earle, *Corsairs*, p. 35.

42 Knight, *Relation*, pp. 28–29.

43 Haedo, *Topografía*, ff. 17, 117.

44 Knight, *Relation*, pp. 28–29.

45 Gómez de Losada, *Trabajos*, p. 83; Haedo, *Topografía*, ff. 17, 117.

46 Gregorio Marañón, "La vida en las galeras en tiempo de Felipe II," in *Vida e historia* (Madrid, 1962), p. 21.

47 Olesa Muñido, *Organización naval*, 2:1154; Haedo, *Topografía*, f. 17; Earle, *Corsairs*, p. 35.

48 AGS, Estado, leg. 1133, ff. 24–25, 48–50, 154–161.

49 Knight, *Relation*, pp. 10, 14–16.

50 Jiménez de Santa Catalina, "Viage," 1:62; Gómez de Losada, *Trabajos*, p. 92; Norman R. Bennett, "Christian and Negro Slavery in Eighteenth-Century North Africa," *Journal of African History* 1 (1960): 77–78. See also Aranda, *Relation*, pp. 23–24.

51 BNM, MS. 2727, f. 44.

52 AGS, Cruzada, leg. 287, n.f.

53 Jiménez de Santa Catalina, "Viage," vol. 2, f. 191.

54 Ibid., ff. 175, 191.

55 Mouette, *Travels*, p. 16; Thomas Phelps, *A true account of the captivity of Thomas Phelps at Machaness in Barbary* (London, 1685), p. 10.

56 John Windus, *A Journey to Mequinez . . . in the Year 1721* in *A General Collection of the Best and Most Interesting Voyages and Travels in All Parts of the World*, ed. John Pinkerton, vol. 15 (London, 1814), p. 469; Julien, *History of North Africa*, p. 258.

57 AGS, Cruzada, leg. 287, petition of Don Diego de Cabañas, September 6, 1693; Mouette, *Travels*, p. 23.

58 Ruth Pike, "Penal Labor in Sixteenth-Century Spain: The Mines of Almadén," *Societas—A Review of Social History* 3, no. 3 (1973): 193.

59 M. Laugier de Tassy, *Histoire du royaume d'Alger* (Amsterdam, 1728), p. 308.

60 Galán, *Cautiverio*, pp. 9, 16; BNM, MS. 2370, f. 411.

61 Haedo, *Topografía*, f. 28.

62 Gómez de Losada, *Trabajos*, p. 94; Haedo, *Topografía*, f. 26.

63 Mouette, *Travels*, p. 10.

64 Ibid., pp. 41–42; Gómez de Losada, *Trabajos*, p. 92; for Don Miguel de Sesa, BNM, MS. 6547, f. 70; for Robert Adams, "Lettre de Robert Adams au Capitaine Robert Adams," November 14, 1625, SIHMA, vol. 2, pp. 591–592.

65 Zuñiga, "Descriptión," f. 131; Earle, *Corsairs*, p. 87.

66 Haedo, *Topografía*, ff. 15, 34; Earle, *Corsairs*, p. 87; Braudel, *The Mediterranean*, 1:436.

67 Haedo, *Topografía*, f. 42.

68 Jiménez de Santa Catalina, "Viage," 1:133.

69 *Relation de trois voyages dans Maroc*, pp. 80, 112.

70 Cervantes Saavedra, *Baños*, pp. 327–328.

71 Gómez de Losada, *Trabajos*, p. 94.
72 Cervantes Saavedra, *Don Quijote*, p. 1416.
73 Gómez de Losada, *Trabajos*, p. 94,
74 Cervantes Saavedra, *Don Quijote*, p. 1416.
75 BNM, MS. 6547, f. 70.
76 Ibid., ff. 23–24, 70, 106; MS. 4390, f. 1.
77 Jiménez de Santa Catalina, "Viage," 1:41; 2:29, 234.
78 Gómez de Losada, *Trabajos*, p. 51.
79 Haedo, *Topografía*, ff. 17, 117–118.
80 Jiménez de Santa Catalina, "Viage," 1:84.
81 Cervantes Saavedra, *Don Quijote*, p. 1416.
82 Gracián, "Trabajos y vida," p. 460; Galán, *Cautiverio*.
83 ACA, Consejo de Aragón, leg. 993, April 28, 1692.
84 Laugier de Tassy, *Histoire*, p. 308.
85 Paul W. Bamford, *Fighting Ships and Prisons: The Mediterranean Galleys of France in the Age of Louis XIV* (Minneapolis, 1973), p. 178.
86 AHN, Estado, leg. 3565, expediente de 1768, September 18, 1767; Vicente Graullera Sanz, *La esclavitud en Valencia en los siglos XVI y XVII* (Valencia, 1978).
87 AGS, Guerra Moderna, leg. 1533, expediente de 1754, August 17, 1754.
88 Ibid., Cruzada, leg. 287, n.f.
89 BNM, MS. 6141, f. 89.
90 Ibid., MS. 3551.
91 Laugier de Tassy, *Histoire*, p. 96.

Chapter 4: Religious Privileges

1 San Juan del Puerto, *Missión historial*, p. 103; BNM, MS. 8293, "Fragmentos históricos de la merced," f. 80; Melchor García Navarro, *Redenciones de cautivos en Africa, 1723–1725*, ed. M. Vázquez Pájaro (Madrid, 1946), p. 19.
2 Jiménez de Santa Catalina, "Viage," 3:67.
3 Aranda, *Relation*, pp. 19, 49; BNM, MS. 3287, f. 334; Zuñiga, "Descriptión," f. 137.
4 Haedo, *Topografía*, f. 42.
5 Gómez de Losada, *Trabajos*, p. 365; Jiménez de Santa Catalina, "Viage," 2:268.
6 Gracián, *Trabajos y vida*, p. 459.
7 Ibid., p. 461.

8 San Juan del Puerto, *Missión historial*, pp. 338–342, 429–431.
9 Ibid., pp. 542–560.
10 Ibid., pp. 610–623, 439.
11 Haedo, *Topografía*, f. 42.
12 Ibid., f. 152.
13 Silvestre, *Fundación histórica*, p. 142; see also BNM, MS. 2370, f. 412; Gómez de Losada, *Trabajos*, p. 362.
14 Haedo, *Topografía*, f. 146.
15 BNM, MS. 2387, f. 334; see also BNM, MS. 3631, f. 28; MS. 4394, f. 17.
16 Jiménez de Santa Catalina, "Viage," 2:124; Silvestre, *Fundación histórica*, p. 144.
17 Quoted by Silvestre, *Fundación histórica*, p. 64.
18 Ibid.
19 Ibid., p. 143.
20 Zuñiga, "Descriptión," ff. 137–138.
21 Quoted by Silvestre, *Fundación histórica*, pp. 65–66.
22 Jiménez de Santa Catalina, "Viage," 1:93.
23 Ibid., 1:131; 2:268; Silvestre, *Fundación histórica*, p. 146.
24 Jiménez de Santa Catalina, "Viage," 1:95–96, 129; 2:268; 3:64; Silvestre, *Fundación histórica*, p. 145.
25 Silvestre, *Fundación histórica*, p. 467.
26 Ibid., p. 464.
27 Ibid., p. 461.
28 Ibid., p. 438.
29 Ibid.
30 Ibid.
31 Zuñiga, "Descriptión," ff. 131, 137–138; Jiménez de Santa Catalina, "Viage," 3:79; BNM, MS. 2370, f. 412; Gómez de Losada, *Trabajos*, p. 362.
32 AHN, Códices, lib. 123B; BNM, MS. 2370, f. 412; Zuñiga, "Descriptión," f. 137; Silvestre, *Fundación histórica*, pp. 81–82.
33 Gracián, *Trabajos y vida*, p. 461; see also Gómez de Losada, *Trabajos*, p. 362; Silvestre, *Fundación histórica*, p. 65; Cervantes Saavedra, *Baños*, pp. 364–365; Zuñiga, "Descriptión," ff. 137–138; Haedo, *Topografía*, f. 65.
34 Gracián, *Trabajos y vida*, p. 461.
35 Cervantes Saavedra, *Baños*, p. 365.
36 Silvestre, *Fundación histórica*, p. 147.
37 Gómez de Losada, *Trabajos*, p. 370.
38 San Juan del Puerto, *Missión historial*, p. 73.
39 Gracián, *Trabajos y vida*, pp. 461, 468.

40 Haedo, *Topografía*, f. 34.
41 Gómez de Losada, *Trabajos*, p. 368.
42 Gracián, *Trabajos y vida*, p. 467.
43 Haedo, *Topografía*, ff. 123, 179.
44 Jiménez de Santa Catalina, "Viage," 2:326, 355.
45 Gracián, *Trabajos y vida*, p. 461; Fisher, *Barbary Legend*, p. 99.
46 Gracián, *Trabajos y vida*, p. 461.
47 Gómez de Losada, *Trabajos*, p. 87.
48 Jiménez de Santa Catalina, "Viage," 1:35.
49 Ibid., p. 42.
50 Haedo, *Topografía*, f. 74.
51 Jiménez de Santa Catalina, "Viage," 2:227.
52 BNM, MS. 3593, f. 112.
53 Gracián, *Trabajos y vida*, p. 461; Gómez de Losada, *Trabajos*, p. 87.
54 The limitations on conversion to Islam by captives did not extend to those who had been redeemed, and apostasy by captives whose rescue prices had already been paid was a serious problem for the friar-redemptors. In 1686, four of the captives redeemed by the Mercedarians converted to Islam and remained in Algiers. BNM, MS. 4363, f. 104. After the Mercedarian redemption of 1713, two of the rescued captives, Antonio del Omo of Orihuela and Tinés Ros of Cartagena became Muslims and remained in Algiers. BNM, MS. 3837, f. 74. In the Mercedarian redemption of 1723 six captives and in that of 1724 two others converted after they had been rescued. BNM, MS. 3549, f. 158; MS. 3589, f. 123. Captives who apostatized after they had been rescued did so in order to live as free men and women in Algiers, since those who converted while slaves were not automatically freed, although their positions did improve considerably. Jiménez alleged that many of them made arrangements with their owners to share the rescue price paid by the redemption. Jiménez de Santa Catalina, "Viage," 3:28.

Chapter 5: The Trinitarian Hospitals

1 Silvestre, *Fundación histórica*; Jiménez de Santa Catalina, "Viage." Silvestre was administrator of the hospital in Algiers in the late seventeenth century. Jiménez's work is a diary of the years he spent at the hospital in Algiers, 1717–1720. The account book kept in Algiers during the late seventeenth and early eighteenth centuries is AHN, Códices, lib. 191B. The books maintained by

the general administrators in Madrid during the latter part of the eighteenth century were found in the uncataloged archive of the Trinitarian monastery in Madrid, "Libro de gasto de los hospitales de Argel y Túnez, que empezó en el mes de Agosto de 1759" and "Libro de recivo de los hospitales de Argel y Túnez, que empezó en el mes de Agosto de 1759." A summary of some of the material contained in these books can be found in B. Porres, "Los hospitales cristianos de Argel y Túnez desde 1759 hasta su fin," *Acta Ordinis SS. Trinitatis* 7 (1968): 677–731.

2 For a discussion of the type of care provided by hospitals in the eighteenth century, see A. E. Imhof, "The Hospital in the 18th Century: For Whom?" *Journal of Social History* 10, no. 4 (Summer 1977), pp. 448–470.

3 Haedo, *Topografía*, f. 37.

4 AHN, Códices, lib. 191B, f. 1. "Fiel copia de los privilegios antiguos que la Ilustre Regencia de Argel tiene concedidos al Hospital de Padres Trinitarios."

5 Jiménez de Santa Catalina, "Viage," 3:67.

6 Silvestre, *Fundación histórica*, pp. 57, 64. Reference to this hospital was made in October 1620 by Friar Antonio Obispo de Sirene, writing from Algiers. "Relación de la gloriosa muerte que los Turcos dieron a Pedro de Torres Miranda . . . en la ciudad de Argel, el año de 1620," RAHM, MS. 9–758, ff. 186–190.

7 Gómez de Losada, *Trabajos*, p. 349.

8 Silvestre, *Fundación histórica*, p. 119.

9 Ibid., p. 118, on seventeenth-century practices; García Navarro, *Redenciones*, pp. 47, 172, on the surgeons brought by the Mercedarians in 1723 and 1724; on Manuel Antonio Suárez and Alejandro San Millán, ATM, "Libro de Gasto," ff. 16, 20v., 37; on Felix Antonio Morales, ibid., f. 58v., and AGS, Guerra Moderna, leg. 1536, expediente de 1776, letter of Friar Antonio Moreno, January 19, 1776.

10 Cano, "Nuevo aspecto," pp. 41–42.

11 AHN, Códices, lib. 191B, ff. 4–85v.

12 Ibid., f. 50.

13 Ibid., ff. 225–235.

14 ACA, Monacales de Hacienda, lib. 2692, "Copia de carta de . . . Fr. Bernardo Pasqual . . . 28 de octubre de 1756."

15 Ibid., "Copia de otra carta del mismo Fr. Bernardo Pasqual . . . 6 de diciembre de 1756."

16 Silvestre, *Fundación histórica*, pp. 49, 121.

17 AHN, Códices, lib. 153B, n.f.; BNM, MS. 2727, f. 30.

18 AHN, lib. 191B, ff. 4–85v.
19 Ibid., ff. 108–181.
20 Silvestre, *Fundación histórica*, p. 119.
21 AHN, Códices, lib. 191B, ff. 250–275; Silvestre, *Fundación histórica*, pp. 121–122.
22 ATM, "Libro de recivo."
23 Silvestre, *Fundación histórica*, p. 48; AHN, Estado, leg. 1617, September 16, 1690.
24 AGS, Cruzada, leg. 287, September 20, 1729; ATM, "Libro de gasto," ff. 7, 8v.
25 ATM, "Libro de recivo," ff. 13, 29.
26 Silvestre, *Fundación histórica*, p. 119; ATM, "Libro de gasto," f. 9.
27 ATM, "Libro de gasto"; AHN, Códices, lib. 191B.
28 AHN, Códices, lib. 191B. f. 1.
29 Silvestre, *Fundación histórica*, prologue.
30 AHN, Códices, lib. 191B, ff. 100–102v.
31 Ibid., ff. 181, 101.
32 Ibid., f. 1.
33 Silvestre, *Fundación histórica*, pp. 110, 119–120.
34 Ibid., pp. 124–125.
35 Ibid., p. 127.
36 AHN, Códices, lib. 191B, f. 8v.
37 Jiménez de Santa Catalina, "Viage."
38 Silvestre, *Fundación histórica*, p. 123; Jiménez de Santa Catalina, "Viage."
39 ATM, "Libro de gasto," ff. 8, 11.
40 Jiménez de Santa Catalina, "Viage," 2:132.
41 Laugier de Tassy, *Histoire*, pp. 295–301.
42 An example of such a conflict and the administrator's intervention can be found in García Navarro, *Redenciones*, p. 81.
43 Windus, *Journey to Mequinez*, pp. 713–716.
44 AHN, Códices, lib. 190B, n.f.; Jiménez de Santa Catalina, "Viage," 4:19.
45 AGS, Cruzada, leg. 287.
46 AHN, Códices, lib. 191B, ff. 86–99, lib. 190B, ff. 8–9; also Silvestre, *Fundación histórica*, p. 119.

Chapter 6: Procedures and Financing

1 F. Gazulla, *La orden de Nuestra Señora de la Merced: Estudios históricos, 1218–1317* (Barcelona, 1934), 1:19.
2 J. W. Brodman, "The Trinitarian and Mercedarian Orders: A Study

of Religious Redemptionism in the Thirteenth Century," (Ph.D. diss., University of Virginia, 1974), pp. 19, 32; Gazulla, *La orden de Nuestra Señora de la Merced,* p. 53; García Navarro, *Redenciones,* p. 11.

3 Gazulla, *La orden de Nuestra Señora de la Merced,* p. 56; García Navarro, *Redenciones,* p. 12.

4 Jesús Ernesto Martínez Ferrando, *Catálogo de los documentos referentes al antiguo reino de Valencia, reinado de Jaime I* (Madrid, 1934), 2:230, no. 1071, cited by Brodman, "Trinitarian and Mercedarian Orders," p. 25.

5 Gazulla, *La orden de Nuestra Señora de la Merced,* p. 51.

6 Brodman, "Trinitarian and Mercedarian Orders," pp. 206, 218.

7 AHN, Códices, lib. 1112, ff. 1, 95.

8 BNM, MS. 3549, f. 32; García Navarro, *Redenciones,* p. 13.

9 García Navarro, *Redenciones,* p. 19.

10 This prohibition was included in the instructions of the Council of Castile found in the following redemption books: AHN, Códices, lib. 138B, f. 11; lib. 136B, f. 7; lib. 140B, f. 7; BNM, MS. 4359, f. 5; MS. 4394, f. 8; MS. 3586, f. 4.

11 AHN, Códices, lib. 128B, f. 10.

12 BNM, MS. 3572, ff. 39, 99.

13 AGS, Guerra Moderna, leg. 1533, expediente de 1752, May 17, 1752; leg. 1531, expediente de 1740, July 13, 1740.

14 AHN, Códices, lib. 138B, f. 17.

15 *Nueva recopilación de las leyes de España* (Madrid, 1772), book VI, title XVIII, laws 1, 3, 5, 6, 7, 8, 9. Stringent penalties were provided for violation of the regulations on the export of specie, including loss of goods and death.

16 BNM, MS. 3573, ff. 21, 33.

17 Ibid., MS. 2974, ff. 13, 15.

18 The one exception to this that I have found is the redemption in Algiers in 1768–1769, which was arranged by the Spanish government and carried out jointly by the two orders.

19 García Navarro, *Redenciones,* pp. 37–38.

20 AGS, Cruzada, leg. 286–289; ACA, Monacales de Hacienda, lib. 2705, Order of Council of the Cruzada.

21 AGS, Cruzada, leg. 286, January 1621.

22 Ibid., leg. 287, n.f.

23 Ibid., leg. 286–289. These are four large bundles of documents containing thousands of petitions for aid, from the early seventeenth to mid-eighteenth century.

24 Ibid., leg. 286.

25 Ibid., October 18, 1659.

26 Ibid., November 25, 1644; October 27, 1627.
27 Ibid., April 15, 1641; AHN, Códices, lib. 133B, ff. 1, 3.
28 AGS, Cruzada leg 287, November 1713; leg. 286, June 1637, and petition of Lorenzo de Mesa.
29 Ibid., leg. 287, January 26, 1702.
30 BNM, MS. 3588, f. 1.
31 AHN, Códices, lib. 139B, f. 12.
32 Ibid., lib. 137B, f. 7; BNM, MS. 2963, f. 6.
33 AHN, Códices, lib. 126B, f. 4; lib. 125B, ff. 35–36.
34 This provision appeared in the instructions issued to each group of redemptors by the general of their order. Examples of these instructions may be found in BNM, MS. 7752, f. 2 and MS. 2974, f. 4, as well as other redemption books.
35 García Navarro, *Redenciones*, pp. 19–20.
36 BNM, MS. 3613, f. 4.
37 Ibid.
38 Ibid.; ibid., MS. 3586. Sánchez' predictions concerning the high prices that would be demanded for captives from the *Margarita* proved only too true. The difficulties encountered in ransoming some of these individuals are discussed in chapter 8.
39 AHN, Códices, lib. 119B, ff. 5, 15.
40 Ibid., lib. 139B, f. 12; lib. 126B, f. 22.
41 BNM, MS. 2963, f. 117.
42 Ibid., MS. 7752, f. 13; MS. 2974, f. 33; M.S. 3593, f. 56; MS. 4394, f. 23; MS. 4359, f. 18.
43 Ibid., MS. 4394, f. 20; MS. 6160, f. 90; MS. 6547, f. 22; MS. 3862, f. 1; MS. 6573, f. 2; MS. 3631, f. 33; MS. 3597, ff. 7, 12; MS. 3586, f. 27; AHN, Códices, lib. 125B, f. 8; lib. 126B, f. 22; lib. 129B, f. 80; lib. 133B, f. 8; lib. 134B, f. 13; lib. 132B, f. 6; lib. 137B, f. 7; lib. 135B, f. 21; lib. 144B, f. 31.
44 BNM, MS. 2974, f. 20; MS. 3588, f. 4; AHN, Códices, lib. 127B, f. 1; lib. 128B, f. 1; lib. 130B, f. 53; lib. 132B, f. 6; lib. 133B, f. 8; lib. 137B, f. 7; lib. 139B, f. 12; lib. 142B, f. 16; lib. 143B, f. 21; lib. 144B, f. 31.
45 AHN, Códices, lib. 139B.
46 García Navarro, *Redenciones*, pp. 19–20.
47 BNM, MS. 3631, f. 38.
48 Ibid., MS. 2974, ff. 27–29.
49 Ibid., MS. 7752, f. 11.
50 For example, a royal decree of 1664 confirmed 21 mercedes granted to one of the Trinitarian monasteries in Madrid over the years, which provided them with an annual income of 1,423,000 mara-

vedís. These included such items as 31,103 maravedís from the *millones* (tax levied mainly on food) of Toledo and 546,440 maravedís from the *alcabalas* (excise tax) of Seville, Córdoba, Cuenca, and Madrid. AHN, Códices, lib. 153B, n.f. Libro 141B in the same section contains a list of the expenses and income of the Trinitarian order during the 1660s and 1670s. Among the sources of income are a number of mercedes.

51 BNM, MS. 3597.
52 Ibid., MS. 3593; MS. 2727, f. 22.
53 Ibid., MS. 2963, f. 90.
54 AHN, Códices, lib. 119B, f. 19.
55 BNM, MS. 3597, f. 7; AHN, Códices, lib. 128B, f. 11.
56 AHN, Códices, lib. 120B, f. 32.
57 BNM, MS. 3631, f. 45.
58 Ibid., MS. 3597, f. 12.
59 Captives in North Africa were frequently able to earn money by operating their own businesses, paying a percentage of the profits to their masters. Sometimes the galley slaves were permitted to share in the booty of the corsairs. Slaves also acquired money by stealing. The traffic in stolen goods was considerable, with the officials of the baños acting as intermediaries. The chief victims were the Jews. Earle, *Corsairs*, p. 88. Adjutorios donated for a captive whose rescue the redemption was not able to negotiate were frequently turned over to him, and these funds were sometimes applied by the captive toward his redemption at a later date.
60 AHN, Códices, lib. 125B, f. 26; lib. 118B, f. 153; BNM, MS. 7752, ff. 45–46.
61 AHN, Códices, lib. 143B, f. 67; BNM, MS. 3593, f. 134.
62 BNM, MS. 3837, f. 71; AHN, Códices, lib. 119B, f. 40.
63 BNM, MS. 6569.
64 See AHN, Códices, libs. 118B, 119B, 122B.
65 BNM, MS. 6547, f. 4.
66 Ibid., MS. 3870, ff. 46–48.
67 AHN, Códices, lib. 126B, ff. 4, 41–42.
68 Ibid., lib. 128B, ff. 1–3, 18.
69 Ibid., lib. 136B, f. 86; BNM, MS. 3631, f. 51.
70 BNM, MS. 3872, f. 20.
71 AHN, Códices, lib. 132B; BNM, MS. 6160.
72 Ibid., Códices, lib. 125B.
73 ACA, Monacales de Hacienda, lib. 2705, papal concessions of September 9, 1690 and July 8, 1725.

74 For example, see BNM, MS. 3572, ff. 326–334; Freytas, "Por la redención de cautivos sobre que no se deve impedir"; la Assunción, "Memorial del general de la orden . . . de la Santíssima Trinidad"; "Impugnación a la carta que impugna las redenciones de cautivos por el Pᵉ Francisco de Rábago" (copy), Biblioteca Municipal de Santander, Colección Pedraja, MS. 239, fols. 26–33. This last document was given to me by Professor Susan Tax Freeman.

Chapter 7: Negotiations in North Africa

1 AHN, Códices, lib. 142B, ff. 91–92.
2 Ibid., lib. 143B, f. 30.
3 Ibid., Estado, leg. 3028, dto. 29, consulta of November 5, 1712; BNM, MS. 6141, ff. 10, 59–89; ACA, Monacales de Hacienda, lib. 2705, n.f.; García Navarro, *Redenciones*, p. 37.
4 BNM, MS. 3572, f. 163.
5 Ibid., MS. 2963, f. 31.
6 AHN, Códices, lib. 119B, f. 142.
7 Zuñiga, "Descriptión," f. 200.
8 For an example of such an occurrence, see García Navarro, *Redenciones*, p. 57.
9 BNM, MS. 3837.
10 Ibid., f. 26.
11 Ibid., ff. 29–30.
12 Ibid., f. 33.
13 Ibid., f. 41.
14 Ibid., f. 49.
15 Ibid., ff. 60–61.
16 Ibid., MS. 3549.
17 Ibid., ff. 91–92; García Navarro, *Redenciones*, pp. 88–94.
18 García Navarro, *Redenciones*, pp. 57, 65.
19 AGS, Guerra Moderna, leg. 1530, letter of Friar Francisco Navarro, Algiers, April 11, 1724; García Navarro, *Redenciones*, p. 155.
20 For an account of this redemption, see BNM, MS. 3589; García Navarro, *Redenciones*, pp. 157–236.
21 García Navarro, *Redenciones*, p. 79.
22 The documentation concerning this case can be found in AGS, Estado, leg. 494, consulta of February 11, 1610; leg. 495, consultas of June 30, 1614 and November 11, 1617; leg. 1880, ff. 54–

55; leg. 1881, ff. 31–32; leg. 1882, ff. 265–280; leg. 1888, f. 12; leg. 1889, f. 26; RAHM, leg. 9–758, f. 90, "Capítulo de una carta que escrivó en la ciudad de Argel en veynte y dos de setiembre del año de 1620 el Padre Fray Bernardo de Monroy." See also Silvestre, *Fundación histórica*, pp. 60–62. None of these sources provide information on the final outcome of the incident.

23 AHN, Códices, lib. 124B; BNM, MSS. 4405, 3870.
24 BNM, MS. 4405, ff. 63–64.
25 Ibid., MS. 3870, ff. 19–20.
26 Ibid., f. 8; ibid., MS. 4405, f. 43; AHN, Códices, lib. 124B, ff. 51–52.
27 AGS, Estado, leg. 1882, f. 273; AHN, Códices, lib. 125B.
28 AHN, Códices, lib. 125B, ff. 54–55.
29 Ibid., ff. 69–72.
30 Ibid., ff. 71–75.
31 Ibid., ff. 26–27, 71.
32 BNM, MS. 4363.
33 The source of all the money for the Cisternes family is not indicated, but in April 1684 the Cruzada, in response to a request from their father and the Council of Aragón, granted them 5,500 reales. AGS, Cruzada, leg. 287; ACA, Consejo de Aragón, leg. 993, expediente, "Esclavos y cautivos," f. 89.
34 BNM, MS. 3872, ff. 33–34.
35 Ibid., f. 84.
36 Ibid., MS. 6547.
37 AHN, Códices, lib. 126B.
38 Ibid., f. 18.
39 Ibid., ff. 20–21.
40 Ibid., Códices, lib. 127B, f. 11.
41 BNM, MS. 3572, ff. 206–212.
42 Ibid., ff. 210–211.
43 Ibid., ff. 214–216.
44 Ibid., MS. 3551.

Chapter 8: The Rescue

1 Haedo, in the last quarter of the sixteenth century, estimated that there were 25,000 Christian captives in Algiers. Haedo, *Topografía*, f. 8. The Mercedarian friar Serafín de Freytas, writing in 1631, claimed that at that time there were more than 20,000 captives throughout North Africa, most of them Spaniards. BNM,

MS. 3536, f. 11. Felipe Palermo, a captive, wrote on September 5, 1656 that there were 35,000 Christian captives in Algiers. AGS, Cruzada, leg. 286. Other observers of the period estimated 25,000 captives of all nations in Algiers alone. John Windus, who visited Morocco in 1721, reported that there were approximately 400 Spanish captives in Meknès at the time. Windus, *Journey to Meguinez*, p. 487. The only reliable figure for Spanish captives in Algiers is for the period 1768–1769, when the last redemption was made in Algiers. At that time about 1,000 Spaniards were rescued and 454 remained in captivity. MN, Colleción Vargas Ponce, MS. 1552, dto. 6, f. 16, February 28, 1769; BNM, MS. 3551.

2 In addition to the record books utilized for the quantitative analysis in chapter 1, I also consulted the following: BNM, MSS. 2974, 3588, 3590, 3592, 3597, 3598, 3608, 3609, 4363; AHN, Códices, libs. 148B, 149B; ACA, Monacales de Hacienda, libs. 2704, 2705.

3 Galán, *Cautiverio*, p. 98.

4 BNM, MS. 3870, ff. 30, 36.

5 Cervantes Saavedra, *Don Quijote*, p. 1416.

6 BNM, MS. 3819, f. 10.

7 Ibid., MS. 3870. f. 19.

8 Ibid., MS. 3593, f. 53; MS. 3572, f. 378.

9 Ibid., MS. 3631, ff. 108, 69.

10 AHN, Códices, lib. 137B.

11 BNM, MS. 4394, ff. 28, 36.

12 Ibid., MS. 3586, f. 73.

13 Ibid., MS. 4390, f. 1; MS. 6547, f. 24.

14 AHN, Códices, lib. 118B, f. 183; lib. 119B, f. 89.

15 Ibid., lib. 118B. ff. 157–158.

16 BNM, MS. 3613, ff. 30, 36.

17 Ibid., MS. 3586, f. 47.

18 Ibid., MS. 3593, ff. 43, 76, 131; ACA, Monacales de Hacienda, lib. 2704.

19 BNM, MS. 3631, f. 107.

20 Jiménez de Santa Catalina, "Viage," 1:86.

21 AGS, Guerra Moderna, leg. 1530, expediente de 1739, leg. 1532, expediente de 1750; ACA, Monacales de Hacienda, lib. 2705, Pedro Ros Valle and Juan Talamanco, April 11, 1737; BNM, MS. 2727, f. 43, letter of Friar Pedro Ros Valle, February 23, 1735; ibid., MS. 3572, f. 374; ibid., MS. 2727, f. 43.

22 AGS, Cruzada, leg. 286, September 24, 1644; ACA, Monacales de Hacienda, lib. 2705, redemption of July 1639; AHN, Códices, lib. 134B, f. 85; ibid., lib. 131B, f. 11.

23 AHN, Códices, lib. 133B, ff. 1, 3.
24 Ibid., lib. 131B, f. 7.
25 Ibid., lib. 133B, f. 8; lib. 134B.
26 MN, Colección Vargas Ponce, vol. XXII, dto. 56, f. 111, "Real cedula de la reyna governadora, 29 enero 1667, a la provincia de Guipúzcoa."
27 BNM, MSS. 3586, 3593.
28 Ibid., MS. 3586, f. 88.
29 AHN, Códices, lib. 135B, f. 62.
30 BNM, MS. 3586, f. 29; AHN, Códices, lib. 139B, f. 15.
31 BNM, MS. 3593, f. 46.
32 Ibid., MS. 3586, ff. 44–45.
33 BNM, MS. 4405, ff. 75, 27, 71.
34 AHN, Códices, lib. 135B, f. 57.
35 BNM, MS. 6160, f. 141.
36 Six percent of the rescued captives surveyed were under twelve years of age.
37 AHN, Códices, lib. 124B.
38 Ibid., lib. 127B.
39 *Gaceta de Madrid.* September 7, 1728; García Navarro, *Redenciones*, pp. 104–105; 186. For 1718, AHN, Códices, lib. 148B, ff. 71–72. For 1717, BNM, MS. 3572, n.f. For 1713, MS. 3837, f. 28.
40 Galán, *Cautiverio*, pp. 113–116.
41 BNM, MS. 3634, f. 45.
42 Ibid., MS. 3597, f. 53.
43 AHN, Códices, lib. 132B, ff. 33–35. The average time in captivity for rescued captives was 5.2 years.
44 BNM, MS. 3597, f. 49.
45 AHN, Códices, lib. 122B, f. 145.
46 Ibid., lib. 139B, f. 125.
47 Ibid., lib. 143B, f. 69.
48 AGS, Guerra Moderna, leg. 1531, expediente de 1739.
49 AHN, Códices, lib. 136B, f. 65.
50 Ibid., lib. 122B, ff. 18–19, 231.
51 BNM, MS. 3572, f. 61; ibid., MS. 3590, ff. 54–126; García Navarro, *Redenciones*, p. 208.
52 ACA, Monacales de Hacienda, lib. 2705, letter from the marqués de la Ensenada to the master-general of Merced, Barcelona, July 29, 1751. For the royal orders concerning the exchange of captives, AGS, Guerra Moderna, leg. 1532, expediente de 1750, October 6, and November 3, 1750.
53 BNM, MS. 3608, ff. 53–54.

54 Ibid., MS. 1635, ff. 2–9.
55 Ibid., MS. 3572, f. 212.
56 Ibid., MS. 3592, ff. 116v.–129.
57 Cano, "Nuevo aspecto."
58 As Professor Peter von Sivers has pointed out, for political reasons it was important that the dey of Algiers not be dependent on the income received from the provinces. "The Turkish Ruling Elite in Algeria," paper read at the Middle East Studies Association, Louisville, Kentucky, 1975.
59 Cano, "Nuevo aspecto," pp. 138–139.
60 N. Barbour, "North West Africa from the 15th–19th Centuries," in *The Muslim World, a Historical Survey*, part 3, *The Last Great Muslim Empires*, trans. F. R. C. Bagley (Leiden, 1969), p. 125.
61 AHN, Estado, leg. 3565, expediente de 1766, letters of May 20, June 3, and July 24, 1766.
62 BNM, MS. 3551, ff. 10, 26; AHN, Estado, leg. 3565, expediente de 1768, letter of Sidi Muḥammad (translation into Spanish), November 19, 1768.
63 For example, see AHN, Códices, lib. 129B, f. 134; lib. 119B, f. 139; lib. 124B, f. 41; BNM, MS. 2963, f. 103.
64 For the frequency of plague in the eastern Maghrib, see J.-N. Biraben, *Les hommes et la peste en France et dans les pays européens et méditerranéens*, vol. 1 (Paris, 1975), pp. 430–439.
65 AHN, Códices, lib. 139B, f. 139.
66 Ibid., lib. 146B.
67 Ibid., lib. 147B.
68 Gómez de Losada, *Trabajos*, pp. 134–148.
69 BNM, MS. 2727, f. 30.
70 Ibid., MS. 3872, ff. 46–47.
71 Ibid., MS. 3592, f. 21.

Conclusion

1 Pedro Fernández Navarrete, "Conservación de monarquías y discursos políticos." In *Obras de Don Diego de Saavedra Fajardo y del Licenciado Pedro Fernández Navarrete. Biblioteca de autores españoles.* Vol. 25. Madrid: Imprenta y estereotipía de M. Rivadeneyra, 1853.
2 Domínguez Ortiz, *La sociedad española*, p. 96.

Bibliography

Primary Sources

Manuscripts
In all cases, I have provided the official names of the archival sections. An item in parentheses refers to the name by which a section is commonly known, or the portion of the section I utilized, and is the designation I have used in the notes. In most instances, this listing does not include individual manuscripts, since so many were utilized. References will be found in the notes.

Archivo de la Corona de Aragón (Barcelona)
    Consejo de Aragón
    Clero Regular y Secular (Monacales de Hacienda)
Archivo General de la Marina (Museo Naval, Madrid)
    Colección Navarrete
    Colección Sanz de Barutell (Simancas)
    Colección Vargas Ponce
Archivo General de Simancas (Simancas, Valladolid)
    Secretaría de Estado
    Guerra y Marina (Guerra Antigua)
    Secretaría de Guerra (Guerra Moderna)
    Comisario de Cruzada
    Varios (Casa de Medina Sidonia)
Archivo Histórico de la Ciudad de Barcelona (Arxiu historic de la Ciutat de Barcelona) (Barcelona)
    Registre de deliberaciones
    Registre de lletres closes
Archivo Histórico Nacional (Madrid)
    Consejos
    Estado
    Códices
Archivo, Monasterio de la Orden SS. Trinidad (Madrid)
Biblioteca Nacional (Madrid)
    Manuscritos

Real Academia de Historia (Madrid)

"Advertimientos del . . . Fr. Ysidro de Valçaçar sobre cosas de Berbería . . . 1608." MS. 9–6436.

Cano, Alonso. "Nuevo aspecto de la topografía de Argel." MS. 2–71.

Castanedo, Friar Antonio de. "Relación del estado de la ciudad de Arjel . . . 1600." MS. 9–2240.

Jiménez de Santa Catalina, Francisco. "Viage de Argel." 7 vols. MS. 9–27–7E 193–199.

Obispo de Sirene, Friar Antonio. "Relación de la gloriosa muerte que los Turcos dieron a Pedro de Torres Miranda . . . en la ciudad de Argel, el año de 1620." MS. 9–758.

"Relación verdadera del martirio . . . de Pedro Borguien, natural de . . . Mallorca, que murió quemado vivo . . . en la ciudad de Argel a 30 de agosto . . . 1654." MS. 9–466.

Published Documents and Contemporary Writings

Actas de las Cortes de Castilla, 1563–1627. 39 vols. Madrid, 1887–1925.

Aguilar, Pedro de. *Memorias del cautivo en la Goleta de Túnez.* Edited by Pascual de Gayangos. Madrid: Sociedad de Bibliófilos Españoles, 1875.

Aranda, Emanuel d'. *Relation de la captivité et liberté de sieur Emanuel d'Aranda.* Paris: Compagnie des libraires du palais, 1665.

Bauer y Landauer, Ignacio. *Papeles de mi archivo: Relaciones de Africa.* 5 vols. Madrid: Editorial Ibero-Africano-Americana, 1922–1923.

Brooks, Francis. *Barbarian Cruelty.* London, 1693.

Castries, Henri de. *Une description du Maroc sous le règne de Moulay Ahmed el-Mansour (1596) d'après un manuscrit portugais de la Bibliothèque Nationale.* Paris, 1909.

Castries, Henri de; Cenival, P. de; Richard, R.; la Veronne, C. de; and Cossé Brissac, Philippe de. *Sources inédites de l'histoire du Maroc.* Première Série: *Dynastie saadienne, France,* 3 vols.; *Angleterre,* 3 vols.; *Pays-Bas,* 6 vols.; *Espagne,* 3 vols.; *Portugal,* 5 vols. Paris, 1905–1961.

Cerdán de Tallada, Thomás. *Visita de la cárcel y de los presos.* Valencia, 1574.

Cervantes Saavedra, Miguel de. *Los baños de Argel.* In *Obras completas.* Edited by A. Valbuena Prat. Madrid: Aguilar, 1970.

Cervantes Saavedra, Miguel de. *Don Quijote de la Mancha.* In *Obras completas.* Edited by A. Valbuena Prat. Madrid: Aguilar, 1970.

Cervantes Saavedra, Miguel de. *El trato de Argel.* In *Obras completas.* Edited by A. Valbuena Prat. Madrid: Aguilar, 1970.

Comelin, F., La Motte, P. de, Bernard, Joseph. *Voyage pour la rédemption des captifs aux royaumes d'Alger et de Tunis fait en 1720.* Rouen, 1731.

Cortes de los antiguos reinos de León y de Castilla. 5 vols. Madrid, 1861–1903.

Dan, Pierre. *Histoire de Barbarie et de ses corsaires.* Paris, 1637.

Fernández Navarrete, Pedro. "Conservación de monarquías y discursos políticos." In *Obras de Don Diego de Saavedra Fajardo y del Licenciado Pedro Fernández Navarrete. Biblioteca de autores españoles.* Vol. 25. Madrid: Imprenta y estereotipía de M. Rivadeneyra, 1853.

Galán, Diego. *Cautiverio y trabajos de Diego Galán, natural de Consuegra y vecino de Toledo, 1589–1600.* Edited by M. Serrano y Sanz. Madrid: Sociedad de Bibliófilos Españoles, 1913.

García Navarro, Melchor. *Redenciones de cautivos en Africa, 1723–1725.* Edited by M. Vázquez Pájaro. Madrid: Consejo Superior de Investigaciones Científicas, 1946.

Gómez de Losada, Gabriel. *Escuela de trabajos.* Madrid, 1670.

Gracián, Jerónimo. "Los trabajos y vida del padre maestro Gracián, desde que salió de Madrid expulso de los descalzos." In *Escritos de Santa Teresa.* Edited by Vicente de la Fuente. *Biblioteca de autores españoles.* Vol. 55. Madrid: Ediciones Atlas, 1952.

Haedo, Diego de. *Topografía e historia general de Argel.* Valladolid, 1612.

Haedo, Diego, de. *Topografía e historia general de Argel.* 3 vols. Madrid: Sociedad de Bibliófilos Españoles, 1929.

Jiménez, Francisco. *Colonia Trinitaria de Túnez.* Tetuán: Ignacio Bauer, 1934.

Knight, Francis. *A Relation of Seaven Yeares Slaverie Under the Turks of Argeire.* London, 1640.

Laugier de Tassy, M. *Histoire du royaume d'Alger.* Amsterdam, 1728.

Marmol Carvajal, Luis. *Descripción general de Africa.* 3 vols. Granada: Rene Rabut, 1573–1599.

Mendoça, Hieronimo. *Jornada de Africa.* Lisbon, 1607.

Mouette, Germaine *The Travels of the Sieur Mouette in the kingdoms of Fez and Morocco, during his eleven years captivity in those parts.* In *A New Collection of Voyages and Travels in all Parts of the World.* London, 1710.

Nueva recopilación de las leyes de España. Book 6. Madrid, 1772.

Phelps, Thomas. *A true account of the captivity of Thomas Phelps at Machaness in Barbary.* London, 1685.

Relation de ce qui s'est passe dans les trois voyages que les religieux de l'ordre de nostre dame de la mercy ont faits dans les états du roy de Maroc pour la rédemption des captifs en 1704, 1708 et 1712. Paris: Chez A.-U. Coustelier, 1724.

San Juan del Puerto, Francisco de. *Missión historial de Marruecos.* Seville: Francisco Garay, 1708.

San Raphael, Miguel de. "Procura general de Roma y redención de Venezia," *Revista del centro de estudios históricos de Granada y su reino.* Vol. 3 (1913), 160–170, 226–240, 323–332. Vol. 4 (1914), 90–96, 190–197, 373–380. Vol. 5 (1915), 112–128. Vol. 6 (1916), 136–146.

Silvestre, Francisco Antonio. *Fundación histórica de los hospitales que la religión de la Santísima Trinidad . . . tiene en la ciudad de Argel.* Madrid: Julian de Paredes, 1690.

Windus, John. *A Journey to Mequinez, the Residence of the Present Emperor of Fez and Morocco . . . in the Year 1721.* In *A General Collection of the Best and Most Interesting Voyages and Travels in All Parts of the World.* Edited by John Pinkerton. Vol. 15. London, 1814.

Secondary Sources

Abun-Nasr, J. M. *A History of the Maghrib.* Cambridge: Cambridge University Press, 1971.

Acción de España en Africa. Vol. 1. *Iberos y bereberes.* Madrid: Comisión histórica de las Campañas de Marruecos, 1935; Vol. 2. *Cristianos y musulmanes de occidente.* Madrid: Ministerio de Ejército, Servicio Histórico Militar, 1941.

Alexandrescu-Dersca, M. M. "La condition des captifs Turcs dans l'Empire des Hapsbourgs (1688–1689) d'après les Mémoires de 'Osman Aga." *Studia et Acta Orientalia* (Bucharest) 8 (1971): 125–144.

Bagley, F. R. C., trans. *The Muslim World, A Historical Survey.* Part 3. *The Last Great Muslim Empires.* Leiden: E. J. Brill, 1969.

Bamford, Paul W. *Fighting Ships and Prisons: The Mediterranean Galleys of France in the Age of Louis XIV.* Minneapolis: University of Minnesota Press, 1973.

Barbour, N. "North West Africa from the 15th–19th Centuries," in *The Muslim World, a Historical Survey,* part 3, *The Last Great Muslim Empires,* trans. F. R. C. Bagley. Leiden: 1969.

Bennett, Norman R. "Christian and Negro Slavery in Eighteenth-

Century North Africa." *Journal of African History* 1 (1960): 65–82.

Biraben, J.-N. *Les hommes et la peste en France et dans les pays européens et méditerranéens.* 2 vols. Paris: Mouton, 1975.

Bono, S. *I corsari barbareschi.* Turin: Edizioni Rai Radiotelevisione Italiana, 1964.

Braudel, Fernand. "Les Espagnols et l'Afrique du Nord de 1492 à 1577." *Revue Africaine* 69 (1928): 184–233, 351–428.

Braudel, Fernand. *The Mediterranean and the Mediterranean World in the Age of Philip II.* Translated by S. Reynolds. 2 vols. New York: Harper & Row, 1972–1973.

Brodman, J. W. "The Trinitarian and Mercedarian Orders: A Study of Religious Redemptionism in the Thirteenth Century." Ph.D. dissertation, University of Virginia, 1974.

Brown, Kenneth. "An Urban View of Moroccan History—Salé, 1000–1800." *Hesperis-Tamuda* 12 (1971): 5–106.

Burns, R. I. *The Crusader Kingdom of Valencia. Reconstruction on a Thirteenth-Century Frontier.* 2 vols. Cambridge, Mass: Harvard University Press, 1967.

Camamis, George. *Estudio sobre el cautiverio en el Siglo de Oro.* Madrid: Gredos, 1977.

Carrera Pujal, J. *Historia política y económica de Cataluña, siglos XVI al XVIII.* 4 vols. Barcelona: Bosch, Casa Editorial, 1947.

Castries, Henri de. "Le Maroc d'autrefois les corsaires de Salé." *Revue des Deux-Mondes* (Paris) (15 February 1903): 833–834.

Clark, G. N. "Barbary Corsairs in the Seventeenth Century." *Cambridge Historical Journal* 8 (1945–1946): 22–35.

Coindreau, Roger. *Les Corsaires de Salé.* Paris, 1948.

Cortés Alonso, Vicenta. *La esclavitud en Valencia durante el reinado de los reyes Católicos (1479–1516).* Valencia, 1964.

Domínguez Ortiz, Antonio. *The Golden Age of Spain, 1516–1659.* New York: Basic Books, 1971.

Domínguez Ortiz, Antonio. *La sociedad española en el siglo XVII.* 2 vols. Madrid: Consejo Superior de Investigaciones Científicas, 1963–1970.

Domínguez Ortiz, Antonio, and Vincent, Bernard. *Historia de los moriscos. Vida y tragedia de una minoría.* Madrid: Biblioteca de la Revista de Occidente, 1978.

Earle, Peter. *Corsairs of Malta and Barbary.* London: Sidgwick & Jackson, 1970.

Elliott, J. H. *Imperial Spain 1469–1716.* New York: New American Library, 1966.

Epalza, Miguel de. "Moriscos y andalusíes en Túnez durante el siglo XVII." *Al-Andalus* 34 (1969): 247–327.

Epalza, Miguel de, and Petit, R. *Etudes sur les moriscos andalous en Tunisie*. Madrid: Dirección General de Relaciones Culturales. Instituto Hispano-Árabe de Cultura, 1973.

Fisher, Godfrey. *Barbary Legend: War, Trade, and Piracy in North Africa, 1415–1830*. Oxford: Oxford University Press, 1957.

Friedman, Ellen G. "Christian Captives at 'Hard Labor' in Algiers, 16th–18th Centuries." *The International Journal of African Historical Studies* 13, no. 4 (1980): 616–632.

Friedman, Ellen G. "The Exercise of Religion by Spanish Captives in North Africa." *Sixteenth Century Journal* 6, no. 1 (1975): 19–34.

Friedman, Ellen G. "North African Piracy on the Coasts of Spain in the Seventeenth Century: A New Perspective on the Expulsion of the Moriscos." *The International History Review* 1, no. 1 (January 1979): 1–16.

Friedman, Ellen G. "Trinitarian Hospitals in Algiers: An Early Example of Health Care for Prisoners of War." *The Catholic Historical Review* 66, no. 4 (October 1980): 551–564.

Garcés Ferrá, Bartolomé. "Propuesta de armada contra los piratas berberiscos entre Holanda y España a mediados del siglo XVII." *Hispania* 8 (1948): 403–433.

García Martínez, Sebastián. *Bandolerismo, piratería y control de moriscos en Valencia durante el reinado de Felipe II*. Valencia: Universidad de Valencia, 1977.

Giménez Soler, Andrés. "El corso en el Mediterráneo en los siglos XIV y XV." *Archivo de Investigaciones Históricas* 1 (1911): 149–179.

Graullera Sanz, Vicente. *La esclavitud en Valencia en los siglos XVI y XVII*. Valencia: C.S.I.C. Institución Alfonso el Magnánimo, 1978.

Guilmartin, John Francis. *Gunpowder and Galleys: Changing Technology and Mediterranean Warfare at Sea in the Sixteenth Century*. London: Cambridge University Press, 1974.

Hess, Andrew C. "The Battle of Lepanto and Its Place in Mediterranean History." *Past & Present* 57 (November 1972): 53–73.

Hess, Andrew C. *The Forgotten Frontier: A History of the Sixteenth-Century Ibero-African Frontier*. Chicago: University of Chicago Press, 1978.

Hess, Andrew C. "The Moriscos: An Ottoman Fifth Column in Sixteenth-Century Spain." *American Historical Review*, 74, no. 1 (October 1968): 1–25.

Imhof, A. E. "The Hospital in the Eighteenth Century: For Whom?" *Journal of Social History* 10, no. 4 (Summer 1977): 448–470.

Ireland, J. de C. "The Corsairs of North Africa." *The Mariner's Mirror* 62, no 3 (August 1976): 271–283.

Julien, C.-A. *History of North Africa.* Translated by John Petrie. Edited by C. C. Stewart. London: Routledge & Kegan Paul, 1970.

Latham, John D. "Towards a Study of Andalusian Immigration and Its Place in Tunisian History." *Les Cahiers de Tunisie,* 5 (1957): 203–249.

Lynch, John. *Spain under the Habsburgs.* 2 vols. Oxford: Oxford University Press, 1964–1967.

Marañón, Gregorio. "La vida en las galeras en tiempo de Felipe II." *Vida e historia.* Madrid: Colección Austral, 1962.

Mas, Albert. *Les Turcs dans la littérature espagnole du siècle d'or.* 2 vols. Paris: Centre des Recherches Hispaniques, 1967.

Mathiez, J. "Trafic et prix de l'homme en Mediteranée aux XVIIe et XVIIIe siècles." *Annales: Économies, sociétés, civilisations* 3 (1954): 157–164.

Olesa Muñido, Francisco-Felipe. *La organización naval de los estados mediterráneos y en especial de España durante los siglos XVI y XVII.* 2 vols. Madrid: Editorial Naval, 1968.

Parker, Geoffrey. *The Army of Flanders and the Spanish Road, 1567–1659.* Cambridge: Cambridge University Press, 1972.

Penz, Charles. *Les captifs français du Maroc aux XVIIe siècle (1577–1699).* Rabat: Institut des hautes études Marocaines, 1944.

Pike, Ruth. "Penal Labor in Sixteenth-Century Spain: The Mines of Almadén." *Societas—A Review of Social History* 3, no. 3 (1973): 193–206.

Pike, Ruth. "Penal Servitude in the Spanish Empire: Presidio Labor in the Eighteenth Century." *Hispanic American Historical Review* 58, no. 1 (February 1978): 21–40.

Porres, B. "Los hospitales cristianos de Argel y Túnez desde 1759 hasta su fin." *Acta Ordinis SS. Trinitatis* 7 (1968): 677–731.

Raurich, Salvador. "Las obras pías de beneficia para la redención de los cautivos." *Revista General de Marina,* 126 (1944): 623–630.

Raurich, Salvador. "La piratería berberisca en las costas de Cataluña." *Revista General de Marina,* 124 (1943): 317–327.

Raurich, Salvador. "La piratería en las costas de España y las Islas Baleares." *Revista General de Marina,* 125 (1943): 667–676.

Reglá, Joan. "La cuestión morisca y la coyuntura internacional en tiempos de Felipe II." *Estudios de Historia Moderna,* 3 (1953): 217–234.

Rodríguez Joulia Saint-Cyr, Carlos. *Felipe III y el Rey de Cuco.* Madrid: Consejo Superior de Investigaciones Científicas, 1953.

Salva, Jaime. *La Orden de Malta y las acciones navales españoles contra turcos y berberiscos en los siglos XVI y XVII.* Madrid: Histórico de Marina, 1944.

Sancho de Sopranis, H. "Cádiz y la piratería Turco-Berberisca en el siglo XVI." *Archivo del Instituto de Estudios Africanos* 5, no. 26 (September 1953): 7–77.

Sancho de Sopranis, H. "El viaje de Luis Bravo de Laguna y su proyecto de fortificación de las costas occidentales de Andalucía de Gibraltar a Ayamonte." *Archivo del Instituto de Estudios Africanos* 9, no. 40 (March 1957): 23–78.

Serrano y Sanz, M. "Literatos españoles cautivos." *Revista de Archivos, Bibliotecas y Museos* 1 (1897): 498–506, 535–544.

Serrano y Sanz, M. "La redención de cautivos por religiosos mercedarios durante los siglos XVII y XVIII." *Revista Contemporánea* 92 (1893): 630–638; 93 (1894): 273–282, 507–518; 94 (1894): 63–80.

Sevilla y Solanas, Felix. *Historia penitenciaria española (La galera).* Segovia, 1917.

Tenenti, Albert. *Piracy and the Decline of Venice, 1580–1615.* Berkeley: University of California Press, 1967.

Thompson, I. A. A. *War and Government in Habsburg Spain, 1560–1620.* London: Athlone Press, 1976.

Valensi, Lucette. "Esclaves chrétiens et esclaves noirs à Tunis au XVIIIe siècle." *Annales: Économies, sociétés, civilisations* 22, no. 6 (November–December 1967): 1267–1285.

Vincent, Bernard. "Les Bandits Morisques en Andalousie au XVIe siècle." *Revue d'histoire moderne et contemporaine* 21 (July–September 1974): 389–400.

Weiner, Jerome B. "Fitna, Corsairs, and Diplomacy: Morocco and the Maritime States of Western Europe, 1603–1672." Ph.D. dissertation, Columbia University, 1975.

Wilhelm, Jacques. "Captifs chrétiens à Alger." *Revue des sciences politiques* 56 (1933): 127–136.

Wolf, John B. *The Barbary Coast: Algeria under the Turks.* New York: W. W. Norton, 1979.

Index

203

COMPOSED BY GRAPHIC COMPOSITION, INC., ATHENS,
GEORGIA
MANUFACTURED BY CUSHING-MALLOY, INC.
ANN ARBOR, MICHIGAN
TEXT AND DISPLAY LINES ARE SET IN CALEDONIA

Library of Congress Cataloging in Publication Data
Friedman, Ellen G., 1939–
Spanish captives in North Africa in the early
modern age.
Bibliography: pp. 195–202.
Includes index.
1. Africa, North—History—1517–1882. 2. Ransom—
Spain—History. 3. Ransom—Africa, North—History.
4. Pirates—Africa, North—History. 5. Spaniards—
Africa, North—History. 6. Slavery—Africa, North—
History. 7. Spain—History—1516–1700. I. Title.
DT201.F74 1983   961'.023   83–47759
ISBN 0–299–09380–8